The Dvořák So
Occasional Public

No.2

A TRIBUTE TO

PETR EBEN

to mark his 70th. birthday year

Edited by Graham Melville-Mason

Burnham-on-Crouch: The Dvořák Society

The Dvořák Society is a Registered Charity, No. 267336

Published by

The Dvořák Society
for Czech and Slovak Music
Registered Charity No. 267336

32, Glebe Way
Burnham-on-Crouch CM0 8QJ
Essex

First published 2000

© The Dvořák Society 2000

ISBN 0-9532769-1-0

Printed by
Colin Cross printers
Leachfield Industrial estate
Garstang, PR3 1PR

The Dvořák Society is grateful to the Czech Ministry of Foreign Affairs, Department of Cultural Affairs for Czechs Living Abroad (MZV-OKKV) for financial assistance with the production of its various publications.

Thanks are due also to Norman Chapman, Karel Janovický, Susan Landale and Graham Melville-Mason for their generous help with translations.

CONTENTS

Preface 3
    by Graham Melville-Mason

Petr Eben: Great Composer in a Life of Service, Humanity and Love . 4
    by Graham Melville-Mason

Music as Message and the Ruling Principles of
                      Petr Eben's Music making 10
    by Johannes Landgren

Petr Eben - A "Romanticist" with a Modern Language............. 25
    by Martin Sander

Petr Eben - The Symphonic Works 29
    by Milan Slavický

The Organ Concertos of Petr Eben 34
    by John Browne

Thoughts on *Laudes* 64
    by Claude Hermitte

Okna - Chagall's Windows According to Petr Eben............. 68
    by David Titterington

Petr Eben's Works for Organ with Other Instruments 80
    by Susan Landale

God's *Gesamtkunstwerk:* Petr Eben's *Faust* 87
    by Janette Fishell

Construction on Improvisation: Eben's *Job* 99
    by Andreas Jacob

Voices from the Whirlwind: Perspectives on Petr Eben's *Job* 111
    by Michael Bauer

Petr Eben's Church Opera: *Jeremias* 134
by Ruth Forsbach

Personal Tributes to Petr Eben 143
by Sieglinde Ahrens,Hördur Áskelsson, Gerd Augst, Theo Brandmüller, Irena Chřibková, Leopoldas Digrys, Guy Erismann, Janette Fishell, Marteinn Fridrikkson, Johannes Geffert, Georges Guillard, Volker Hempfling, Jan Hora, Niels Henrik Jessen, Andreas Kempin, Kamila Klugarová, Susan Landale, Lothar Mohn, Karel Paukert, Christian Praestholm, Peter Schwarz, Wolfgang Sieber, Peter Stadtmüller and Alena Veselá

Discography 184
by Peter Herbert

Pictures
Chagall Windows at the synagogue of the Hadassah-
Hebrew University Medical Centre, Jerusalem .... Plate 1
Opposite page 68

Petr Eben with Susan Landale, Prague 1977 .... Plate 2
opposite Page 80

Petr Eben with Ruth Forsbach, Remscheid 1994 .... Plate 3
opposite Page 134

Petr Eben during the recording of *Faust*, 1981 .... Plate 4

Petr Eben rehearsing *The Labyrinth of the World and the Paradise of the Heart*, Greyfriars Kirk, Edinburgh 1990
.... Front cover and Plate 5

Cartoon of Petr Eben by Nenad Vitas, *Prague Post* 1993 .... Plate 6

Petr Eben at the organ in his study in Prague 1998   Plate 7

Petr Eben with Graham Melville-Mason and Susan Landale,
Paris 1999 ....Plate 8

PREFACE

In 1999 Petr Eben celebrated his seventieth birthday. Susan Landale, organist of St. Louis des Invalides in Paris, had the idea to get international organists to write short tributes to be published in *L'Orgue*, since that journal had marked his fiftieth birthday with an issue largely devoted to his organ music. In the event, *L'Orgue* felt unable to publish these tributes and the Dvořák Society for Czech and Slovak Music, of which Petr Eben is a Patron, then offered to include them in an Occasional Publication, expanded to include larger articles on his music, as the Society's own tribute to mark his 70th. birthday.

Although the intention was to publish this volume in Petr Eben's special birthday year, such is the love, affection and esteem in which he is held by musicians all over the world that many people expressed a wish to contribute. Particularly gratifying was the desire of some to write at length and so contribute more to published Eben scholarship. The number of tributes received, expressing such personal warmth, extraordinary individual feelings and immense gratitude will surprise nobody who has had the privilege of knowing Petr Eben as a colleague and true friend. For those of us with the great good fortune to have shared in his friendship over many years and to have had regular contact with him, we have experienced so many facets of Petr's human qualities, his unswerving faith, his strength in adversity, his creative genius and his devotion to his family. That which is Eben the man is reflected in the loving support of his wife Šárka and in the lives of his three sons, Kryštof, Marek and David, now rubbed off also onto their wives and I am sure will be carried forward into the next generation.

Even with a year's delay, there remain some friends who were unable to complete essays in the time but whose contributions to Eben scholarship would be significant. It is intended to publish these in future issues of *Czech Music*, the journal of the Dvořák Society for Czech and Slovak Music. The contents of this little volume come with the love of its authors, who write on behalf of the many for whom Petr Eben's music speaks with its special message. Petr has often remarked that our age is profoundly lacking in gratitude. These pages should serve to demonstrate that there is no lack of gratitude from us for Petr Eben, the man, his life and his works.

Graham Melville-Mason

PETR EBEN:
GREAT COMPOSER IN A LIFE OF SERVICE, HUMANITY AND LOVE

by Graham Melville-Mason

Petr Eben shares with his nation's President, Václav Havel, the distinction of being the Czech Republic's most loved and highly respected figure in its cultural life, having also the distinction of being its leading internationally recognised contemporary composer.

Petr Eben is best known in Britain for his fine works for the organ, yet his output embraces all forms except, so far, the symphony. He was born on 22nd. January 1929 in Žamberk, in North Eastern Bohemia. His parents were teachers and the family moved to Český Krumlov in South Bohemia, where he spent his childhood years. Here he found his early keyboard talents pressed into service during the war, in the absence of the adults on military service, playing the organ of the church of St. Vitus, even though his legs could hardly reach the pedal-board. In the hours alone in the organ loft, he was able to explore the tonal and colouristic possibilities of the organ and this was to be an experience which triggered the way much of his later musical activities would take him. Early experience of chamber music playing also came at this time, when he learnt much repertoire, both original and arrangements of major orchestral works, in a piano trio with his father and brother. At the same time he wrote some of his first compositions which were songs and instrumental works for the family to perform. External musical experience was limited, the Germans having confiscated the radio and public concerts being rare events. Among those rare musical occasions he recalls hearing the great German tenor, Julius Patzak, singing Mozart and the union of music and movement in the dancing of Harald Kreuzberg. Both Mozart, in the orchestral *Pražské nokturno (Prague Nocturne) (1983)* and dance in the *Biblické tance (Biblical Dances) (1990-91)* for organ, especially in its version with dancers, have been later manifestations of these early impressions.

Although the family embraced the Catholic faith, the fact that his father was a Jew meant that, in 1943, he was ostracized by friends and expelled from school. After a period working for a printer and then on a building site, he spent the rest of the war years in the concentration camp at Buchenwald.

For such an intelligent lad, these formative and impressionable years brought an early maturity of thought and conscience, many facets of which have remained with him to this day. One of these is his total understanding of the organ, both as composer and performer, from the hours he spent exploring its wonders in the organ loft at Krumlov. Another and more profound stems from his experiences in Buchenwald. Here, as a teenager, he came face to face with life and death, mans' inhumanity to man as well as mans' capacity for faith and sacrifice. He remembers vividly holding the hand of his brother as they stood in the camp showers, expecting gas to engulf them and the relief when it really was water that rained down. The succeeding daily contact with death and suffering brought him an early understanding of faith and the importance of life, with hope in survival. In one of his early works, the *Suita balladica* for 'cello and piano of 1955, he reflects on this period and says of the work that:

> "It is a remembrance of the dead in the mass graves and...a testimony of the wonderful faith of human beings. Faith and hope cannot be killed, the spirit cannot be defeated by external events".

It was this same philosophy, this same faith and inner strength, that sustained him through a further forty years of political oppression.

After the war Eben resumed his schooling at the Music School in Český Budejovice and then entered the Prague Academy of Music and Dramatic Arts in 1948, studying piano with František Rauch. In 1950 he commenced composition classes there under Pavel Bořkovec, graduating in 1954. It was only at this time that he began to widen his limited knowledge of the French Impressionist composers and heard the music of Schönberg, Prokofiev and Stravinsky for the first time, rather as Martinů had done on his coming to Prague earlier. The post-1948 impact of the Communist hold became even more restrictive after 1950 and access to contemporary music of the west became even more cut off. His natural ability as a teacher was recognised immediately and he was appointed as a lecturer in the history of music at Charles University in 1955. To Bořkovec Eben gives the credit for his sense of form and discipline, eschewing the increasingly unfettered "freedoms" of much contemporary writing. From his piano and organ studies came an easy keyboard facility and a fine sense as an accompanist, fed by his interest in the *Lieder* writers, Schubert and Brahms. He fell foul of the political authorities when he announced his intention of playing Martinů's *Piano Concerto No.2* for his graduation, only to be told that the parts were not available. Using his initiative, he obtained a set of orchestral parts and only then was he told that he still could not perform the work as Martinů was a politically unacceptable "Western" composer. This only served to strengthen his life-long antipathy to this brand of Socialism and his refusal to write music which would be acceptable to the authorities just in order to obtain performances.

His success with his students ensured that he was retained throughout the next thirty-five years, although the promotion long due to him was denied because of his refusal to join the Communist Party and his open continuation of attending church with his family Sunday by Sunday. After the 1989 Revolution, when the students demanded the removal of many of their former Party Member teachers, they balloted for those who they wished to be their future professors. One name was common on all ballot papers - Petr Eben. From November 1989, he was been called upon to fill many important positions in Czech musical life. In addition to his professorial positions at Charles University and the Academy of Music, he was President of the Prague Spring Festival for the first five years after the Velvet Revolution. Typical of his modest nature, he refused to allow any work of his to be performed at the Festival while he held that office. He holds a number of honorary positions with various musical organisations at home and abroad, not the least of which are those associated with religious music at home and that of Patron of the Dvořák Society for Czech and Slovak Music in Great Britain.

In spite of the difficult years, Eben continued to develop his individual style true to his beliefs and slowly the quality of his work became recognised abroad. Along with the precepts Bořkovec instilled in him, there was kindled also an interest in Czech folk music from his student days, with expeditions collecting folksongs in Moravia as Dvořák, Janáček and Novák had done before him. Some of these found their way into *Písně Těšínska (1952)* and *O vlaštovkách a dívkách (1959-60)*, as well as some of his song settings for children. The church environment at Krumlov sowed the seeds for his later study of plainchant. In spite of the political constraints, an awareness of Eben's music, especially that for the organ, slowly grew outside the sealed borders of Czechoslovakia. Little by little especially German and British contacts were established and the occasional visits to Prague by "western" musicians would include a meeting with Petr Eben, even though this was often quite dangerous for him and closely monitored by the authorities. At times, during the forty years of Communist control, restrictions were slightly eased, as in 1968. Occasional visits to German organ festivals eventually were allowed but his biggest opportunity came in the academic year of 1978-9, when he was allowed to take up the position of visiting professor of composition at the Royal Northern College of Music in Manchester.

In addition to Czech folk sources and plainchant influence on his thematic material and although, in one sense, his music may be considered conservative, there is a distinctive originality threading through each composition. His sense of tonality has a tonal freedom about it and yet any flirtation with more modern techniques, aleatorical, serial or atonal, has been brief. Bitonality often plays an important part in his writing and any highly developed chromaticism finds resolution in a radiant openness. The tritone also plays an important rôle in his exploration of tonality. Rhythm is central to Eben's music, with the use of ostinato featuring strongly to support the moving melodic lines, repetition of motifs and sequential writing also being hallmarks of his style. From his experimenting years in the organ loft at Český Krumlov also comes his incredible facility as an improviser, features of which find their way into his compositions, notably his three major organ works on literary texts.

His output contains many fine works for organ, including two *Concertos (1954)* and *(1982)* and the major solo compositions, *Faust (1980)*, *Job (1987)* and *The Labyrinth of the World and the Paradise of the Heart (1991)*. Based upon Goethe, the Bible and Comenius respectively, the last two originally were massive organ improvisations, an art of which Eben is a rare master. All three cycles should be performed with the spoken texts. Of his other very approachable organ compositions, any organist who has Eben in his repertoire will have enjoyed the *Sunday Music (1958-9)*, with its famous *Moto ostinato* movement, and *Laudes (1964)* while, if lucky enough to have two organs in the building, *Mutationes (per organo grande e piccolo)(1980)* will provide a challenge. Shorter but equally attractive recital or voluntary pieces are the *Festive Voluntary on Good King Wenceslas (1986)*, the toccata and fugue *Hommage à Dietrich Buxtehude (1987)* and *Four Biblical Dances (1991)*. This last named work is also impressively moving in its choreographed form. Requests and commissions continue to pour in from organists everywhere. Works such as *Momenti d'organo* came in 1994 and this was followed by *Hommage à Henry Purcell (1994-5)* and *Versio ritmica (1996)*. *Campanae gloriosae* was written in 1999 for Trier Cathedral and makes use of the notes of the cathedral's bells.

Where an instrumental soloist also is available, Eben's contribution to the repertoire is equally valuable - notably with trumpet in *Okna*

(Windows)(1976) based on the Chagall windows in the synagogue of the Hadassah Medical Centre near Jerusalem. Eben himself said:

...the window as a source of light, as a view from the material world surrounding us into the world of the imagination. Once I saw Chagall's windows and they left in me the memory of floods of colours and blazing forms bathed in fiery light.

For percussion and organ he wrote *Landscapes of Patmos (1984)* and for trombone and organ *Two Invocations (1988)*.

The kind heart of Petr Eben makes it difficult for him to say "No" when commissions for yet more organ works pour in. Yet he longs to write more orchestral and instrumental music and hoped that his retirement from university life would allow him the time to achieve that wish. His first opera was commissioned by the National Theatre in Prague just before the Revolution, the request being renewed a few years later, resulting in the church opera *Jeremias (1996-7)*, believed to be the first composed church opera since the three by Benjamin Britten. However, his intention at the moment is firmly on more orchestral and choral works. Among his orchestral works to date, the best known are *Vox clamantis (1969)*, which requires three solo trumpets spatially placed, *Noční hodiny (Night Hours) (1975)* and *Prague Nocturne (1983)* written for the 1984 Salzburg Festival and using a Mozart sized orchestra to which he adds an important part for celeste. For the Czech Philharmonic centenary in 1996, Petr Eben was one of four Czech composers commissioned to write major orchestral works. His *Improperia* was the successful result. Now Raphael Wallfisch has commissioned a *Violoncello Concerto* from him and we await such a potentially exciting outcome with impatience.

His many choral works include religious compositions and those of apparent secular nature in which he disguised church melodies to hoodwink the Communist authorities! *Pragensia (1972)* is a work which displays his interest in the Renaissance, using Prague based sources of that period, accompanied by instruments of the time, some of which are played by the singers. The *Missa cum populo (1982)*, as its name implies, allows for congregational participation. In 1992-3 he wrote *Posvátná znameně (Sacred Symbols)* for the opening of the restored Salzburg Cathedral, making use of the four organ lofts - two for organs and one each for wind and percussion. In 1998 he wrote his *Bilder der Hoffnung* for the German Catholic meeting in Mainz, interspersing unaccompanied choral passages with short organ pieces.

He has more than a dozen song cycles to his credit, of which the early *Písně k loutně (Songs with Lute) (1951)*, written as an engagement present for his wife, is particularly attractive, while the *Song of Ruth (1970)* for alto and organ or piano is an *eulogy to devotion and faithfulness beyond the grave.*

In more recent years his considerable list of chamber music compositions has been enhanced by a number of works to receive international acclaim, notably the *String Quartet (1981)* written for the Smetana Quartet, the *Piano Trio (1987)* and the *Piano Quintet (1991-2)* commissioned by the Nash Ensemble. Following Petr Eben's year at the Royal Northern College of Music, British musicians have been well served by him. *Job* was dedicated to David Titterington and the *Four Biblical Dances* written for Susan Landale. Of his smaller piano output, William Howard is the recipient of the Kafka based *Letters to Milena (1990)* and the author received *A Cry for the Spirit (1992)*, an improvisation on *Veni Creator Spiritus*, as a sixtieth birthday present.

Ask anyone to name a living Czech composer and the answer is likely to be "Eben". He is considered already by many to be the next in the line of Smetana, Dvořák, Janáček and Martinů. As to that, only time will tell. What is certain is that his humanity, humility and strong Catholic faith have sustained him through years of persecution and personal suffering to emerge as one of the leading figures to whom his countrymen turn with confidence and love in the difficult times of new found freedom. His sincerity as a man manifests itself in every note of music that he writes. His belief is that, in composing, intellect and heart must combine. Petr Eben is a modest man of wide learning and with a very big heart, a heart which embraces not just his music but his fellow man, as all who come into contact with him feel and accept with deep gratitude.

MUSIC AS MESSAGE AND THE RULING PRINCIPLES OF PETR EBEN'S MUSIC-MAKING

by Johannes Landgren

Improvisation and the mysterious inspirations which attend its successful execution lie at the heart of Petr Eben's musical ideology. Improvisation is perhaps the most unmediated form of musical discourse, one which, particularly in Eben's case, draws on context and is constantly influenced by the unique circumstances of individual performance: the organ, the audience, the church and, as was the case in the Lyra Pragensis concerts, the political and social atmosphere. The power of improvisation, both as a generating compositional tool and as a medium for communicating meaning to an audience, plays a central rôle in Eben's view of his mission as a composer. For Eben, music must communicate something to its audience; it must have a message. This view of the musical act is consistent with his own recollections of the Lyra Pragensis concerts:

> *Ich muß wieder sagen, daß ich eigentlich damals diese Abende, diese Konzerte (Lyra Pragensis), als eine wichtige Botschaft angesehen habe und ich habe mich darüber sehr gefreut. Und aus diesem Grund habe ich dort eine Zeit gearbeitet...Ich muss gestehen; ich glaube wirklich das war, so zu sagen, das Honorar, das ich von oben bekommen habe, weil ich sonst kein großes hatte, aber daß der liebe Gott und der heilige Geist mir dann wirklich eine ganze Reihe von guten Themen haben einfallen lassen. Ich konnte da wirklich nur zwei Tage vor dem Konzert hinkommen. Und da hatte ich den Text vor mir und es kamen wirklich Einfälle, die für mich sehr wichtig waren. Und diese Einfälle habe ich dort notiert, aber nur die Themen und Motive.*[1]

The purpose of this article is to try to outline the nature of Eben's aesthetic beliefs and to examine the ways in which they have moulded his mature

---

[1] Eben, P. Prague, 1st. March 1995.

musical language and what implications they may have for the performance practice of his works.

1. Eben's Musical Ideology

It is imperative to Petr Eben that music must convey some meaning and each creative act must somehow move the listener: *For me music should in some way have a function to serve people.*[2] Even when the musical discourse is complex and employs modern compositional techniques, his view is that it should be expressively meaningful: *Dass wir...mit dieser zeitgenössischen Sprache wirklich eine Botschaft ausdrücken können.*[3]

What Eben refers to as *die dienende Funktion der Musik (serving the function of music)*[4] provides the basis for his view of the composer and the performing musician. That music can only serve its audience in context means for Eben that composition is not a creative act of an isolated musician nor is performance separable from its surroundings but rather music making in general is the result of a creative interaction between composer, interpreter and listener.

Yet if music is to be able to attain this function it must, in Eben's view, serve not only its audience but more importantly God. For him, this is a reciprocal relationship for artistic creation - a witnessing of the rôle of the Holy Spirit in the invention of the thematic material for the Lyra Pragensis improvisations - would not be possible without the spiritual element. In his music then, Eben seeks to communicate not only to his audience but to God as well; the underlying message is communicated through the ever-present spiritual dimension of his music. For Eben there is no conflict between the imperatives of individual artistic expression (itself pervaded by religious belief) and the necessity of comprehensibility to listeners. Thus the "serving function" seems to be an expression of a symbiosis between Eben's religious beliefs and a necessity to communicate this faith, where the artistic activity and the urge for technical perfection work in the service of musical communication. In the preface to *Laudes*, Eben formulates his musical *Credo* as follows:

---

[2]Eben, P.: Prague, 1988.

[3]Eben, P.: Prague, 1st. March 1995.

[4]Eben, P.: Prague, 1st. March 1995.

Our century is full of ingratitude - ingratitude to people around us, to the world and above all to the Creator Himself. Everyone hears demands, complaints, discontent and rebelliousness but nowhere is there a trace of gratitude. So perhaps the most pressing concern of art must be to praise, because otherwise "the very stones will cry out".[5]

Laudes becomes the symbol of man's reflection of the artistic perfection as it is embodied in the creation of the world and in the cosmic proportions of the universe, which are represented in the numerical proportions evident in the formal structure of *Laudes*. The "serving function" of music and the creative potential of the art is always subordinated to the Creator of the universe. In *Laudes* Eben uses Gregorian Chant for much of the thematic material, since its liturgical origins provide the perfect medium for conveying this message. The piece reflects Eben's Christian faith and his belief in Christ's victory over death but this message is not meant to exclude those outside the faith but rather would be recognizable to them as well, since it presents an archetypal narrative of struggle and triumph. Thus his message is not confined by its religious inflections, even though the spiritual pervades his music.

What is perhaps most striking in Eben's work is that this communicative element informed his music even during the long period of his career when political conditions might have been expected to limit his ability to convey meaning to his audience. The notion of music as message was both a means of asserting artistic independence from the State and offering a spiritual alternative to an enforced secularism. Of course, in contrast to novels and poetry, the nature of musical discourse made it easier for Eben to thwart attempts to censor his work. This was especially the case with his improvisations which, because they are not written down, are perhaps the most destabilizing of musical acts. Thus, during the Communist era, Eben saw his music as offering the public a message which was not sanctioned nor even allowed by the State. He said:

In den 40 Jahren ohne Freiheit konnte man verschiedene Dinge überhaupt nicht often sagen. Das bedeutete also, man konnte sie weder in der Zeitung lesen noch im Fernsehen sehen oder im Radio hören. Die Kunst hat die Möglichkeit gehabt diese Dinge auszudrücken und von allen Bereichen der

---

[5]Eben, P.: Preface to *Laudes*; London, United Music Publishers, 1964.

> *Kunst hat gerade die Musik, glaube ich, die grösste Möglichkeit gehabt, weil sie nicht so intensiv wie z.B. die Literatur und die darstellende Kunst zensuriert wurde. Schon von Anfang an haben wir das eingesehen. Wir hatten daher die Möglichkeit, mit unseren Kompositionen die Menschen anzusprechen und ihnen eben das zu bringen, was zu dieser Zeit überhaupt nicht möglich war.*[6]

The interplay between composer and listener further encouraged his musical ideology and his thoughts on the period demonstrate both the importance of giving music a message and of having that message understood. Eben has remarked on the symbiotic relationship between the composer and the listener, particularly during periods when artistic freedom is severely curtailed:

> *Am wenigsten konnte die Zensur in die Musik eingreifen und so war es gerade die Aufgabe der Komponisten, die unterdrückten Botschaften wenigsten in ihren Tönen auszudrücken. Und es war unglaublich, wie dankbar die Zuhörer für jede Andeutung waren, wie hellhörig sie für jedes Wort oder jeden Ton aus den verbotenen Bereichen waren. So führte diese Situation zu einer anderen Richtung: Musik als Botschaft.*[7]

Petr Eben's basic ideology remained intact after the Velvet Revolution in 1989. Since then his artistic beliefs could be expressed more freely and openly.

Eben's aesthetic principles immediately suggest comparison with earlier views of the composer which prevailed before the nineteenth century, where the music was meant to serve a specific purpose or even a certain patron, where the musical act was subordinated to the function that that act was meant to fulfil. Thus, there may be a tendency by modern musicians and critics to dismiss Eben's ideas as encouraging the composer to be subservient to the demands of the listener, not to mention the demands of the marketplace. This conception of artistic expression was given paradigmatic formulation by Arnold Schoenberg when he argued that:

---

[6]Eben, P.: Prague, 1st. March 1995.

[7]Eben, P.: *Aufstieg*, a lecture given in Darmstadt, 2nd. December 1993.

Those who compose because they want to please others and have audiences in mind are not real artists. They are not the kind of men who are driven to say something whether or not there exists one person who likes it, even if they themselves dislike it. They are not creators who must open the valves in order to relieve the interior pressure of a certain creation ready to be born. They are merely more or less skilful entertainers who would renounce composing if they did not find listeners.[8]

The romantic search for "inner truth" and cultural conceptions of an ideal musical genius which is utterly free from debasing, extra-musical interference was encouraged by notions of autonomy; music became a way of exploring the inner, psychological universe, an introverted and even solipsistic view of musical creation which sought to eradicate interaction between artist (the composer), the art work (the music) and the receiver (the listener). "Adjustments" in the musical structure, derived from the listener's perspective, were thought to compromise the aesthetic values. This meant that the communicative aspect and the use of extra-musical references were severely denigrated.

After the Second World War, primarily through the influence of the Darmstadt School, the arbitrary criterion of autonomy, coupled with the urge to reach an objective truth, were seen by many as a necessary antidote to the manipulative nationalistic tendencies in music-making, most notably the cynical, propagandist views on music held by the Nazis.

However, conditions for composers in Western Europe were quite different from those of their contemporaries in the countries of the Warsaw Pact, where prevailing aesthetic beliefs, as well as political life in general, opposed notions of artistic autonomy. Here the regulating force at all levels of music-making, as well as in other arts, was the state enforced social realist cultural policy, which assigned aesthetic value according to the utility of an art work with respect to "the people" as defined by the State. In other words, the criteria which served as aesthetic standards for the acceptance of an artist or composer in Western Europe were, conversely, reasons enough for rejection or even persecution behind the Iron Curtain.

Eben was, of course, aware of the influences from the Darmstadt School and recognized its valuable contributions to musical life after the war:

---

[8]Schoenberg, A.: in Cook, N.: *Music, Imagination and Culture*, p.182.

> *Wir haben uns immer bemüht, auch wenn es bei uns schwer zu erreichen war, die anderen Autoren - zum Beispiel auch die zweite Wiener-Schule und dann natürlich auch Bartók, Stravinskij und so weiter - all diese Sachen zu kennen und davon zu wissen und damit auch sozusagen umzugehen. Aber der Effekt sollte nicht der sein, daß wir uns präsentieren, sondern daß wir die zeitgenössische Sprache haben und mit dieser zeitgenössischen Sprache wirklich eine Botschaft ausdrücken können.*[9]

Earlier he had said:

> *I think there was a very strong and big difference in the fifties, where you could find that, while Darmstadt and the whole of modern music was going in only the Webern or Post Webern directions, here was the real opposite and you had to write music which was for the masses, where they really wanted you to write in a very harmonic style.*[10]

Although he did not directly reject those developments associated with the Darmstadt School, they did not accord with his own aesthetic principles, based as they were on service to the listener. In any case, Eben's views on music militate against the, by now, hackneyed view of artistic autonomy: "art for art's sake". Concepts of autonomy, originality and heroic refusals to compromise one's own artistic values have been used as reductive factors in adjudicating aesthetic value since the nineteenth century, so that to admit an affinity for your listener has often been seen as a sort of compromise.

Yet Petr Eben is by no means a panderer, as he has noted in his description of the composition of what would become his most widely played organ cycle, *Nedělní hudba (Sunday Music)*:

> *It was written in the fifties and that was a time where, in our country, the church was persecuted. The priests, religion and also the organ were not very much liked, the organ because it was the instrument which was bringing spiritual ideas. So the Government did not like the organ as an instrument and they even forbade all organ concerts and so nobody was writing for*

---

[9]Eben, P.: Prague, 1st. March 1995.

[10]Eben, P.: Prague, June 1988.

the organ because there was no chance to perform such works. But for me the organ was - and still is - an instrument which brought me such a lucky time in my youth, where I could forget the troubles of war, so I wanted to write for the organ. I did not consider whether the composition would be performed or not. I simply felt that I must write it. I was very astonished that this work, which I thought would be lying on my table and nobody would play it, suddenly became the most well-known composition and was performed in all the states and in very many countries of the world. The work has been recorded on many CDs and gramophone records, so sometimes you never know how a composition will finish. The third movement, "Moto ostinato", is something which has a spiritual character. It is in the rhythm where my idea of the content was that it should be a sort of a battle between good and evil; a mediėval battle, where one row of soldiers are coming in a strict order. So it is very strict in the form from an apocalyptic view.[11]

His desire to communicate a message does not then, in his view, conflict with his artistic integrity. If a musical work is to be based on artistic "truth" it must derive from freely expressed personal creativity. However, if the semantic content of musical expression is to be retained, this creativity will necessarily seek intelligibility and attempt to offer a comprehensible musical object to the listener.

For Eben, the desire to compose is not in this case an act of pleasing others but represents an inner necessity, itself activated by religious belief. Eben's sincere love of composing and his humanitarian outlook are the determining factors in his aesthetic credo: a musical altruist, he seeks to communicate his own love of humanity, as well as God's, by remaining true to himself. He is, above all, a Christian composer. It would be impossible, in his view, to pursue an arcane and elitist musical course and still be able to communicate something to his audience through his work. The fulfilment of the "serving function" is not dependent on the popular success of a work but by the degree that it communicates God's love to the listener.

---

[11] Eben, P.: Göteborg, 28th. May 1993.

2. The Musical Message

The often indefinite aspect of music allows it, in the opinion of Petr Eben, to function spiritually:

> *Nicht nur ein text oder ein gewähltes musikalisches Zitat hat die Fähigkeit eine Botschaft zu überreichen, sondern die Musik selbst ist eine Kunst, deren Abstraktion der Spiritualität nahe ist und sie ausdrücken kann.*[12]

The communicative function is, then, related to spiritual reality, where the status of music is not reduced to the delivery of simple semantic units but attempts to convey a more global religious belief, something like an universal affect, such as that expressed in the move from struggle to triumph in the fourth movement of *Laudes*, which is itself determined by these beliefs.

In his lecture at Darmstadt in 1993, Eben emphasised that the dramatic experiences of his life and his religious faith have had a substantial impact on his music-making:

> *Ich bin weder Philosoph, noch Theologe und Theoretiker nur im Bereich des Musikhantwerks und so kann ich mich an diesem Gesprächskreis nur als Komponist beteiligen. Als ich mir die einzelnen Themen des zur Diskussion vorgeschlagenen Gesamtprozesses durchlas, wurde ich mir bewusst, dass gerade die Elemente "Wandlung und Aufbruch" einen Cantus Firmus in meinem Werk bilden, der in vielen Kompositionen ziemlich markant ausgedrückt ist. Und als ich darüber nachdachte, wie ich zu dieser Thematik kam, traten mir vier wichtige und ausschlaggebende Momente in meinem Lebenslauf vor die Augen, welche diese beiden Elemente mit sich brachten und so meine Kompositionen beeinflussten.*
>
> *Ich will Ihnen nun also durchaus nicht mein Curriculum vitae schildern, sondern nur von diesen view Momenten sprechen und ihrem Zusammenhang mit einigen konkreten Werken...*[13]

---

[12]Eben, P.: Prague, 1st. March 1995.

[13]Eben, P.: *Aufstieg*, lecture in Darmstadt, 2nd. December 1993.

At this point he referred to four important events: An experience from Žamberk at the age of four; the German occupation; an experience from the Buchenwald concentration camp and the political oppression from 1948.

For Petr Eben, music is always of its time and should reflect its surroundings, seeing the separation of life and work as a convenient fallacy.

3. The Musical Drama and the Rôle of Improvisation

The graphic and plastic arts we perceive in quite another way than music. We can look at the picture without a time limit. But music is bound with time...[14]

Eben emphasizes the musical identity as a temporal art, a process subordinated to the conditions of time and the contexts of performance. The awareness of this temporal process is an important feature concerning Petr Eben's view on music-making, whether dealing with improvisation, composition or interpretation. Because improvisation is a form of musical creation which comes into being in real time, the creative act itself is synchronous with its reception by the listener. Eben believes that the improviser is constantly interacting with his surroundings through intuition and that the inspirations of the moment are facilitated by preparation of thematic material and registrations. However, in the performance itself, the process of music making is subordinated to the same temporal conditions as those of the listeners. This improvisatory approach is related to Eben's basic ideology where the communicative aspects and the listener-oriented function are essential parts of the music making process. In this way the actual creation of music in time is a natural consequence of this awareness, since the "serving function" is dependent upon all contextual aspects.

4. The Interrelation Between The Musical Language and the Basic Ideology

Eben's belief in the communicative power of music does not mean that he has a proscriptive view of musical style. He said:

---

[14]Eben, P.: Prague, 2nd. March 1995.

Wenn ich von der Botschaft der Musik spreche, meine ich durchaus nicht, daß diese in einem traditionellen Stil sein sollte; das, was aber diese Musik beeinflussen muß, ist der geistliche Inhalt und die Zuwendung an die Zuhörer.[15]

Rather his is a metaphysical approach in which religious belief and artistic integrity will allow him to make his message comprehensible. In addition, although his musical language is complex, particularly in its far-reaching polytonal features and his methods of thematic development, it is nonetheless accessible. This should not be taken to mean that his musical language is a debased form of expression, a surrender to public approval. It is wellknown that his musical style did not receive the approval of the Czech Composers' Union. Further, he was among the few leading international composers who did not adopt serial techniques, although some of his thematic inventions, particularly in the 1960's, were somewhat influenced by these procedures. His is an unique voice and his resistance to modern trends is a reflection both of his artistic independence and his musical ideology, the latter centring on the need to communicate with the listener.

5. Harmony

Because Petr Eben believes that the function of music should be oriented towards the listener, his use of bi- or polytonality seems to be a choice founded in part on the demands of comprehensibility. Bitonality is certainly more accessible than complex serial structure, even for a very trained listener. However, his output spans a wide range with respect to tonal complexity.

Eben's harmonic practice, at its most complex in *Laudes* and tending towards greater stability in *Nedělní hudba* and *Job*, is ideally suited to his collaborative improvisations with other instruments. In such cases bitonality results from the conditions of music making, so that the compositional practice is inseparable from the instrument on which the work was conceived. Polytonality seems, in Eben's case, to be inseparable from context and Jygen Kerz notes the improvisational origins of his tonal practice:

---

[15]Eben, P.: Prague, 1st. March 1995.

Diese Art bitonale Klänge zu erzeugen weist ebenfalls auf einen improvisatorischen Charakter hin.[16]

The generative harmonic principles of Eben's art spring from the contexts of performance, so that the communicative ideology that activates his musical language is a product of the symbiotic relationship between audience and musician, creation and reception.

6. Melody

Eben's use of already existing thematic material relates directly to his communicative aesthetic. In this way thematic materials of liturgical origins become recognizable to both the listeners who identify with the religious source and those who do not, when it returns at later stages of a movement. Intelligibility governs his approach to the choice of thematic material. The delivery of this material also helps Eben to organize coherent formal structures. Repetition and recognition play an important rôle in his compositional practice:

> *I think that for the form and structure of the composition it is necessary to work with motifs or themes. Also for the listener it is a help in understanding the music. Therefore I think that the a-thematic style is not near to my conception.*[17]

Eben's method of mathematical transformation of the thematic material also seems to be quite comprehensible, since this technique retains the shape of melodic figures, so that even in altered form they can be recognized by the listener on their return. This kind of developing variation is controlled by the harmonic flow between tonal centres, themselves determined by Eben's polytonal language. Form and relatively stable harmonic background of the thematic material provide a kind of rhetorical basis for the communicative act, forming a framework for the coherent utterances of his vast melodic talents.

7. Rhythm

The irrepressible energy of many of Eben's organ works delivers its message by pure insistence. The elemental rhythmic quality of much of his

---

[16]Kerz, J.: *Der Orgelzyklus Hiob von Petr Eben - Eine Analyse*, Düsseldorf, 1990.

[17]Eben, P.: Prague, 2nd. March 1995.

music to a large extent explains its accessibility: witness the enduring appeal of his most famous organ composition, the *Moto Ostinato*, the third movement from *Nedělní hudba*, a piece which, according to its composer, evokes a battle between good and evil, that is to say it is pervaded by religious belief. The rhythmic vitality of his music also draws inspiration from Czech folk music but more significantly it derives from his improvisatory style, as in his frequent use of ostinato patterns and the birhythmic structures of *Job*, originating from the Lyra Pragensis performances. In these concerts Eben exploited rhythmic energy to depict the texts, as for example in the fragment which would become the sixth movement of *Job* where the ostinato dramatises the biblical passage: *When the Lord answered Job out of the whirlwind*. The link between the rhythmic motif and the pictorial element is a consequence of the rhetorical and communicative approach, which is a ruling principle in Eben's improvisational aesthetic and in his ability to enact vibrant musical dramas.

8. Sound

Although the indications of registration that Eben provides in his organ scores are often very detailed, he is also extremely sensitive to the qualities of individual instruments and aware of the differing performing conditions in churches and concert halls. Eben not only includes alternative registrations but encourages the performer to adapt these detailed sound visions to match the organ on which his music is to be performed. This is also true of his tempo indications:

> The advice given as to the stops to be used should be read only as suggestions, depending of course on the organ in question. They are merely intended as indications of my thoughts on the mood of individual passages. Nor are the given metronome markings meant to be adhered to too strictly, since they too may have to be adjusted according to the acoustics of the building in which the organ is to be played.[18]

9. Form/Structure

The structure of Eben's music is generally clearly articulated and the rhetorical disposition of the movements are coherently presented to the listener. As Eben has noted, it is essentially through form that musical

---

[18] Eben, P. Preface to *Hommage à Henry Purcell*, Schott, 1995.

meaning is communicated, particularly by means of repetition. For this reason, many of his compositions show a symmetrical structure and rely for their cogency on the recall of prior material. Without well-considered formal layout, itself dependent on his methods of thematic elaboration, Eben says that he would not be able to convey universal affects to the listener. As indicated, his temperament tends towards the romantic but his highly individual style is anchored by tonal centres and clear formal configurations. For Eben, without form there can be no communication. Thus his formal structures, such as variations, passacaglias and clearly organized narrative movements, are related to his belief in the serving function of music.

10. Conclusion

Petr Eben's musical language does not demonstrate significant differences between the "accumulated" compositions based on improvisations and the primarily "composed" works. Rather, the similarities between these two types of works overshadow the differences in formal layout and thematic elaboration. However, the actual differences remaining might be related to the different conditions and extra-musical contexts which inhere in Eben's instrumentally idiomatic approach, his constant adjustments to his surroundings and immediate influences, which often directly affect the compositional. Eben describes this contextual approach, as well as the importance of extra-musical factors, in his account of the composing of *Okna*.

> *As I view works of art in various fields, I always feel very strongly that all art is one; an ecstatic expression of the reality around us and in us and at the same time a constant struggle to capture something more, something behind that reality. Every expression, musical, literary or visual, is merely one element of this one art, whether it be expressed by brush, chisel, words or tones...*
>
> *I wrote this cycle of the windows because the Gallery of Cheb asked me to compose something for a series of compositions inspired by fine arts. In this moment I thought about the Chagall Windows which I had seen on slides, maybe ten years before. I could see the windows before my eyes. I had the image of them so in my head that I was really fascinated by*

them. Then I went to the library and there I could get a book where they were printed in colours...[19]

This quotation illustrates the importance of surroundings for Eben's musical invention and the direct relationship between his art and extra-musical factors. For Eben there is no such thing as the music itself; the autonomous art work for him is a myth.

Petr Eben's aesthetic concept, where the definition of "music as message" and "the serving function of music" are regulating forces, of course could be controversial. Eben's views on the meaning of composing and musical creation are to a large extent formed by his dramatic experiences at the end of the Second World War. Expecting imminent death in the showers at Buchenwald, the sixteen-year-old Eben suddenly was forced to reconsider the nature of life and the reasons for his own existence. This experience only strengthened his urge to compose and to communicate his powerful beliefs to others. As a result, his individual creative process is always encompassed by the larger gift of God's creation:

> *In a sense of artistic creation that must be connected to some humble recognition of its ancillary function. This means neither composing only on liturgical texts, nor a swift and obedient reaction to political events. What I am speaking of is the endowing consciousness that is to be found in Teilhard de Chardin's writings. The creation of the world is never finished but continues in an ever more splendid way and we can help it towards completion with every honest deed.*[20]

Consequently, in both sacred and secular contexts, Eben's music is an act of making visible or audible a new aspect of God's creation. Even where sacred elements, such as Plainchant or biblical programmes, are not used, his music evokes universal effects, recognizable hermeneutical structures which communicate a moving message to the listeners, independently of their religious beliefs. Eben's concept of music making might be described as a "Laudes-ideal" where praise is defined as the aim to create art that

---

[19]Eben, P.: Prague, 2nd. March 1995. *Okna (Windows)*, for trumpet and organ was written in 1976. Only in 1999 did Eben finally have the opportunity to visit the Chagall Windows at the Hadassah Medical Centre synagogue in Jerusalem.

[20]Eben, P.: in Dehner, Jan., *Contemporary Composers 1992,* Chicago & London, St.James Press.

ranges beyond all possible dogmas and acts of political coercion. The ultimate optimism of Petr Eben's richly creative music draws not only on faith and the urge to communicate that faith but also on the vibrant inspirations of audience, architecture, biblical texts, folk music, Gregorian Chant and the endless resources provided by good thematic material, a gift which he sees from the Holy Spirit. It is not surprising, in the light of Eben's musical ideology, that improvisation offers him a profound and energetic means of musical service and that the act of composing is equally a product of context, experience and faith.

PETR EBEN - A "ROMANTICIST" WITH A MODERN LANGUAGE

by Martin Sander

Ich melde mich ja zu den Romantikern...[1]

Beyond any doubt, Petr Eben is a "modern" composer. Many new and original musical ideas impart to his tonal language its unique characteristics. However, he also adheres to some important principles which elsewhere have been discarded as old-fashioned or as being "romantic" in a negative sense. For the understanding of Eben's music they are of basic importance, as he has managed to combine the value of these fundamentals with his modern tonal language into a very personal style.

In the first place, all of his music carries an expression and has a meaning which the composer wanted the notes to convey. He chooses his musical means according to what he wishes to express - not the other was round. Nowhere does Eben constrain himself by some abstract principle of construction, nor would he allow any passage to slip into arbitrariness or indifference. Consequently his music requires the full personal and emotional participation of the player. One has to understand this demand against the background of the mainstream philosophy of music in the second half of the twentieth century. For several decades many composers, and especially organists, have been following an ideology best described by the demand of placing the work into the foreground and keeping oneself in the background. That ideology identifies the work with its architecture, whose objective qualities should not be obscured by any interference from subjective additions. In marked contrast to the coolness resulting from such objective interpretation, there is no artificial distinction between the work and the interpreter's self in Eben's music. As Eben wrote, he himself *never writes without inner excitement which, consequently, must be felt also by the interpreter.*[2]

---

[1]Personal communication from the composer, 5th. August 1988. *I enlist with the romanticists...*

[2]*op cit. Und ohne diese innere Erregung schreibe ich nie, deshalb muß sie wohl eben auch beim Interpreten zu spüren sein.*

The great subject for Petr Eben is the development of the human soul. This lies at the very core of his music, as he himself frequently points out in the introductions to his works, which are partly contained in the printed editions and partly distributed personally to those asking for them. The purpose of all the programmatic effects, which he builds in so masterly a way into his works, is never a mere description of the external situation. Rather, the sometimes quite drastic description of the surroundings serves to make the drama comprehensible, going on inside the human heart. Several allusions to French-style *Toccatas* and some other elements of his writing might seem to place Eben closer to the French as well as, quite naturally, the Czech schools. However, since his music derives its most important driving force from the innermost human feelings and processes, it is very much related to the German Romanticism as well. Apart from Petr Eben, the century just past probably has seen only Max Reger exploring and describing mental and spiritual development with similar resolution.

The realization of this positively "romantic" emotional attitude achieved through Eben's musical language can be studied very well in his organ works, from the very first cycle onwards. The third movement, *Moto ostinato*, of *Nedělní hudba (Sunday Music)* of 1957-59 is described in the foreword as a

> *reminiscence of a fight between Good and Evil in the human heart, before the combined positive forces of the personality get the upper hand in the Finale.*[3]

Four movements, each starting in a different atmosphere, demonstrate the transformation of the opening mood into grateful praise in Eben's following cycle, *Laudes* (1964). The composer describes these initial moods as

> *amazement in front of the sublime Majesty in the first part, standing silent before the nascent mystery in the second part, dramatic strife and anxiety in the third part and nebulously fateful searching and straying in the last part.*[4]

---

[3]Eduard Herzog, in the Foreword to Petr Eben: *Nedělní hudba (1958)*, Supraphon, Prague, 1988.

[4]Petr Eben, in his remarks on *Laudes*.

By taking the interpreter and the listener along with the elevation of these feelings into thankfulness and praise, the music aims at countering the ingratitude of our century, where we find

> everywhere claims, complaints, discontent and even revolt - only no trace of gratitude.[5]

One and a half decades later, in the *Faust* suite, Eben

> sought...to express, through his handling of the instrument, the poles of Good and Evil...and the struggle of these conflicting elements within Faust's own character.[6]

Related to *Faust* by the common subject of *the wager between Satan and God on the fate of a human being*[7] and written another decade later, the organ cycle *Job* (1987) represents perhaps Eben's most contrasted and refined work with respect to the exploration of an inner development. Here, the composer sometimes even resists temptation to depict the external action; rather it is Job's reaction, his feelings upon the fate befalling him, which are expressed by the music. This is already obvious from the grouping of the biblical verses in such a way as to make it a suite of emotions rather than of stories. The titles of this suite first lead us all the way from the rough theme of Job's *Destiny (I)* through his *Faith (II)* and *Acceptance of Suffering (III)* down to Job's *Longing for Death (IV)* and his deep *Despair and Resignation (V)*. At the turning point of the cycle, *Part VI*, *Mystery and Creation* gives a *vivid picture of the creation as depicted by God to Job*.[8] What appears to be most important here is again not the external programme but rather Job's reaction, his bewilderment, symbolized by *mysterious pianissimo chords, contrasted with a questioning flute phrase*.[9] *Penitence and Realisation (VII)*, where Job's understanding is illustrated by the wonderful symbol of the plainsong *Veni Creator Spiritus*, leads to the final redemption in *God's Reward (VIII)*.

---

[5] *ibid.*

[6] Susan Landale, in the Foreword to Petr Eben: *Faust (1979-80)*, United Music Publishers, London, 1983.

[7] Petr Eben, in the Preface to *Job*, United Music Publishers, London, 1989.

[8] *ibid.*

[9] *ibid.*

For several other works, Eben did not derive his primary inspiration from themes lending themselves so obviously to the study of human spiritual evolution. Nevertheless, especially in his four-part cycles, the relation of the respective third and fourth parts follow similar lines of development as established in *Nedělní hudba* and *Laudes*. Thus the cycle *Okna (Windows)* of 1976 for trumpet and organ was inspired by Marc Chagall's glass windows of the Synagogue of the Jerusalem University Hospital. However, the lively *Blue Window* and the pastoral *Green Window* are followed by a *Red Window* whose aggressiveness does not seem to completely match the ostensible model of a *sun-set above the sea with two fish leaping over it in a dramatic turn*.[10] Nor does the last part, the *Golden Window*, appear to find its full explanation in the shining and solemn atmosphere Eben saw in Chagall's window. Obviously, Eben's music interprets the colours in a much stronger way than his words may suggest. The colour Red, which for anybody living in a Communist country inevitably must have evoked associations quite different from Chagall's red window, appears to set the stage for a dramatic fight, before the majestic Gold finally erupts into victorious triumph.

Even in the *Biblické tance* of 1990-91, explicitly intended to be *less severe in mood*[11] than *Job*, the dramatic Part III, *The Dance of Jephtha's Daughter*, derives its emphasis from the emotional development, leading from the joyful dance, *interrupted by the anticipation of a threatening theme*[12] to the *daughter's lament on her imminent death*[13] and to the ultimate sadness of the funeral music, marking the end of this remarkable dance. And again, in the fourth and last part, the joy of *The Wedding in Cana* has a similar relieving effect as in the finales of Eben's earlier cycles.

Petr Eben's music is very special in our time in its power to captivate musicians audiences alike. I am strongly convinced that it is the "romantic" - or should that rather be "timeless" - aspect here described and lying at its core which really makes his music speak to the unconscious parts of our personalities, taking us along with the development it wants to evoke.

---

[10]Petr Eben, in remarks on *Okna*.

[11]Petr Eben, in the Preface to *Four Biblical Dances*, United Music Publishers, London, 1993.

[12]*ibid.*

[13]*ibid.*

PETR EBEN - THE SYMPHONIC WORKS

by Milan Slavický

Side by side with the rich and various output of Petr Eben, his symphonic works seem, at first glance, to form a relatively small group, especially when compared with the long list of his vocal or organ compositions. Nonetheless, seen in the context of his whole *oeuvre*, they are among his most important. Each of them sprang from a clear programmatic baseline. All were also written at some distance in time from each other, thus making it possible to follow each step in the development of Eben's musical language with clarity.

Eben's symphonic output began in a sense, with his graduation work, his *Organ Concerto No.1*, subtitled *Symphonia Gregoriana* and dating from 1954. This is a four-movement composition, almost an hour long, drawing on the Gregorian plainchant. To its twenty-five year old composer it was an important experience in the art of combining the sound of the orchestra with that of the organ, a combination with its own very specific demands on the composer's imagination since the organ, unlike most solo instruments, is able to cover the whole range of orchestral sound itself. This work, written at a time when his country was in the throes of the greatest political repression and persecution of anything connected with religion, was also a significant pointer to his future career and lifelong direction, through which also his firm belief remained unbowed.

During the 1950's and 1960's he used the orchestra in several vocal works, as well as in his *Piano Concerto*. However, his first purely orchestral work, written in 1969, was *Vox Clamantis* for three trumpets and orchestra, a thirteen minute piece in a single movement. Eben had just celebrated his fortieth birthday and using all his experience with orchestral sound he produced a mature work of a standard found in the best of not only Czech but also European composition. The year of its compositions was significant for the birth of its idea. The end of the 1960's saw several new works react to the crushing experience of the Soviet invasion of Czechoslovakia in August 1968, Karel Husa's *Music for Prague* being perhaps the best known among them. As time went on, more works reacted then to the growing hopelessness of the years of political "normalisation", of which Miloslav Kabeláč's *Symphony No.8 [Antiphonies](Op.54)* of 1969-70 is a typical example. *Vox Clamantis* is a mature work which expresses a powerful idea by means of modern orchestral sound. Its idea has, in fact, been the leading motif of Eben's work throughout his life, bringing fresh and living hope during periods of depression and despondency: *Straighten out the paths for the coming of the Lord.* Here the *vox clamantis* is the voice calling in the wilderness and meant to be that of John the Baptist. The development of the music reflects the idea of a gradual winning of certainty and strengthening of hope. The three trumpets, placed high on the concert platform, are gradually united in a single voice; the two main musical ideas, quotations from a Gregorian *Sanctus* and from the mediæval Czech chant *Hospodine pomiluj ny (Lord have mercy),* are similarly treated. They are symbols not only of a thousand years of Czech national culture but also of its firm roots in the universal Christian tradition.

Eben's next work for orchestra was written six years later. Entitled *Noční hodiny (Night Hours),* it is a symphonic concerto for wind quintet, tenor tuba, string orchestra, piano and percussion, written in 1975 to a commission by the Leipzig Radio. In 1987 its composer was to produce a version with children's chorus. In contrast to the strong impact of *Vox Clamantis,* whose one movement format is easy to follow, this new work consists of five movements and takes twenty-five minutes to play. It is more colourful and more varied, as is the style of its composition. Its basic idea is a musical portrayal of five phases of night, in which people amuse themselves, love and dream, listen to the night sounds and finally wake to face a new day. Eben's style is basically tonal but several more stylistic planes are integrated into it in order to portray everyday life during the particular periods. There is an imitation of jazz, an old night watchman's song, a chromatic arrangement of the folk song *Lásko, Bože, lásko...(My love, God, my love...)* and so on. Other new features make their appearance, such as collage, aleatorics, "dual zoning" (that is separate strands of music sounding together), quartertones and onomatopśia (for example, the ticking of the clock in the fourth movement, gradually growing louder and louder). This polystylistic development corresponds to a similar trend in the other areas of Eben's output. For instance, his *Pragensia,* written three years earlier, contains a number of elements, ranging from dodecaphony and aleatoric passages to many echoes of old music and of the techniques of Renaissance composers. The work stands out among his output to date as stylistically most colourful and diverse.

After an eight-year pause came the single movement *Pražské nokturno* (1983). In contrast to the earlier work, it reduced the multiplicity of stylistic features to a much narrower range in keeping, once again, with its basic programmatic idea. It lasts eighteen minutes and was written to a commission by the Salzburg Festival. It sets out to look at Mozart's personality through the eyes of a late twentieth century musician. Eben focuses on a certain melancholy in Mozart's final years, rather than the proverbial brilliance and spontaneous joy of his music generally. It is for this reason that he prefaces the score with a quotation from a letter written by Mozart half a year before his death in which he speaks of his feelings of sadness and depression. Eben gets to the core of his chosen idea by scoring the work for a Mozartian orchestra, by incorporating a number of special instrumental effects, as from the opening chords, which start as simple triads but are gradually "sharpened" by the addition of more and more discordant notes, to the "French octaves" in the woodwind, ornamentation etc., but also by adopting two Mozartian themes - the opening of the *Fantasia in c minor (KV.475)* of 1785 for piano, which he uses in the dramatic middle section, plus a *Minuet in A♭ (KV.109b)*, composed by Mozart in London in 1762 when he was eight years old and quoted at the end of the work on the celesta at an independent tempo as a breath of nostalgic air of the purity of childhood. The tonal language of the work is broadened to include elements of polytonality. In order to heighten the feeling of anxiety, Eben also uses quartertones in the upper strings, as well as his well-tried "dual zone" method.

In 1995, twelve years after the *Pražské nokturno*, came Eben's next symphonic work, his *Improperia*, commissioned by the Czech Philharmonic Orchestra for its centenary and first performed in Prague during that jubilee season. The work lasts about twenty minutes and is in three movements: *Con emozione crescente, Andantino timoroso* and *Allegro impetuoso*. It is a sum of Eben's symphonic style to date. Its basic idea, the *Improperia* of the Good Friday liturgy, is the Saviour's reproaches to His chosen people which have not always and devotedly followed His path. The work differs from Eben's earlier pieces in a number of ways. It does contain certain elements of multi-style writing, such as the saxophone solo in the middle movement, and it draws on the composer's favourite source of quotations - the Gregorian chant, as in the Good Friday liturgy heard in the last movement. Yet, of all his symphonic works this, on the whole, is the most homogeneous. Its three movements are made up of broad, continually developing stretches of music within an extended tonal system, eschewing the various colour, sound and structural embellishments of the *Noční hodiny* or the *Pražské nokturno* and keeping to a traditional kind of sound and terse working out of the thematic material. The use of the Gregorian chant is typical of Eben and his lifelong path. The impressive coda of the final movement is built up from a section of the chant to the words *Svatý Bože, smiluj se nad námi (Holy God, have mercy upon us)*.

Taking Petr Eben's symphonic, or more strictly orchestral, output from 1969 to 1995 together, several features common to all these compositions come to the fore. First, they all have a clear programme, in each case formulated by the composer in writing and projected into the musical structure of the composition. Next, they all endeavour to integrate a wide span of stylistic planes into the work, including a number of quotations which make clear sense to the listener and which spring from the depths of the European musical tradition, ranging from the Gregorian chant to imitations of present day popular music. Lastly, they each have a well-targeted function which dictates the way the quotations or quasi-quotations are used - always in a palpable, literal sense flowing from the programmatic base of the work.

For the sake of completeness, it is necessary to mention works in which Eben integrates the symphony orchestra into a large frame. *Organ Concerto No.2* of 1982, together with *No.1 (Symphonia gregoriana)* are dealt with in greater detail by John Browne in these pages. Of his concerted works so far, that leaves the *Piano Concerto* dating from 1960-61, whose first interpreter and inspirer was the composer's own piano teacher at the Prague Academy, František Rauch. It is in three movements, lasting roughly twenty-six minutes, which, on the one hand, adheres to traditional concise thematic work, especially so in the first movement, while, on the other, seeks new and less conventional ways of writing for the solo instrument, for example in the way that the whole of the second movement is built up from trills and tremolos. The orchestra appears in a more independent rôle only at the beginning of the second movement whereas, for the rest, it forms a counterweight to the dominant piano.

Finally there are the cantatas and oratorios in which Eben employs the orchestra. The first two of these are cantatas belonging to his earliest period as a composer. They are the folk-like *Balady (Ballads)* for soli, mixed chorus and orchestra *(O svatých a hříšnících (Saints and Sinners)* written between 1953 and 1957, being first performed in 1958), consisting of three parts. The first, *Porada*, is on a folk poem of Karel Jaromír Erben, the second, *Balada rytířská*, is on Silesian folk poetry, while the third, *Dívka a džbán*, is on Czech folk poetry. The other is the similarly conceived *Píseň o kalině (The Song about a Guelder-Rose)* for soli, male and female choruses and orchestra of 1960. The oratorio *Apologia Sokratus* for baritone and alto soloists, children's and mixed choruses and orchestra of 1967, in contrast to the two earlier cantatas, is a work of deepest consequence. Plato's text in defence of Socrates, set to music in its original Greek, had inspired the composer to write one of the most significant works of his middle period. The work lasts nearly forty minutes and is divided into three movements prefaced with a prologue. It leans heavily on its vocal forces, with the orchestra supplying the necessary support. The orchestral sound is reduced by the omission of the upper strings but at the same time it is enriched by the inclusion of several stringed and percussion instruments such as the piano, harp, cimbalom and xylophone.

Eleven years later, in 1978, came a new cantata, *Pocta Karlu IV (Homage to Charles IV)* for male voice choir and orchestra. Eben wrote it for the six hundredth anniversary of the death of the Emperor and founder of Charles University in Prague. He used the words of the foundation charter of the University, setting them in an austere archaic style corresponding to the text's character and age.

In 1992-93 Eben wrote the large-scale oratorio *Posvátná znamení (Sacred Signs)* for soprano and baritone soloists, mixed chorus, children's chorus, organ (two organs *ad libitum*), wind ensemble and percussion. The work lasts half and hour and was written for Salzburg Cathedral. The composer distributed the musical forces among the cathedral's four choir galleries, thus making its layout part of the overall effect of the work. He used texts from both the Old and New Testaments, as well as from the liturgy, introducing each movement with quotations from the writings of Romano Guardini. The work's centre of gravity is the multi-faceted vocal component, while the instrumental element is reduced to woodwind, brass and percussion instruments with rich input from the organ. Where the availability of two instruments and the space allows it, the organ part can be split into two mutually corresponding parts.

Petr Eben has always considered his orchestral writing to be important, sometimes regretting the success of his organ and choral works in as much that this has resulted in more and more requests and commissions in these areas, thus precluding the opportunity to write more for the orchestra. Therefore news of a recent commission of a *Violoncello Concerto* from him gives cause for great expectations.

THE ORGAN CONCERTOS OF PETR EBEN

by John Browne

The *Concerto for Organ and Orchestra (Symphonia Gregoriana)[Organ Concerto No.1]* of 1954 has been described by the composer as *an extended symphony with a concertante organ part*[1] and was written as Petr Eben's graduation piece from the Prague Academy of Music. Eben [2] acknowledges his understanding of musical form and architecture to his teacher Pavel Bořkovec and aspects of this neo-classical influence can be seen in the traditional four movement symphonic structure of this work.[3] Janette Fishell[4] further sees the influence of Bořkovec in the sonata form first movement, where the first theme returns as an organ *passacaglia* leading to the development section (Ex.1) and with the inclusion of a solo organ fugue in the recapitulation of the second theme.

---

[1]Preface to the score of *Organ Concerto No.2*, London, United Music Publishers, 1988.

[2]In interview with the composer, 1989.

[3]Šeda, Jaroslav, (translated by J.A. Hanc) in the Preface to *Concerto for Organ and Orchestra*, Prague, Panton, 1961.

[4]Fishell, J.,: *The Organ Music of Petr Eben*, unpublished dissertation, Illinois, Northwestern University, 1988.

Ex.1 *Organ Concerto No.1*: First Movement

This *Concerto* demonstrates a number of characteristics of Eben's own emerging style: bi-tonality, *ostinati*, the integration of plainchant themes and tertiary relationships. An example of bi-tonality can be seen in the first movement where the first theme, an organ *ostinato* on D♭, becomes the accompaniment for the c minor second theme in the strings:

36

Ex.2 *Organ Concerto No.1*: First Movement

The use of plainchant forms a threat running right through Eben's organ output and the second movement of *Organ Concerto No.1* is based on the plainchant Litany of the Saints.[5]

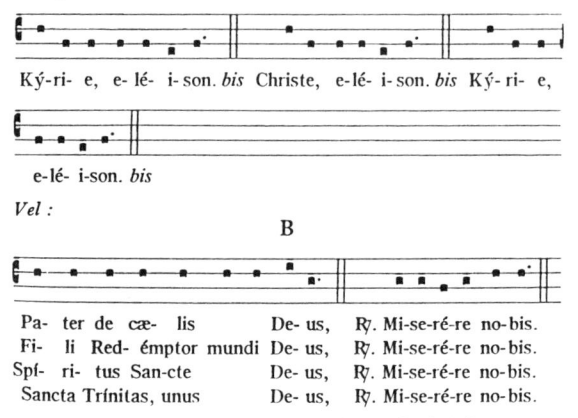

Ký-ri- e, e- lé- i- son. *bis* Christe, e-lé- i- son. *bis* Ký- ri- e,

e-lé- i-son. *bis*

Vel :

B

Pa- ter de cæ- lis   De- us,   ℟. Mi-se-ré-re no-bis.
Fi- li Red- émptor mundi De- us,   ℟. Mi-se-ré-re no-bis.
Spí- ri- tus San-cte   De- us,   ℟. Mi-se-ré-re no-bis.
Sancta Trínitas, unus   De- us,   ℟. Mi-se-ré-re no-bis.

Ex.3 *Litaniæ Sanctorum (Litany of the Saints)*

The chant is treated as a series of dialogues following the plainchant original. This reaches a climax on a pedal G and leads *attacca* into the e minor third movement, an example of a tertiary relationship, which is based on the *Agnus Dei* from the same liturgy, set very simply on divisi strings.

Agnus De- i, qui tol-lis peccá- ta mundi. ℟. Mi-se- ré-re

no- bis. *ter*

Christe, audi nos. *bis* Christe, ex-áudi nos. *bis* Ký-ri- e, e-lé-

i-son. Christe, e-lé- i-son. Ký-ri- e, e- lé- i-son.

Ex.4a *Litaniæ Sanctorum (Litany of the Saints)*

---

[5]Landale, Susan,: The Organ Music of Petr Eben, in *The American Organist*, December 1979.

Ex.4b *Organ Concerto No.1*: Second Movement

The brilliant *Allegro vivace* finale derives its thematic material from a motif stated in octaves by the orchestra and the work ends on a note of exuberance.

The commission to write an organ concerto for the inauguration of the new organ in the ORF (Austrian Radio) Concert Hall in Vienna in 1983 gave Eben an opportunity to write a true concerto for organ and orchestra. Composers in the late twentieth century have found a number of solutions to the textural problems of writing a concerto for an instrument which can match an orchestra both in dynamic range and colour. Francis Poulenc in his *Organ Concerto* of 1938 and Andrzej Panufnik in his *Metasinfonia* of 1978 used only strings and timpani to balance the full range of the organ, whereas the concertos of Anton Heiller (1964) and Paul Hindemith (1962) carefully integrated the organ with a full orchestra. The *Organ Concerto No.2* of Petr Eben, written in 1983, like the *Concerto* of 1953, avoids the woodwind and is scored for 2 horns, 2 trumpets, 2 trombones, timpani, percussion and strings.

Organ Concerto No.2 can be divided into two main sections but forms an integrated four movement symphonic form. The first section contains an opening *Allegro*, slow movement and short *Scherzo*, framed by an Introduction and Coda of spaced out chords. The second section is the *Finale*, in which *runs and grace-notes give bite and aggressiveness to the main themes* and where *pulsating quavers provide a rhythmical underlay to the virtuoso stylisation of the organ part.*[6]

In the introduction of *Organ Concerto No.2* a mood of tense expectation is created by the organ and orchestra dialogue of irregularly spaced *Maestoso* chords. A sustained *klangfarbenmelodie* type solo line alternating between non vibrato vibraphone (i.e. fans off), solo violin, trumpet and viola links these chords which contract, five bars before Fig.3[7], to form one of the main themes of the work (Theme 1) based on an old Slovak melody:[8]

---

[6] In the Preface to the score of *Organ Concerto No.2*.

[7] The rehearsal figure number references refer to those in the full orchestral score and not those in the published organ short score.

[8] The words of this Slovak folk song are *Vyletel vták hore nad oblaky, mal on perie nado všetky vtáky, nado všetko stvorenie.* (*A bird was flying over the clouds. He had feathers more beautiful than all the other birds, than all the other creatures*).

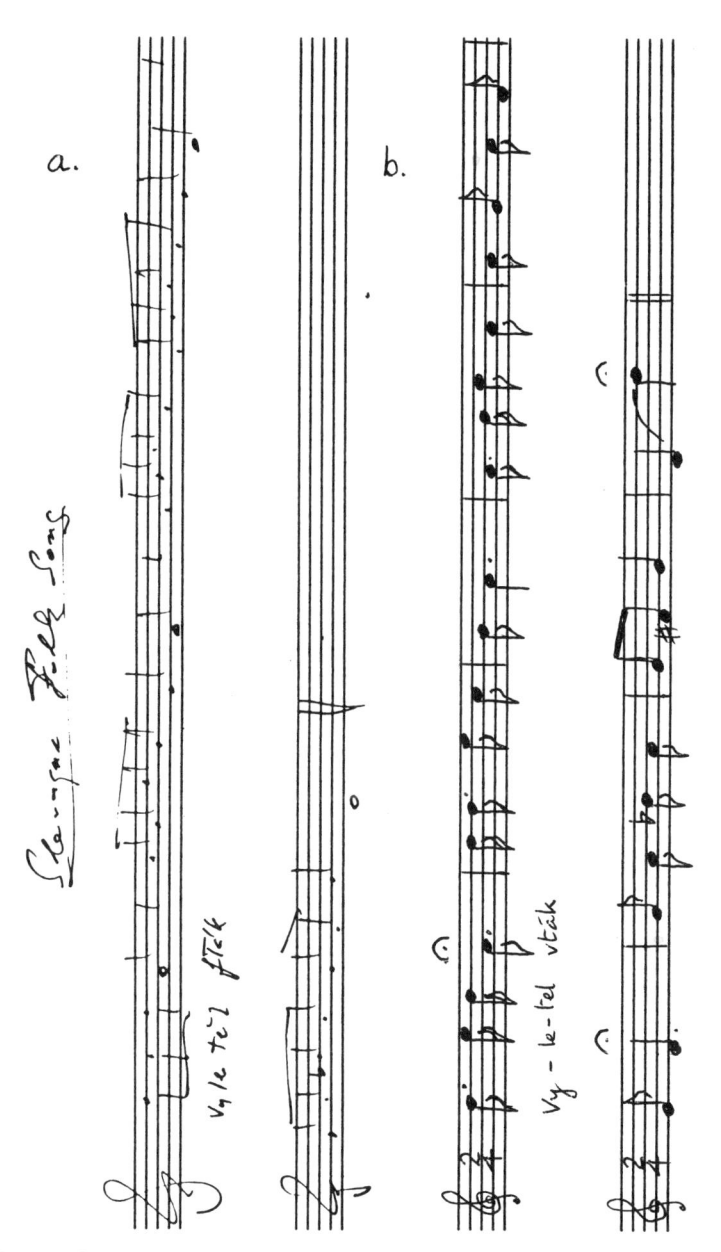

Ex.5 *Slovak Folk Song* (a. composer's manuscript, b. according to Mikuláš Schneider-Trnavský)

The two contracted chordal statements of Theme 1 on D, five bars before Fig.3 and at Fig.16, provide the main tonal areas of the movement. The first statement on the organ, now without reeds, is repeated and extended as an accompaniment to Theme 2 which is introduced *Agitato* on the upper strings playing in unison. Groups of chords alternate between organ, now with 16 foot registers, and strings again polarised against Theme 2 in a bi-metric texture in the second statement.

This bi-metric/aleatoric technique is comparable to that used by other contemporary European composers, such as Lutosławski, and emphasises the distinction between the three elements of organ, strings and brass. Eben consciously places these elements on different planes, contrasting them in thematic material and in time signatures and tempi. In other places he divides the melody and accompaniment between both partners, so that either the organ or the orchestra takes the rôle of a melodic instrument. Figure 1 demonstrates the distribution of the two main themes between the three orchestral elements:

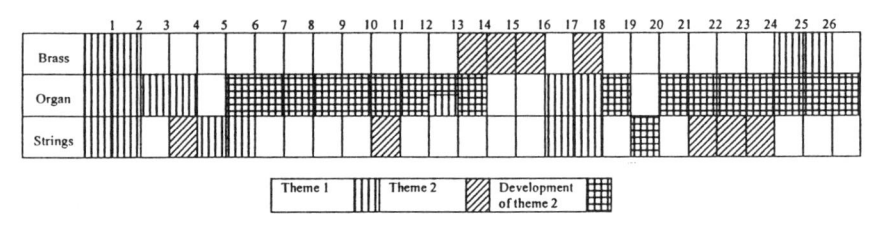

Fig.1 Orchestral distribution of themes in the First Movement of *Organ Concerto No.2*

Theme 2 (Ex.6), announced by unison upper strings, is characterised by an upbeat and a perfect fifth. It is repeated up a tone before unfolding contrapuntally to involve the whole string section. The theme can be divided into four motives that provide much of the material for development in the first section of the *Concerto*.

43

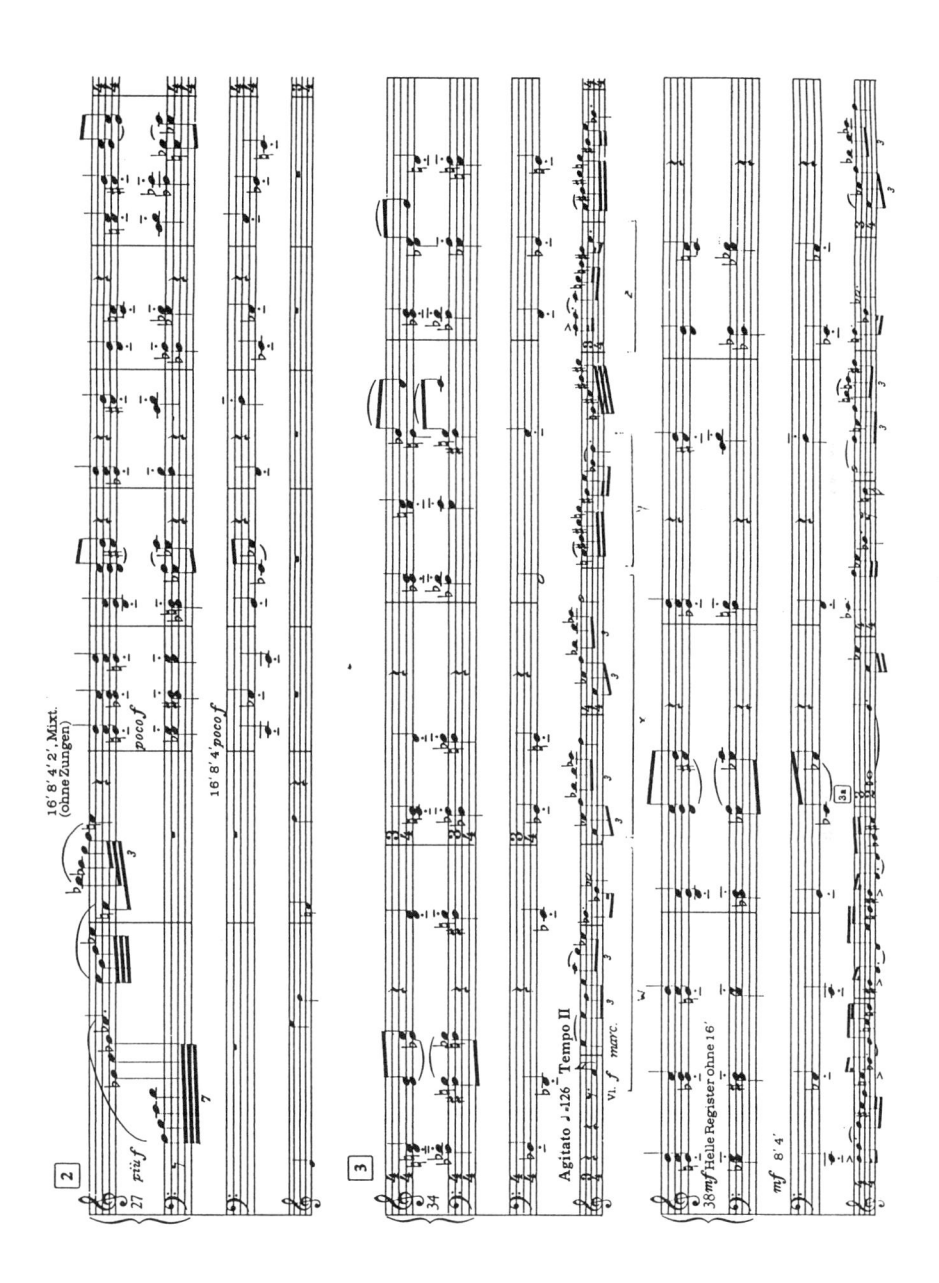

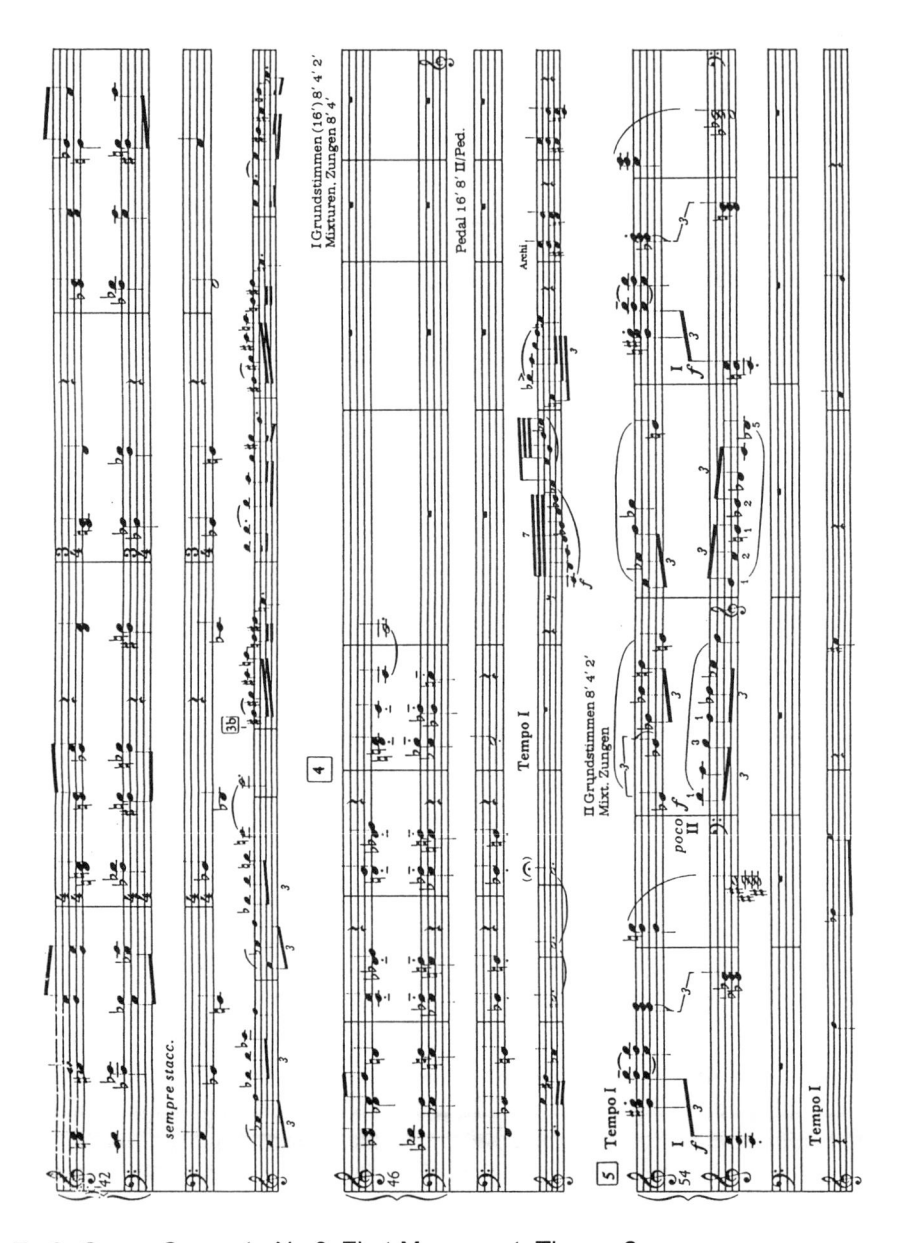

Ex.6 *Organ Concerto No.2:* First Movement, Theme 2

The motifs are transformed in a number of different permutations:

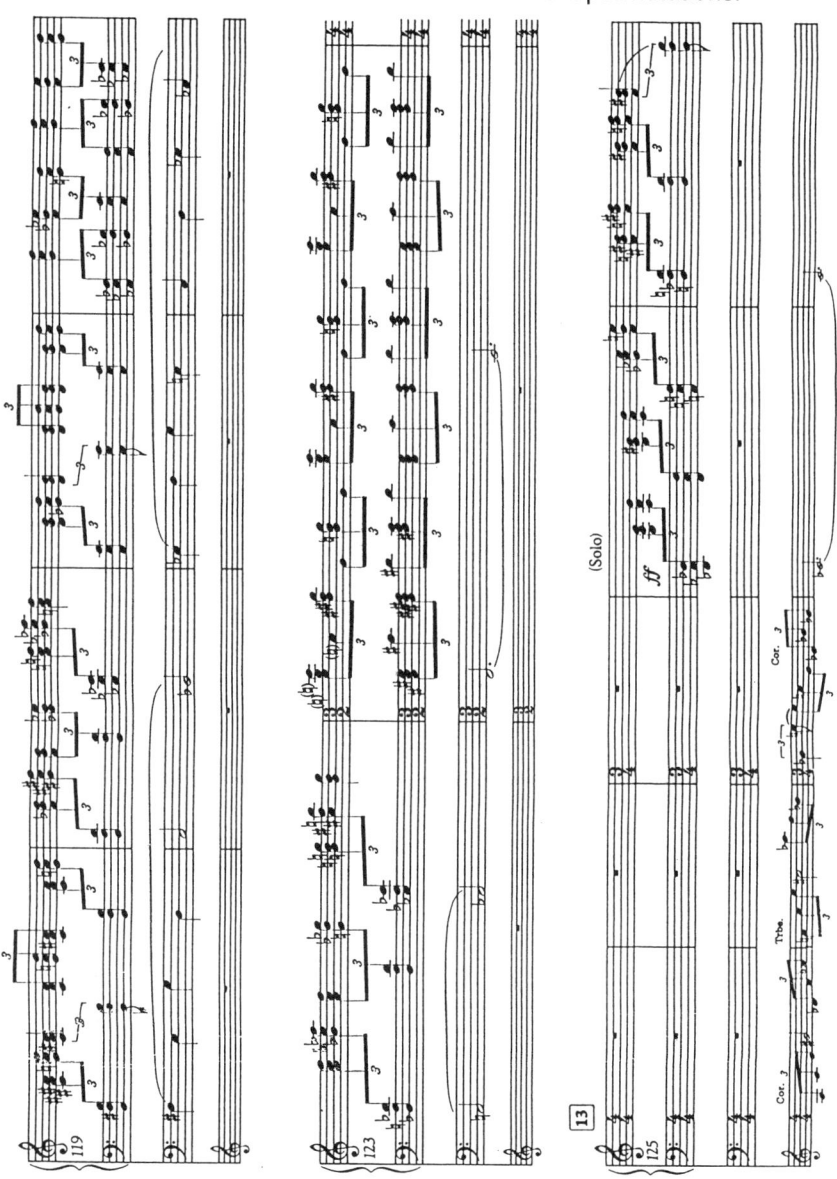

imitation by the brass:

Motif X is:

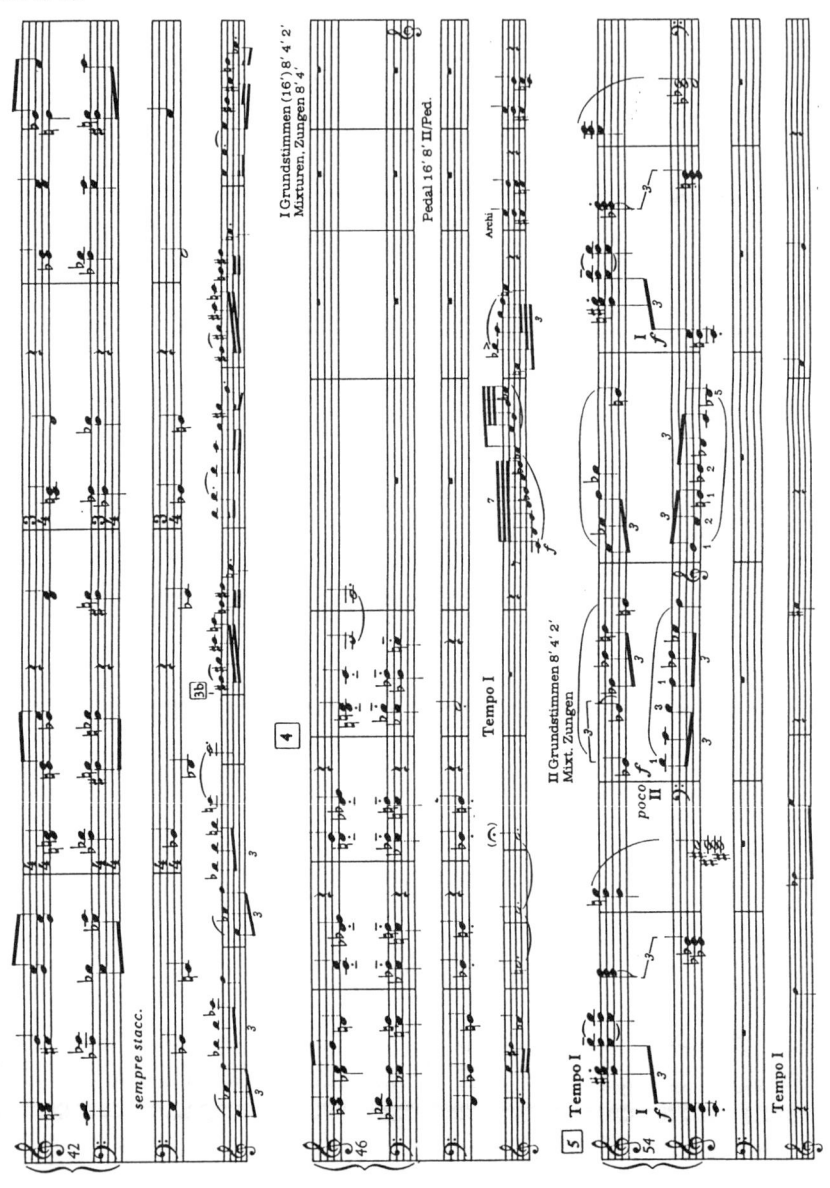

chromatically altered:

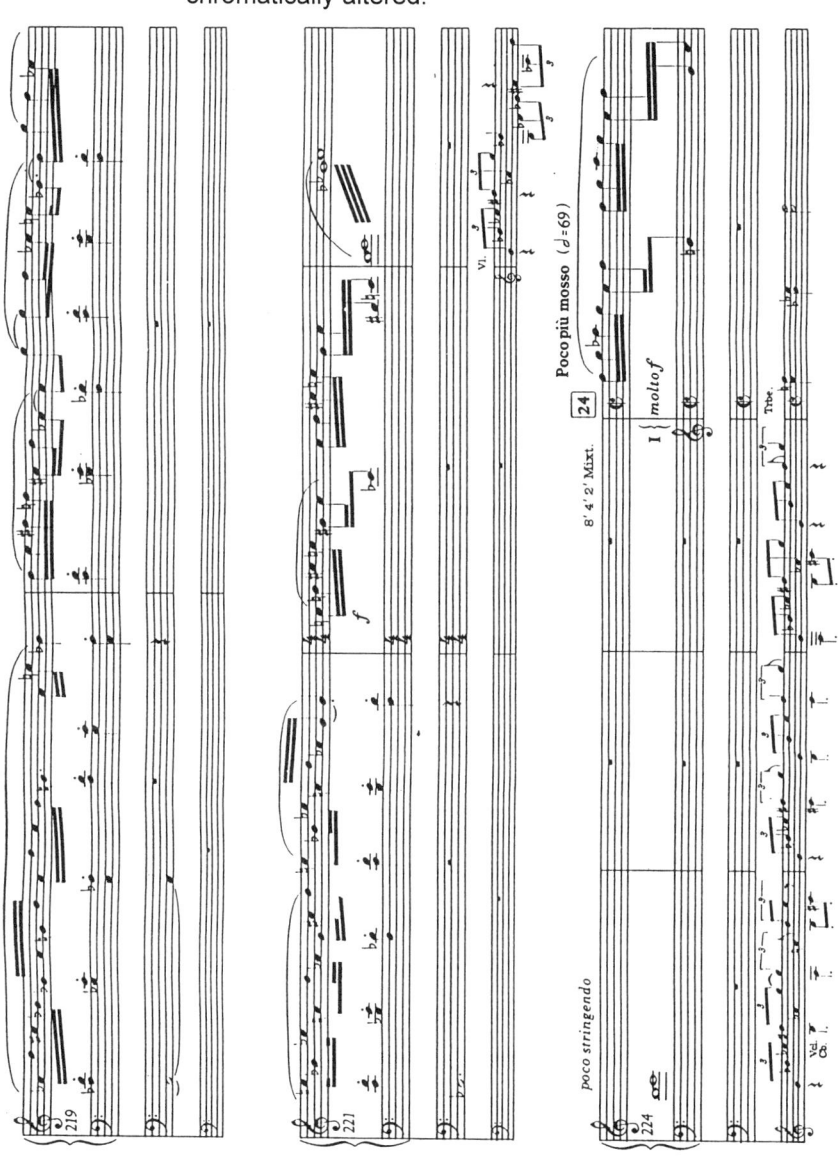

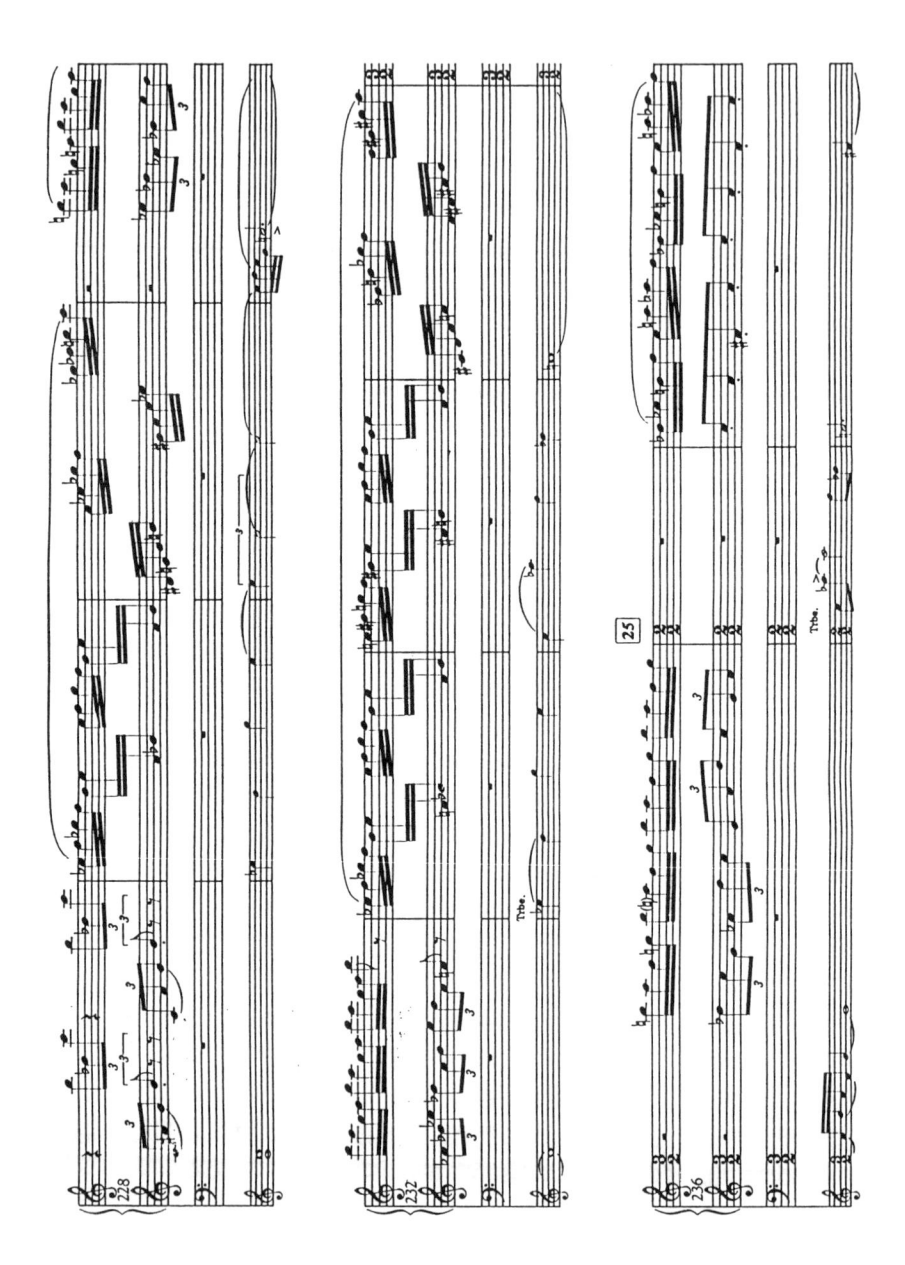

and combined with other material.

Motif Y forms the material for a short section at bar 217 (Fig.23):

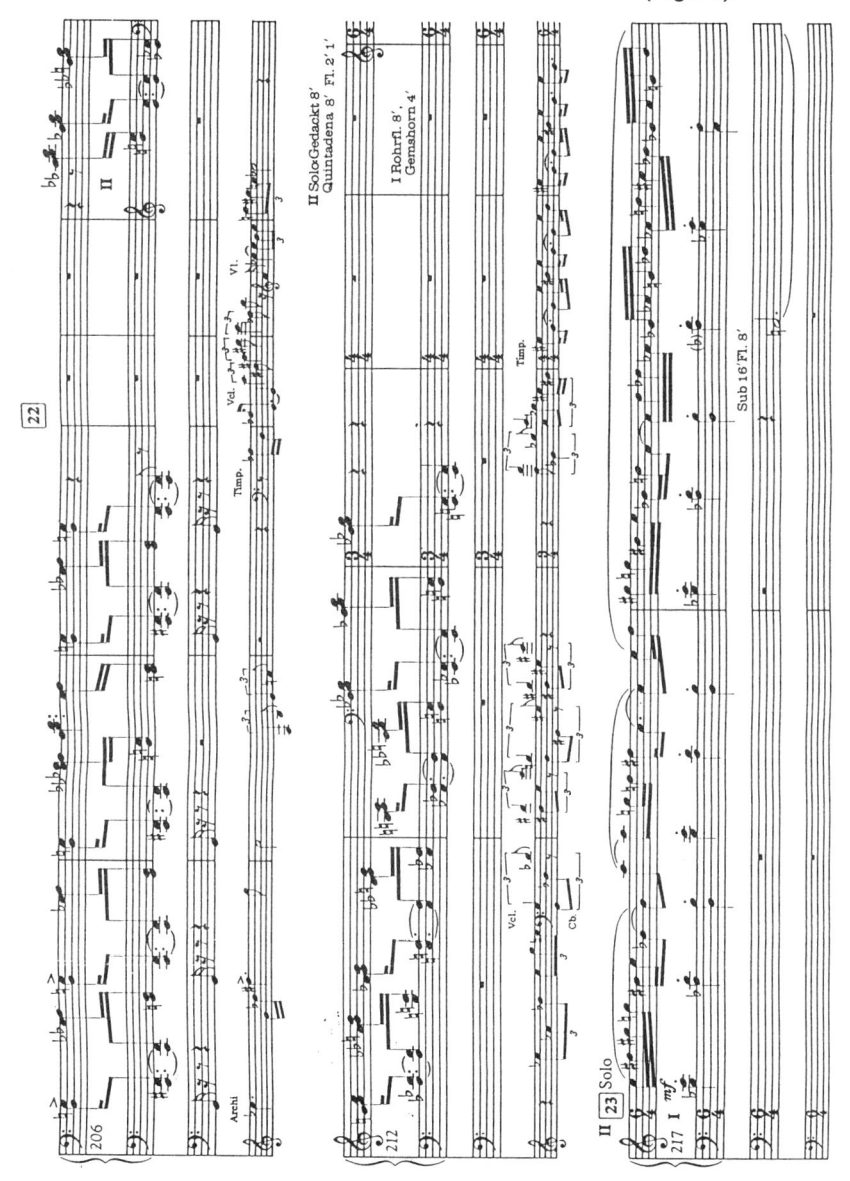

and the short *scherzo* in the second movement (Fig.8).

Motif Z maintains its identity through its rhythm and melodic contour, despite alteration of its melodic intervals:

seen, for example, at Fig.19 in the orchestral writing.

A sense of melodic unity and cohesion is achieved in the first section of the *Concerto* by the use of these different thematic elements presented in a chain of overlapping entries.[9] Besides the long-term relationships outlined here, there are also many short-term connections that bond the musical structure into an evolving musical web.

In contrast to the juxtaposition of blocks of sound in the first movement, the second movement is a melting and mixing of organ and orchestral colours. The two are often indistinguishable. After a long sustained chord, the first two phrases of Theme 1 (Ex.7) are extended sequentially with the addition of folk inspired ornamentation, reminiscent of Balkan pipes and Slovak Fujaras, often outlining the intervals of a seventh.

---

[9] In interview with the composer, 1989.

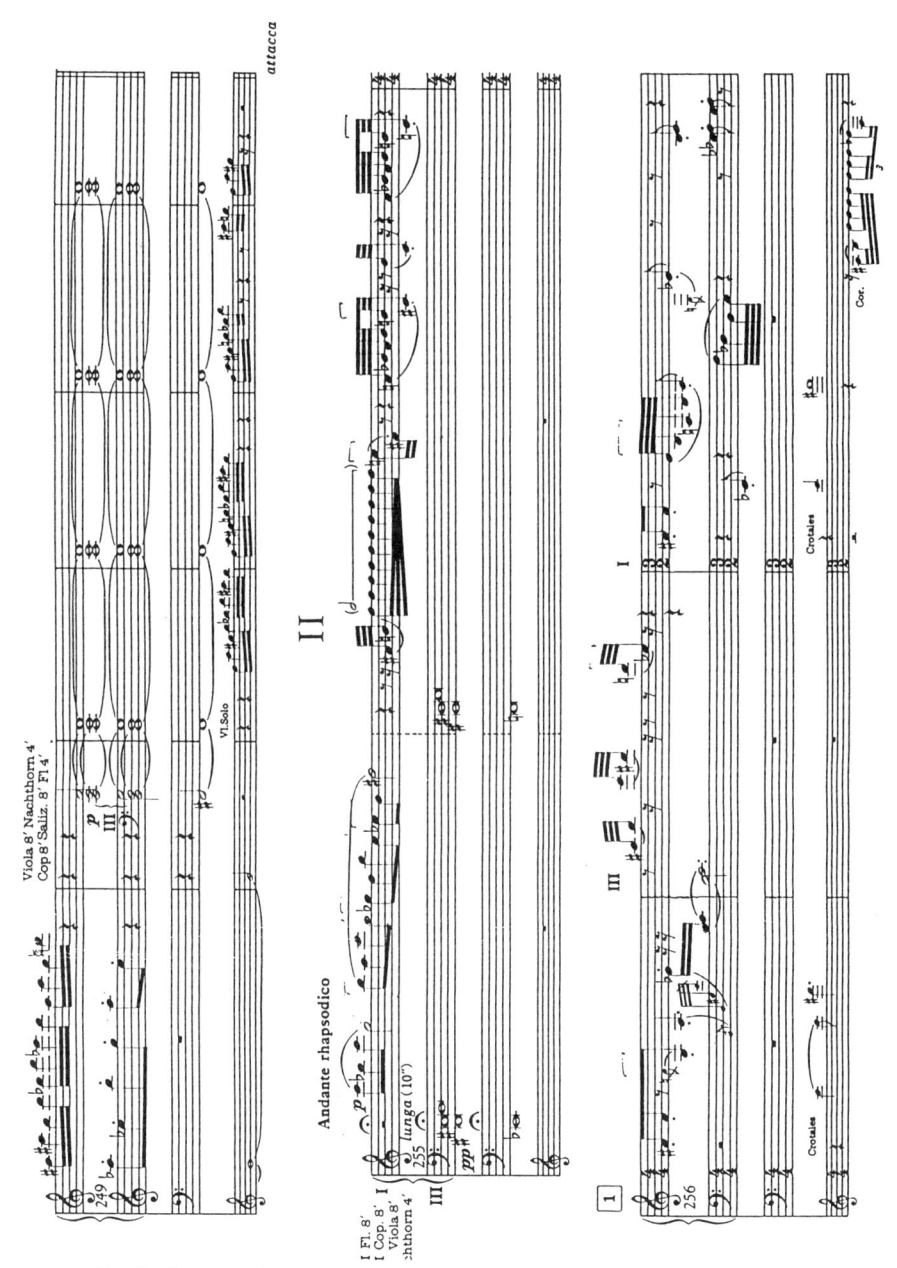

Ex.7 *Organ Concerto No.2:* Second Movement, Theme 1

This material is developed in a variety of ways, including a dialogue between the organ and horn at Fig.1, as an *ostinato* at Fig.2 and this *ostinato* combined with a chromatically altered version of Theme 1 at Fig.4. Eben uses a number of unusual colouristic effects, including crotales, temple blocks, bongos, innovative organ registration and original orchestral scoring, such as the sinister string chords framing the organ part at Fig.2, to blend the worlds of organ and orchestra.

A link into the *Allegretto scherzando* section is provided by a series of overlapping string lines again based on sevenths, two bars before Fig.8. This section almost forms a third movement and is based on motif Y from Theme 2, incorporating the ornaments and sevenths from the folk influenced slow movement.

The theme is built from a repeated two-bar unit repeated three times, melodically extended and then developed as an *ostinato* by the strings against the folk material with tritone *glissandi* on the timpani and double basses. This leads, via another string link in the form of a *ritardando* four bars before Fig.13, to the recapitulation of the opening material. The expectation of the prolonged rests at the start of the *Concerto*, such as after the quavers at bar 13, is resolved here in the Coda, from Fig. 13 in the Second Movement. The rests are filled by fragments of melodic material from the slow movement on the vibraphone, viola, percussion, organ (Flute, 8 foot) and solo violin.

The *finale* opens with an explosion of sound to introduce the main theme which is rhythmically aggressive and characterised by runs and grace notes. Drive and emphasis is added to the irregular groupings of this theme by a motif on the timpani outlining a tritone, for example at Fig. 2 and Fig.4. The employment of the timpani in this movement provides an example of the use of motifs to bind this movement together. For example, the percussion rhythm at Fig.1 provides the rhythm for the trumpet and horn chords which are set against the main theme on the organ at Fig.2. An interesting textural effect is provided by the violins from Fig.2, which occasionally depart from a smooth *legato* line to add high grace-notes to the organ part.

Ex.8 *Organ Concerto No.2*: Third Movement

The second principal section of the movement is characterised by the rapid oscillation of notes between different sections of the organ, which is a typical characteristic of the composer's organ style. From Fig.8 this is used as an *ostinato* against a theme in the strings which is repeated and then rhythmically distorted.

A new motif (Ex.9) appears on the trumpet at Fig.11 and is taken forward in counterpoint to the main theme at Fig.13, appearing in various rhythmic guises.

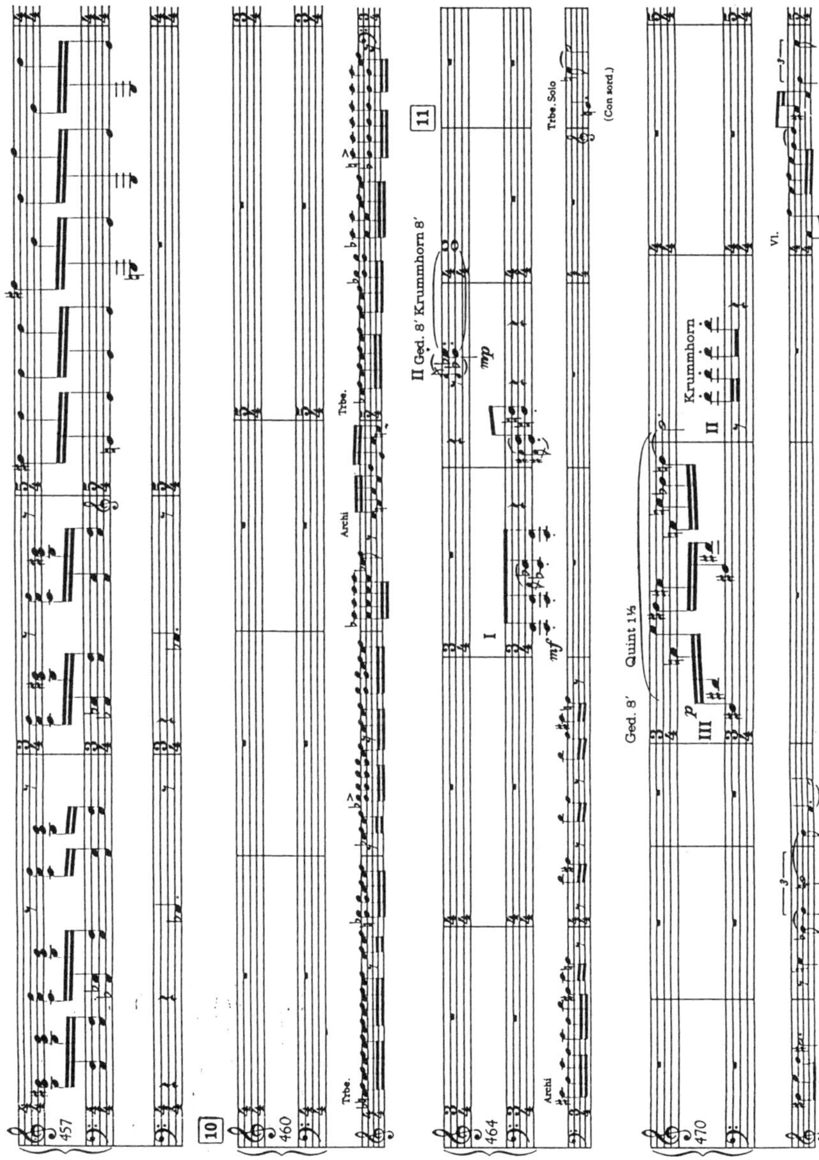
457
10
460
Trbe.
Archi
Trbe.
11
II Ged. 8' Krummhorn 8'
mp
I
mf
464
Trbe. Solo
(Con sord.)
470
Ged. 8'
Quint 1⅓
III
p
Krummhorn
II
Vl.

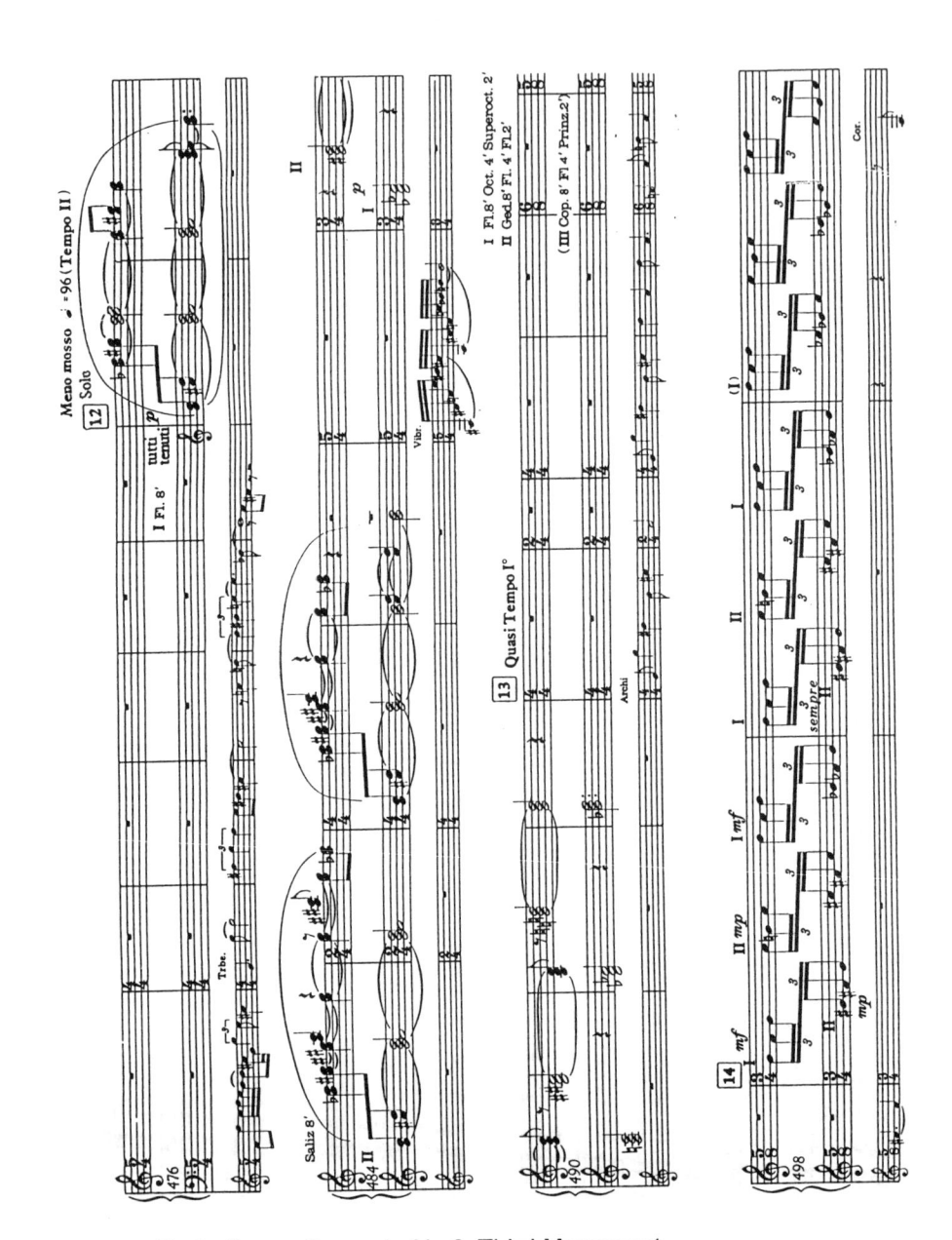

Ex.9 *Organ Concerto No.2*: Third Movement

Statements of this theme on G at Fig.13 and Fig.15 frame a contrasting organ section and demonstrate the use of linear relationships in this movement. A section based on a series of *ostinati* sections leads to what Eben terms as an "organ outcry"[10], melodically outlining a diminished octave, two bars before Fig.17:

---

[10]In interview with the composer, 1989.

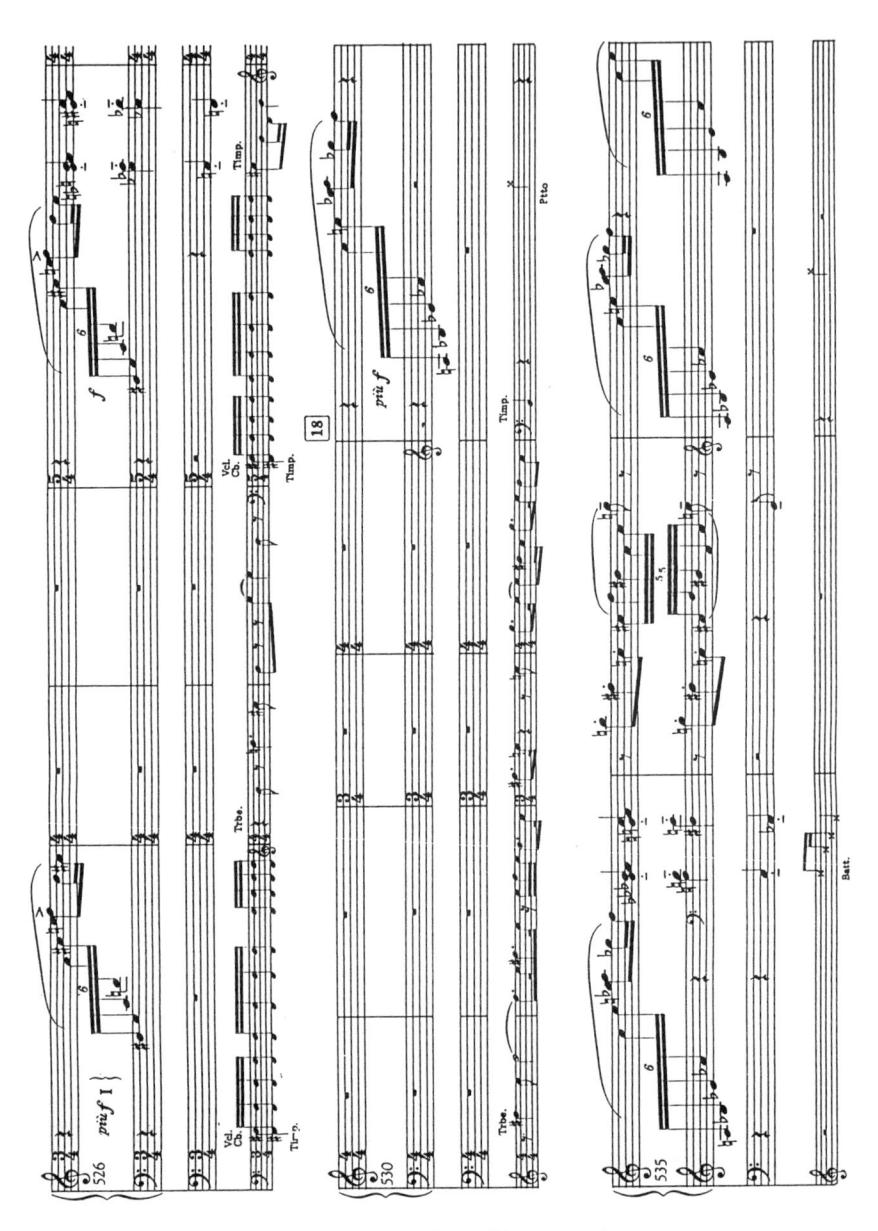

Ex.10 *Organ Concerto No.2*: Third Movement

This "outcry" is combined with a descending seventh figure on the timpani, providing a link with the first movement, developing a series of jagged figures related by stepwise and tertian moves. This culminates in the Coda at Fig.24, where the irregular groupings and time signatures of the *finale* are resolved into duple time. There is almost a military feel here, with the use of the side drum. Several themes are recalled here, including the trumpet motif from Fig.11, the *glissando* motif from the main theme and a chromatically altered version of the folk song from the First Movement, which is combined melodically with the trumpet motif at Fig.29:

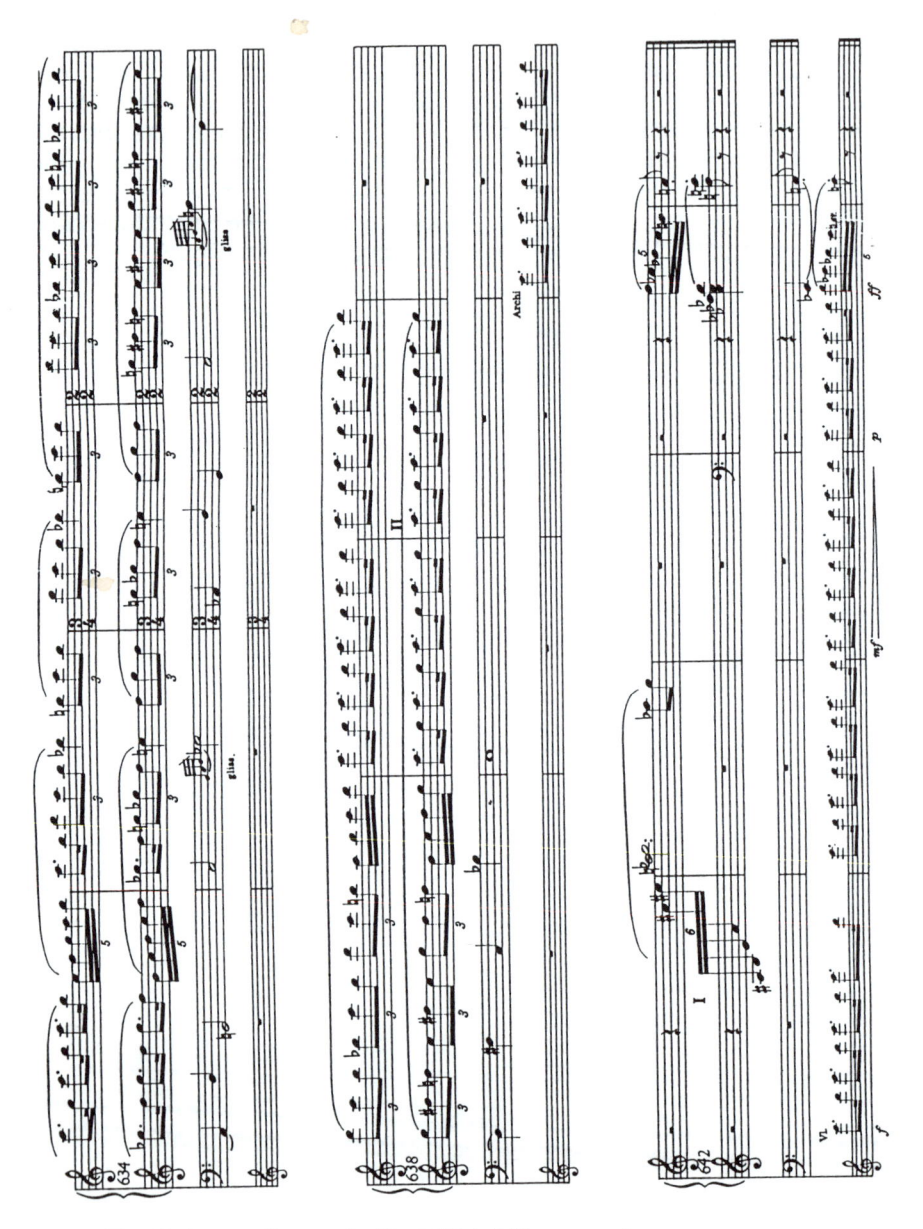

Ex.11 *Organ Concerto No.2*: Third Movement

The interval of the final "outcry" is expanded to an octave, leading to the final *fortissimo* tritone cadence which frames the movement on A, demonstrating a long-term tertiary relationship to the F of the first two movements.

The *Organ Concerto No.2* demonstrates many characteristics of Petr Eben's style: the use of *ostinati*, tertiary relationships, exploitation of timbre and the use of folk music. However, there are also characteristics of a mature and developing composer in the judicious use of dissonance, the consideration of organ timbre on dissonance, the interplay of organ and orchestra and an almost organic development and combination of themes into a truly integrated symphonic structure. This, combined with the more experimental aspects of rhythmic folk notation and bi-metric textures, makes the *Organ Concerto No.2* a serious addition to the organ concerto repertoire, ideally suited and conceived for the modern concert hall.

THOUGHTS ON LAUDES

by Claude Hermitte

Laudes: divine praise and glorifying of Jesus Christ; musical elements and spiritual meaning.

My "Credo" is to convey a message...

In his cycle *Laudes* for organ, Petr Eben entrusts to his favourite instrument the expression of one of his deepest convictions:

Today's world voices only reproach and discontent, so it is Art that must assume the urgent task of opening a spiritual path to man and confronting him with the eternal mystery of Christ.

Thus, for Eben, music must have a purpose and is not merely abstract or decorative. It must speak to the listener, incite him to reflection and provoke in him a reaction. In this way it meets a veritable need of mankind. In the music of Petr Eben, sincerity and expressiveness combine in communicating a profound inner radiance. It was this sincerity, so strongly perceived at our first meeting, which inspired me to undertake this study.[1]

One of the ever-surprising things about Petr Eben is the *joy* which, even in the shortest telephone call, emanates from his voice and personality, as though reflecting a life full of happiness and creativity in a world of peace and light. It is a joy which may indeed seem childlike or naïve (is not a child's naïvety vital to the adult mind?) but which radiates vitality and strength and is luminous, vivifying and always positive. His voice gives courage in adversity and a new energy to overcome distress. Like his music, it can even draw tears of joy as it evokes the beauty of the world and the intense desire to live. This voice which echoes on the telephone like the harmonies which fill the cathedral of Sv.Vít in Prague, is a voice that is striking in its simplicity (so necessary in today's over-sophisticated society), a voice which reminds us of basic values and encourages us to follow the path of sincerity and truth. Like a ray of sunshine through the prevailing

---

[1]This article is made up of extracts from an extensive doctoral thesis of 1998: *Petr Eben, 20th. century harmonist; tradition and message in Czech contemporary music.*

cloud, it reinforces our will to strive for a better and more compassionate world.

Like his voice and his personality, the music of Petr Eben never fails to enrich the listener, bringing him comfort, strength, renewed energy and inspiration. It thus transcends the mere rôle of sound and awakens a particular resonance in each member of its audience. In tune with the eternal charm of the Vltava as it flows through the centre of Prague, it shares the atmosphere of the *city of a hundred spires*.

Composed in 1964, after the *Organ Concerto No.1* (1954) and *Nedělní hudba (Sunday Music)* (1956), *Laudes (Praise)* is Eben's third work for organ and his second for the solo instrument. It was first published in Prague in 1966 by Panton in the second volume of the series *New Compositions for the Organ*, with works by Miloslav Kabeláč, Otmar Mácha, Karel Reiner, Klement Slavický and Miloš Sokola. In subsequent editions the cycle was published separately, by Panton in 1975 and by United Music Publishers, London, in 1979.

Its message is one of praise and thankfulness to the Creator amid the ingratitude of the world today. In his introduction to the work Eben writes:

> *I believe that our century is profoundly lacking in gratitude; gratitude to those around us, to life itself and above all to its Creator. There are complaints, grievances, contention and perhaps even indolence but no gratitude at all. So perhaps the most urgent task of Art is to praise, otherwise "the stones would cry out".*

The characteristics common to each movement are carefully explained by the composer:

> *In each movement you will find two ideas, two parts; the first setting the mood and atmosphere from which Praise will spring up in the second. Similarly, each movement has its own Gregorian theme.*

We can see at once the importance of the structure of each movement in its rôle of conveying the sense of the music: each *Laud* is conceived in a *crescendo*, which ensures the continuity of the Act of Praise and leads the listener towards the divine light, recaptured and eternal.

In the first movement, the rhapsodical and majestic *Largo* is followed by a *Con moto (quasi doppio movimento)* in which the *Praise* is voiced by the Easter *Alleluia*, rising step by step towards its original plainsong form. After a brief *cadenza*, the two ideas unite in a triumphant conclusion.

The calm and concentrated *Lento* of the beginning of the second movement, on a Gregorian *Gloria patri*, is followed by a joyful *allegro* and an outburst of Praise in a dance rhythm. A return to the "secret silence" of the opening concludes the piece.

The *Fantastico* of the third movement is mysterious and strange; the *agitato* section offers Praise in an ecstatic improvisation on the jazz trumpet.

The final movement opens with a sombre *Gravemente*, whose sinister chords are slashed by violent interjections of the Gregorian melody *Christus vincit (Christ has vanquished)* reduced to its barest skeleton. In the *piu mosso* the theme gradually emerges towards the final triumph.

Petr Eben considers his musical language as a veritable means of communication, expressive, sensitive and vibrant. His principal source - and particularly in *Laudes* - is the Gregorian chant which, through the centuries, has allied faith and musical practice. The choice of themes in *Laudes* and the order in which they appear are significant.

First movement: the Easter *Alleluia*, a song of thanksgiving to Christ for his sacrifice, radiant and glorious Praise after the suffering endured, bidding us to praise and magnify the Lord of Majesty.

Second movement: *Gloria patri (Glory be to the Father)*, glorifying God in silence and meditation. In this movement Eben also introduces a chorale melody, stemming from another liturgical tradition, which he combines with a rhumba rhythm in an enthusiastic burst of Praise.

Third movement: *Lauda Sion (Praise O Sion thy salvation)* praising the city of God's Temple. Here the song of Praise seems to interrogate the divine mystery and then venerate the work of God's hand.

Fourth movement: finally the *Christus vincit*, the praise of Christ victorious, reigning for eternity. In His image, Praise breaks out in spite of suffering and adversity and triumphs over all.

Another important source of Eben's inspiration is that of folk music, which he has researched in detail and harmonized extensively in a number of volumes. He thus draws attention to the rich heritage of his native country and initiates a free use of folk song in some of his most significant compositions. Also to be found in his music, whose source is traditional and has particular reference to the organ, is improvisation. An example is to be found in the opening of the first movement of *Laudes*.

Other characteristics of Eben's style are: carefully chosen colours, subtle registrations - even seeking electro-acoustical effects, chromaticism, expanding of tonal harmony, free use of bitonality and atonality. A master of traditional counterpoint, he also employs rapid manual changes for *sforzando* and echo effects.

He exploits the art of variation in *Laudes* at several levels:

- variation on a repeated bass (*passacaglia* - *Laudes III*)
- combining or mixing two themes in different tempi (*Laudes III*)
- variation of melodic intervals (*Laudes I*)
- moving between modal and tonal harmony (*Laudes I*)

Frequently his bimetrical approach permits a simultaneous musical development on two planes: in two keys (*Laudes IV*), in two or more rhythms (*Laudes III*), or two melodies (*Laudes II*). Eben, in so many ways an innovator, explains this bimetrical technique:

> *I see here a way of taking a step forward. If one were to compare it with other forms of art, perhaps the closest would be the Cubist technique in which the subject is projected simultaneously from different angles, enabling one to see its different sides. Today, now that the ear has become more accustomed to such things, I think it is possible for the listener to follow two simultaneous levels in a piece (of course only from time to time, otherwise it would be tiring and lacking in contrast) and this not only in the sense of loud/soft or low/high but on equal planes, designed to be heard together.*

Nevertheless, the music of Petr Eben, despite its many technical and analytical qualities, largely transcends the means employed by the composer. His music belongs to the realm of expression, going far beyond the simple appreciation of the ear. The remarkable strength of its message springs from the deep sincerity of its author and in his profound faith in the beauty of creation and in the good in mankind.

OKNA - CHAGALL'S WINDOWS ACCORDING TO PETR EBEN

by David Titterington

I believe that our century is profoundly lacking in gratitude: gratitude to those around us, to life itself and above all to its Creator. There are complaints, grievances and perhaps even indolence but no gratitude at all. So perhaps the most urgent task of Art is to praise, otherwise the stones would cry out.

With these words, written in 1964 as a preface to his organ work *Laudes*, Petr Eben reveals the quiddity of that creative force that has inspired a canon of works which will ensure him not only a secure place in the annals of Czech music history but as a worthy successor to the mantle of that great triumvirate of Dvořák, Janáček and Martinů.

Whilst the organ music may constitute but a modest fraction of his total output, Petr Eben has, however, been a faithful and seminal figure in the development and history of twentieth century organ composition. For almost fifty years a constant stream of works for organ have appeared, each hall-marked by its acute awareness of texture, registration and an absolute technical command of the instrument, yet often surprisingly varied in style and subject. For him: *...it is most important to listen to the architecture, the colours, the drive...even if it is a long space* (sic) *of music.*[1] Eben may have eschewed the experimentalism of the 1950's and of the pioneering "Cologne School", of which Ligeti and Stockhausen were the rising stars - *out of the tangible we have created the intangible* - as one of their contemporaries wryly noted, preferring instead to draw on his own rich heritage and culture as a basis for his own musical and intellectual inspiration. It is an inspiration that has, in part, been tempered and influenced not only by those harrowing years as a teenager survivor of the Buchenwald concentration camp but also by a deep and unshakeable Catholic faith and a love of his fellow man.

Writing from Český Krumlov in October 1990, Eben is clearly conscious of how these influences have shaped both his life and work:

---

[1]Personal communication, 20th. August 1988.

Blue for Ruben

Green for Issachar

Red for Zebulon

Gold for Levi

Plate 1   Chagall Windows at the synagogue of the Hadassah-Hebrew University Medical Centre, Jerusalem

> ...in this church (kostel sv. Víta) started my musical career. Now the TV is producing here my composers portrait (sic) and I am glad that I can from this place thank the Divine Creator for the scenarium of my life with its coda of freedom.

In 1976 the first of a series of works for organ and solo instrument appeared - *Okna (podle Marca Chagalla)*.[2] *Okna* is a work that had been long in gestation:

> I had been asked for a long time to write a work for organ and trumpet but somehow didn't have a subject.

That subject was to be found in a book detailing the stained glass of Marc Chagall and in particular the windows of the synagogue of the Hadassah Hospital in Jerusalem.[3] The impact of these "visual arts" evoked in Eben a strong and elemental response, as he himself explained:

> It is possible to comprehend the title of the cycle in the symbolic sense of the word: window as the source of light, window as direction of the view from the twilight of the room to the sky, where the clouds are moving from the concrete reality surrounding us to the world of the imagination.

The scoring for trumpet and organ, perhaps the most perfect and thrilling of all duo combinations, led Eben to experiment not only with matters of texture but also with the indigenous possibilities of each instrument. The trumpet shifts with ease from mellifluously haunting melodies to jagged, screeching fanfares, from the blues to the careering Russian *troika*, while the organ provides a multi-dimensional source of sound with its symphonic range creating a perfect foil. Uppermost in Eben's mind was to address the usual problem of co-ordination.

> My experience with the difficulties of various instruments playing together with the organ - the retard of the organ sound, the distance of the soloists and the dispersion of the acoustic source - partially determined the specific method of

---

[2]*Windows (according to Marc Chagall)*. If translated, the title in English is usually given as *Chagall Windows*.

[3]Leymarie, Jean,: *The Jerusalem Windows: M. Chagall*, New York, George Brazillier Inc., 2nd.Ed., 1973.

composition; it led to a mostly free rhythmic structure of both parts, meeting only in the crossways of syrrhythmic places...

The inclusion of aleatoric sections in each of the four movements is a cleverly contrived solution for both instruments. Liberating one from the other enables both to function as "soloists" yet secure in the knowledge that, at prescribed points in the score, they will come together. This musical serendipity ensures that each performance has not only a spontaneity but also a freshness and vitality that is usually absent from more conventional scores.

The four movements of *Okna* represent a different window, each with a dominant colour. The first is *Blue (Modré okno) [Con moto]*.

Reuben, thou art my firstborn, my might, and the beginning of my strength, the excellency of dignity, and the excellency of power; Unstable as water.... (Genesis 49, vv.3-4)

From the window, the birds in the air and the fish in the water swirl in the undulating and restless organ accompaniment. The trumpet, taking up the opening somewhat plaintive four-note motif, unrelentingly carries the music forward. Chorale-like organ sequences cut in and out of the texture, louder and increasingly persistent whilst the trumpet trills and swoops ecstatically:

*) Je-li použito I/p, hraje levá ruka alt
*) Wird die Pedalkoppel I/p benützt, spielt die linke Hand die Altstimme

Ex.1 *Okna: Blue Window,* Figs. 7 to 9

The sheer momentum of this movement contrasts with the pastoral image of the second, Green, window *(Zelené okno) [Andantino pastorale]*.

> *Issachar is a strong ass couching down between two burdens: And he saw that the rest was good, and the land that it was pleasant;...* (Genesis 49, vv.14-15)

Eben describes this movement as an *oriental pastorale* which is given over to the trumpet in a lazy, blues inspired solo. This is a reverie of contentment and a celebration of nature, in contrast to the movement which follows.

The Red window, *(Červené okno) [Risolouto e drammatico]*, was described by Susan Landale as *a symphony of blazing reds* and this explosive movement in sound and colour is the longest and most developed movement of the work.

> *Zebulun shall dwell at the haven of the sea; and he shall be for an haven of ships; and his border shall be unto Zidon.* (Genesis 49, v.13)

Each instrument spars one against the other, exploiting the total dynamic range and compass of both trumpet and organ. This is Eben at his most creative. The writing for the organ explores every conceivable permutation of pitch, texture and rhythmic device, often simultaneously. In particular it is interesting to note here how this movement recalls similar devices as found, for example, in the third movement of *Laudes* - undulating left hand figurations set against an almost improvised right hand solo. In the earlier work this is conventionally notated, whilst in *Okna* the aleatoric notation yields almost the same effect:

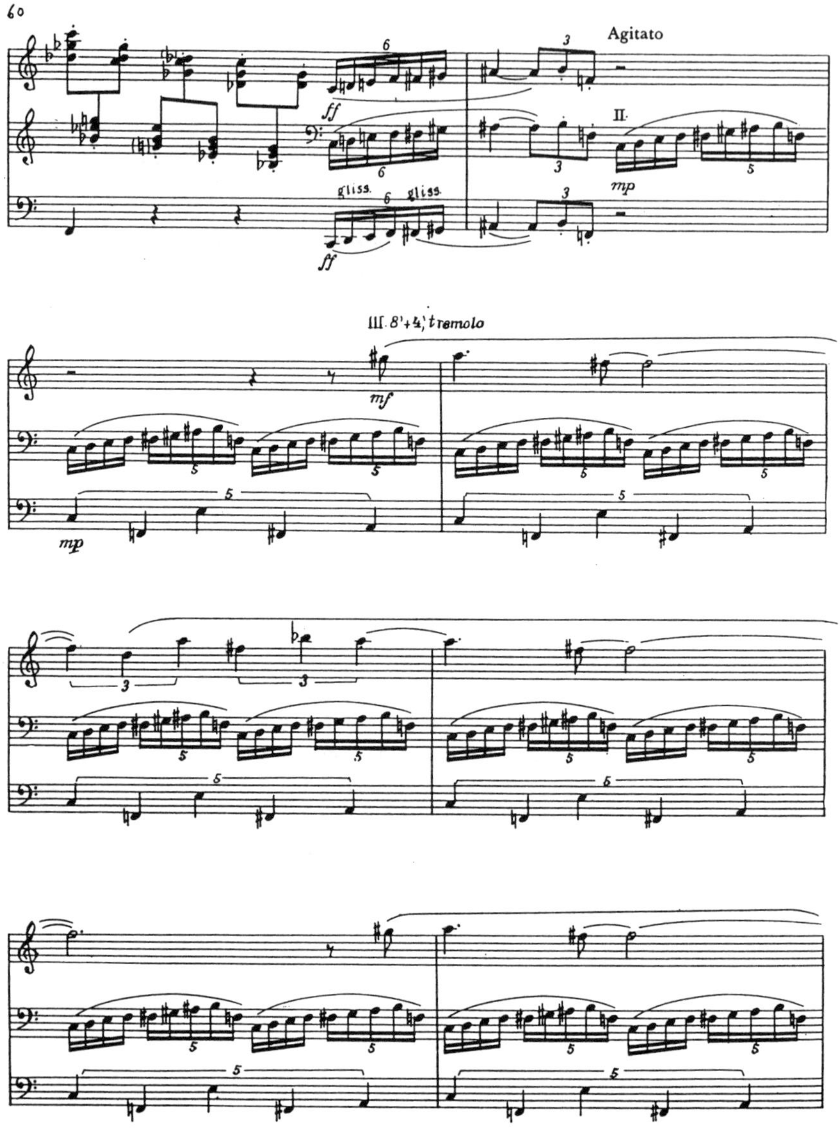

60
Agitato
ff
gliss.
gliss.
II.
mp
III. 8'+4', tremolo
mf
mp

Ex.2 *Laudes:* Third Movement *(Fantastico),* Bars 60-75

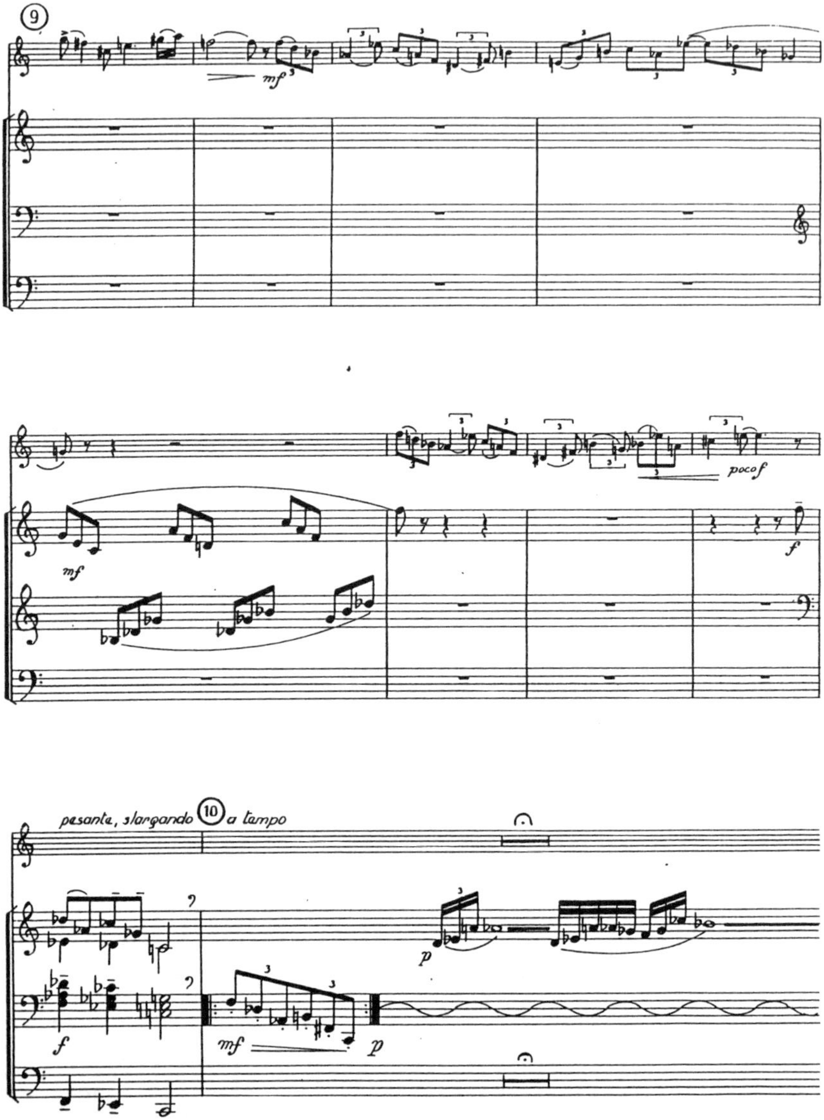
9
mf
poco f
mf
f
pesante, slargando
10
a tempo
p
f
mf
p

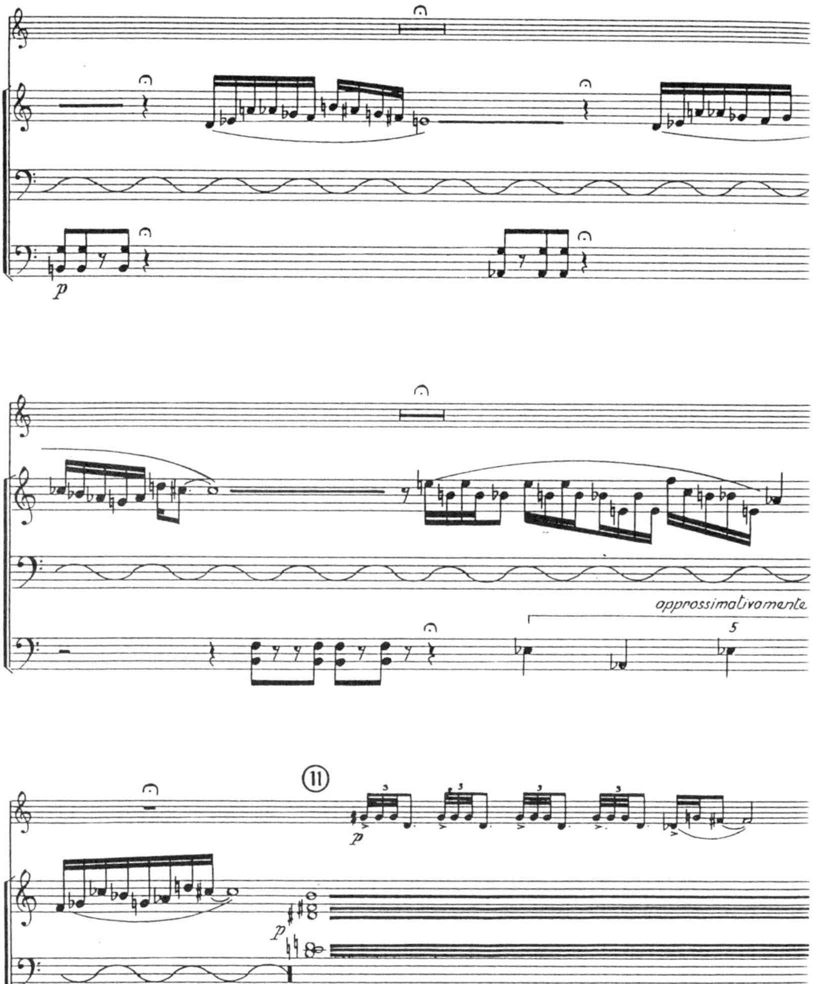

approssimativamente
11

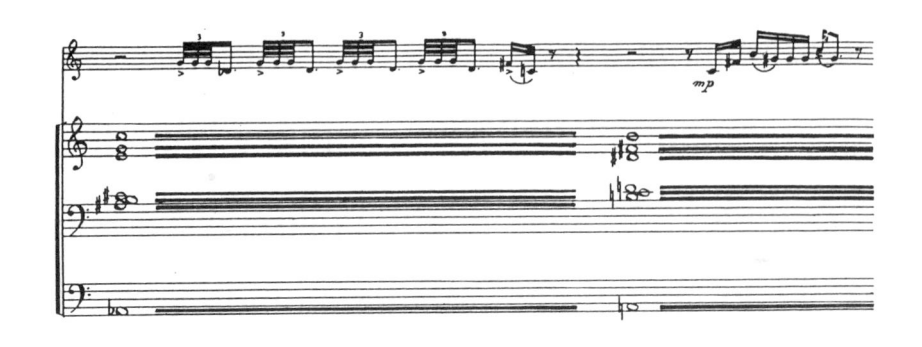

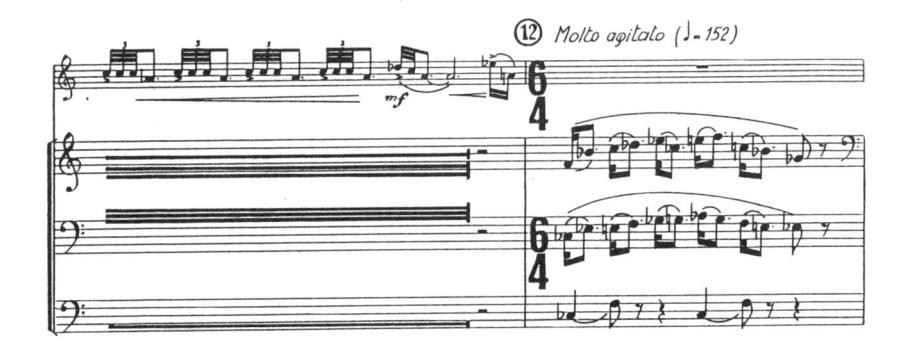

Ex.3 *Okna: Red Window,* Figs. 10 to 12

The final *Gold* window *(Zlaté okno) [Festivo]* - Levi of the twelve tribes of Israel - is the most spiritual of the work in which improvised chant figurations on the trumpet, described by Eben as *a collage of various synagogue chants rather than quotations*, are superimposed onto the well-known theme of Tchaikovsky's *Overture 1812*, itself a direct quote from the Russian Orthodox liturgy and no doubt included as a tribute to Chagall who had been born in Vitebsk. The slow, solemn opening section, like a great ritual bathed in golden candle light "like flamboyant hyacinths", as Chagall described this visual image, yields eventually to a closing and lively *troika*, in which organ and trumpet rally figurations which lead to a glorious and blazing peroration.

Okna has become an important milestone in the development of the trumpet and organ genre, not only from the perspective of technique and idiom but also the genius of realizing the absolute potential of two diverse yet complementary instruments. As Nadia Boulanger pertinently remarked: *A great work is made out of a combination of obedience and liberty.*

PETR EBEN'S WORKS FOR ORGAN WITH OTHER INSTRUMENTS

by Susan Landale

The four movements which make up *Okna (Windows)* of 1976, for trumpet and organ, which must be counted among Petr Eben's masterpieces, has been followed by a number of works for organ with other instruments, all of which date from the nineteen eighties. The choice of instruments is significant. As a composer with a deep knowledge of the organ with its strong and weak points, he is conscious of the limitations imposed upon the organist in a partnership with instruments of softer colours or a smaller dynamic range. Anxious that the resources of the organ should always be used as fully as possible, his favourite choices are brass or percussion. In the *Duo* (7b) which ends *Mutationes* his handling of the two organs carefully avoids the danger of the great organ drowning the smaller one.

Mutationes per organo grande e piccolo

This work was completed in 1980, with the concluding *Duo* added in the following year. During 1979 Eben received two commissions; one from the Welsh Arts Council for an organ work, the other from Universal Edition in Vienna for a set of easy pieces. Attracted by the challenge of using two organs, which was something that he had experienced already from a visit to Oliva cathedral in Poland, he decided to write a single work exploiting the contrasts between two instruments, in style and difficulty, played separately on two instruments or from a single console. The first performance, without the final *Duo*, was given at the Cardiff Festival on 10th. December 1980 by John Scott. On a tour of the United States of America in 1984, the author played the cycle with the composer using one organ for both players.

Mutationes is a set of six pieces in which the players alternate, plus a seventh piece in which the two organs are united. By omitting the finale and ending with a repeat of the first movement, the work may also be played by one organist using one or two organs. The pieces for large organ are written in a virtuoso style, using Eben's characteristic free polytonal harmonic language and registered for mixtures or full organ. The small pieces, on the contrary, are tonal, in the key of A, being more lyrical, even

Plate 2   Petr Eben with Susan Landale, Prague 1977

scherzando which is unusual in Eben's style and comparatively easy for the player. The registration is more detailed, using a more Baroque palette: mutations and softer solo stops. For this cycle Eben also employs a structure which differs from his other works. The climax of *Mutationes* is in the centre, the third piece for great organ, around which he places the shorter movements, framing the whole with the lively rhythm of the first movement and concluding *Duo*.

1. *Impetuoso*: for large organ. An ostinato rhythm of Balkanic origin carries the piece forward with relentless drive. A fleeting quotation from the plainsong *Veni creator* is heard towards the end.

2. *Allegretto* for small organ. A simple melody in a minor is accompanied by repeated chords over a tenuto pedal and gently animated by the little group of semiquavers present in the theme.

3. *Veemente* for manuals only. The second piece for large organ is a brief outburst of arpeggio figures cascading around a progression of bare fifths. These, as they settle on F♯ and C♯, gradually dominate the arpeggios and bring them to a halt.

4. *Scherzando* for small organ. An ostinato of staccato chords accompanies a slow, slightly angular melody, heard in turn in the tenor, soprano, alto and pedal.

5. *Rapsodico* - the centre piece and climax of the suite. The third movement for large organ is in three main sections. A rhetorical recitative of chords over a tenuto cluster in the left hand and pedal followed by an *allegro* of pulsating triplets accentuated by rapid manual changes leads to a third section introduced by a shortened version of the recitative in which the chords are treated *arpeggiando*, leading the final *solenne* in which the arpeggio figuration lends tension and excitement to the theme in bare octaves.

6. *Grazioso* for small organ. This is the last piece for the lesser instrument and is a graceful pastorale. The theme is heard three times, interspersed with short episodes based on fragments of the melody.

(7a. = 1. *Impetuoso*)

7b. *Duo.* A sparkling finale in which the problems of co-ordinating two organs, often at a considerable distance from each other, are resolved in several ways. These are the obvious "echo technique" using the instruments in dialogue, the "solo and accompaniment" texture in which the ostinato figuration of the latter is often independent of the solo part and lastly transparent rhythmical passages in which scintillating notes and chords are tossed, as it were, from one player to the other. The Balkanic rhythm of the first movement is taken up again in the coda and brings the work to its conclusion.

Landscapes of Patmos (Krajiny patmoské) for organ and percussion

Written in 1984 to a commission of the Bach Society in Heidelberg to celebrate the tercentenary of the birth of Johann Sebastian Bach, it was given its first performance in the Lutherkirche, Heidelberg, as part of the Bach Festival there on 31st. May 1985. The organist was Wolfgang Dallmann and the percussionist was Wieland Junge.

Commenting on the score and the choice of instrumentation, Petr Eben says:

The combination of organ and percussion is one of the rare ensembles in which the organ can fully display its resources without being restricted to the softer stops. A duo for these instruments had tempted me for a long time...The tonal possibilities offered by such a combination suggested an atmosphere both festive and dramatic and this led me to the Book of Revelations. I soon, however, became aware of the difficulties of expressing all the richness of its contents in a few movements for two players. I therefore narrowed my horizon to five single images from the Apocalypse, written by St. John on the Greek island of Patmos, hence the title Landscapes.

The events and symbols of the writings of St. John, in their pictorial expression of the Eternal City and the Last Judgement, are diffused into the music in an analogical rather than a literal way. As for the percussion instruments, my choice has been determined by my knowledge of the difficulties, all too often encountered, of narrow, winding stairs and small organ galleries. I have therefore avoided using bulky instruments such as timpani, vibraphone and marimba.

The main solemn movement, The Temple, is placed centrally, as the third of the five movements. It is framed by two short movements, sharing the same thematic material and having as their subjects symbols that are close to the Throne: The Elders and The Rainbow. The outer movements, The Eagle and The Horses, portray the living creatures which herald the dramatic events.

In the last movement, Landscape with Horses, I have used two Gregorian chants. The fateful horses are characterized by the descending movement of the Dies Irae, which eventually gives way to the redeeming Victimae paschali which, with its ascending melody, appears almost as an inversion of the Dies Irae.

The three main movements (first, third and fifth) concentrate on three contrasting timbres: tom-toms and drums in the first movement, metallic sounds of tam-tam, cymbals, bells and glockenspiel in the third, while the wooden sounds of temple blocks and xylophone are heard in the last. In the shorter movements the colours are mixed. Great care should be taken to ensure that both organ and percussion are perfectly balanced in sound and colour. The work is a duo for equal partners; the percussion should not be too present and penetrating, nor the organ too distant.[1]

The movements are:

1. **Landscape with Eagle**

   The fourth living creature was like a flying eagle

---

[1] A fuller description may found in the composer's Introduction and Notes on Interpretation in the published score: *Landscapes of Patmos*, London, United Music Publishers, 1988.

2. **Landscape with Elders**

   Round the throne were twenty-four thrones, and seated on the thrones were twenty-four elders, clad in white garments, with golden crowns upon their heads.

3. **Landscape with Temple**

   Then God's temple in heaven was opened, and the ark of His covenant was seen within His temple.

4. **Landscape with Rainbow**

   The throne was surrounded by an emerald rainbow.

5. **Landscape with Horses**

   Then I saw heaven opened, and behold a white horse. He who sat on it is called Faithful and True, and in righteousness he judges and makes war.
   Then came a red horse and He who sat on it received the power to take away the peace of the earth, and to Him was given a great sword.
   Then I saw a black horse appear and He who sat upon it held the scales of justice.
   Then I saw a pale horse and He who sat on it was called Death, and Hell followed with him.

Two Invocations (Dvě invokace) for trombone and organ

The *Two Invocations* were written in 1988 for a festival in New Prague, Minnesota where, in the St. Wenceslas Church, one can still hear Czech hymns sung in their original language. The first movement was give there on 4th. December 1988 with Joel Blahník playing the trombone and M. Sedio the organ. The complete work received its première in Prague on 20th. April 1990 in Sv. Mikuláš, Malá strana, with the trombonist Jan Votava and the organist Jan Kalfus.

Eben takes the Baroque version of the most famous Czech hymn, the *St. Wenceslas Chorale*, which was sung throughout the Middle Ages at the coronation of the Czech kings and has continued to accompany the Czech nation to the present day, being sung as a second anthem during times of oppression and now returned to the churches. The chorale is thus the main theme for this set of variations. Petr Eben made the following comment on this work:

> Furthermore, this work gave me the opportunity to write a piece in which the regal majesty of the trombone's sonority is combined with the organ to invoke our heartfelt devotions and prayers. This is particularly so in the variations of the first movement, where the melody retains its diatonic form. In the second movement, where the theme appears in a chromatic form, the historical character of the chorale inspired me to express the dramatic and tragic moments in our history and celebration in the long-awaited victory of our freedom.

The first movement starts softly and mysteriously on the organ, using the first notes of the chorale in a cluster-like figure in the lower register. The trombone enters with the chorale melody and the variations gradually gain momentum, culminating in a toccata-like cadenza for the organ and a final broad statement of the theme by the trombone.

The second movement opens in a more chromatic vein, not without a certain vehemence. The second variation introduces a new rhythmical motif of two semiquavers which later become increasingly fragmented and dramatic. In the final sections the organ takes up a toccata-like figure in ternary rhythm then, after an emphatic trombone solo, plunges into a brilliant cadenza in semiquaver septuplets. The trombone joins in a restatement of the chorale and the two instruments combine to bring the movement to a triumphant conclusion on the chord of A major.

Three Jubilations (Tres Iubilationes) for two trumpets, two trombones and organ

The *Three Jubilations* were written in 1987 and first performed on 18th. July that year in King's College, Cambridge by Thomas Trotter and the King's Trumpeters, on the occasion of a Congress of organists. The outer movements were composed originally as the *Prelude* and *Postlude* to the *Missa cum Populo*, itself commissioned by Radio France and given its première in Avignon in July 1984 under the direction of Abbé Georges

Durand. The longer middle movement, written in 1987, completes the set. Introducing the cycle, Petr Eben writes:

> *For the first movement, Preludium, I have chosen two Gregorian themes: the Asperges me (Wash me with hyssop, and I shall be clean) which is sung traditionally at the opening of the Mass, and Psalm 50, Misere mei, Deus (Have mercy upon me O Lord).*
>
> *The Asperges me is first introduced by the brass and then taken up by the organ in a rhythmic and aggressive style. In the middle section the organ continues with this theme, while the first trumpet and then the trombone introduces the psalm. This section is conceived bi-rhythmically, with brass and organ working in independent tempi. The movement concludes with a return to the opening formula and a final reference to the plainsong melody in the brass.*
>
> *The second movement quotes the Czech chorale Vigilanter melodum. It is introduced by the brass, shared between the instruments and set in a free mode which alters the intervals of the melody. The theme is then taken up by the organ, still in its modal form, the brass intervening with series of quick repeated notes to which the organ replies with repeating chords on the reeds. In the central section of the piece a new theme is introduced by the brass and answered by the organ. Finally the original chorale melody returns, this time in its diatonic form, which the organ accompanies with a joyful toccata.*
>
> *The Postludium takes for its theme the Gregorian Ite missa est, traditionally sung at the conclusion of the Mass. It is announced by the first trumpet, shifting the melody a semitone higher in each bar, followed by the theme played by all the brass in the same key. Brass and organ alternate throughout the movement and then unite for the festive conclusion.*

GOD'S *GESAMTKUNSTWERK:* PETR EBEN'S *FAUST*

by Janette Fishell

*...man in his dark impulse always
knows the right road from wrong*

Goethe's *Faust*

Humanity's eternal dilemma of choosing right from wrong in the face of temptations, both alluring and fierce, is a theme that provides the spiritual basis behind Eben's most ambitious organ cycles, *Faust* and *Job*. While the central moral question in the latter is why bad things happen to the innocent, *Faust* addresses the catastrophic result when humans yearn for equality with God. The temptation and ultimate redemption of both Faust and Job are themes that have obviously found and urgent resonance for this composer who has, like so many innocent people, suffered at the hands of men who reckoned themselves God's equal.

The task of communicating a drama as richly woven as the legend of Faust, with its profound spiritual truths, stories of human betrayal, humour and misery, necessitated a large musical canvas. It required a kind of *Gesamtkunstwerk*, a "total work of art", in which the genesis of all musical theme, gesture, rhythm, colour and form spring from Goethe's text, the theatrical imagery inspired and supported by it, spiritual concepts and visual art. The result is Eben's most undeniably dramatic and programmatic organ work. The vivid nature of this music, with its overt references to the text and characters of Goethe's drama, have earned it a unique place in Eben's *oeuvre*. Yet it is this aspect of the work that has perhaps made it susceptible to some degree of misunderstanding, for more than one person has become so distracted by the humorous, bizarre or burlesque moments of Eben's *Faust* that the unifying spirituality of the work is missed.

A complete performance of Eben's *Faust* provides the theological framework that enables the listener to make sense of its disparate musical elements. The deeper spiritual underpinning lives side-by-side with the sinister or fanciful; indeed, the spiritual is *completed* by the presence of the human. As when Satan tempted Jesus Christ, we are taken to the pinnacle of the Temple and the top of the mountain where we look upon the entire human drama and see the spiritual battles that rage in every heart. We see that life is both cathedral and circus, Eucharist and tavern, love and hate. If we find both charm and vulgarity in the pages of Eben's *Faust*, then we must also look deeper to see the transcending divinity behind it. It is this Christological duality, the enigma of being both truly human and truly divine, that makes it God's *Gesamtkunstwerk*.

Historical Background and an Overview of Musical Style Elements

The work is an adaptation of Eben's stage music for a Viennese production of Goethe's play, mounted by the Burgtheater and composed in 1976. It is not an arrangement of the incidental music but a new work that takes its inspiration and motivic material from the music written for the staged production. In that original music the organ was included as part of the orchestra where it played an important symbolic and musical rôle.

> *I worked with the director to portray the organ's split personality. We wanted this to symbolize the struggle between Good and Evil within Faust's own soul.*[1]

Musically this was achieved by juxtaposing the solemn and festive side of the organ, that is to say its "sacred" side, with the trivial vulgarity of the barrel organ representing its "profane" side. Visual effects further reinforced this theme on the stage. In the section of the play which inspired *Requiem* (Movement VII), an organ was surrounded by pious church members who sang the sequence for the dead, *Dies Irae*. Without warning, the next scene introduces a ghastly witches' dance. The sacred church organ mutates into a barrel organ and the pious choristers throw off vestments and become demonic hags who dance to burlesque tunes at their Black Sabbath on *Walpurgisnacht* (Movement VIII).

All movements, except the last, are taken from the massive first part of Goethe's text and each bears a title that clearly links it with a specific scene in the play. They are:

    I   Prolog
    II   Mysterium

---

[1] Petr Eben, in conversation with the writer, September 1984.

III	Lied des Leiermannes	(Song of the Beggar with the Barrel Organ)
IV	Osterchöre	(Easter Choirs)
V	Studentenlieder	(Student Songs)
VI	Gretchen	
VII	Requiem	
VIII	Walpurgisnacht	(Walpurgis Night)
IX	Epilog	

Eben's predilection for combining music and other art forms, such as the recitation of text, is well documented. Not surprisingly he encourages the inclusion of appropriate passages from Goethe's text when performing *Faust*.[2] Mention should be made also of the stunning artwork by the Czech artist Ordřich Kulhánek that graces both front and back covers of the United Music Publishers edition, for it captures the very essence of Faust and is the visual equivalent of Eben's perceptive and evocative music.[3]

Sound

Eben's relationship to the organ is, by his own admission, a non-traditional one. He has played the organ since childhood but has never received formal training as an organist, so his approach to the instrument and its colours is freed from potential constraints of traditional pedagogical attitudes or performance practices. This serves the composer well in *Faust* since a novel approach to sound is in keeping with the dramatic and highly communicative nature of the piece. The composer's registration indications reach a level of meticulous detail not seen previously since his *Nedělní hudba* of 1957-9, reflecting the fact that he conceives music and colour simultaneously.[4]

The most compelling aspect of sound in this work is the link between colour and programme. Traditional use of the organ's colours contrasts with less orthodox practices such as the use of a manual 16' or 4' + 2' without 8' fundamental. The composer creates a unique soundscape in which

---

[2]For a more detailed discussion of Eben's interest in combining art forms, see Landgren, Johannes: *Music, Moment, Message*, Göteborg, Göteborg University Press, 1997.

[3]Eben, P. : *Faust for Organ*, London, United Music Publishers, 1983.

[4]Petr Eben, in conversation with the writer, September 1984.

traditional colours are contrasted with bizarre combinations evocative of the barrel or theatre organ, including honking reed registrations reminiscent of the regal, gap registrations such as 8' + 1', richly diverse mutation complexes and even instructions such as ...*use mysterious, even bizarre colours.*[5] The use of bright registrations, such as chorus stops through *plena*, or high ranges, often seem to suggest heaven and dark registrations, such as broad foundations, 16' flue or reed stops, or low ranges, in turn suggest hell.

As in nearly every one of Eben's organ works, *Faust* contains passages marked by rapid manual changes, a technique that contrasts colour, rhythm and articulation. One of the most difficult aspects of performing any of Eben's larger works, of which *Faust* is no exception, is accomplishing the requisite registration changes without disturbing the forward motion of the musical line. The ideal organ on which to perform this music is a three manual and pedal instrument with at least one enclosed division, a large number of mutations and reeds, as well as sensitive mechanical key action that facilitates the performance of complex rhythms.

Harmony

One detects a change in the composer's harmonic language that can be seen as developing gradually in his work after *Laudes* of 1964. While the highly chromatic, compactly dissonant language of that early work has not been totally abandoned, we see the clear emergence of what will become his mature style: a pervasive use of tertian sonorities, used in bi-tonal relationships and planed in a more impressionistic manner, plus the reliance upon contrasts between densely dissonant and more transparent consonant sections.

Bi-tonality is undoubtedly the most immediately identifiable aspect of Eben's harmonic vocabulary and one that breaks from traditional common practice while still remaining aurally acceptable to the listener. Often the harmonic regions combined are related by the interval of a second or augmented fourth, creating a rather piquant harmonic effect. In fact, the pervasive melodic and harmonic use of the tritone in *Faust* led the writer to ask the composer whether such an inclusion was a hidden reference to the medićval notion of *Diabolus in musica*. While he answered that it was merely a product of his exploration of a harmony not yet exhausted in past

---

[5]Eben, P.: *op.cit.* Notes on the Registration.

styles, the aural connotation that the augmented fourth carries with it provides an unmistakably demonic reference.

As already noted, he makes use of parallel triadic structures that often do not function within one key but migrate between numerous tonal centres and quartal/quintal (4th. and 5th.) harmonic and melodic structures as a way of breaking free of tertian sonorities, while still remaining aurally comprehensible. Interestingly, *Faust* contains two rather rare occurrences of serial technique, passages that, in their tonal austerity, provide a musical note of judgement that reflects an important aspect of the Faustian legend.

Melody

In this work one is constantly reminded of the lyrical nature of Eben's writing, even when the melody is cloaked in extreme dissonance or punctuated with rests. The sources of melodic material in *Faust* mirror the drama itself: sacred chant and chorale musically and symbolically do battle with the profane drinking songs and demonic incantations that were originally sung in the stage version. Gregorian chant is elemental to both Eben's faith and his compositional style.

> *There are three features of Gregorian chant which are so attractive for me: Firstly the simple, and at the same time, the monumental unison, which in the present time is contrasting with the complicated language of modern music; secondly the pliability of the harmony, which allows various possibilities, how to accompany the melody in my own style; and thirdly the rhythmic freedom, which is liberated from the iron dictate of the regular parts of the bar.*[6]

These tunes occur as simple statements and harmonized in Eben's characteristic language of quartal/quintal chords or parallel triads. In some of the most vivid sections of the work a sacred theme undergoes thematic transformation as it is juxtaposed with the profane.

It should be remembered that, as was the case with all of Eben's pre-1989 works, *Faust* was composed and published in the days when overt religious references were dangerous, due to the atheist stance of the Czechoslovak Government. Sacred themes were not labelled in the score yet, to fellow

---

[6] Eben, P.: as quoted in Landgren, J. *op.cit.*

musicians and devout Christians for whom the sacred themes held meaning, these tunes sang out a faith that witnessed to the ultimate triumph of good over evil.

Rhythm

I have a taste for rhythm.[7]

Eben's innovative approach to rhythm is, perhaps, the most immediately engaging aspect of his music. Whether the effect is one of indomitable repetition or rhapsodic freedom, the composer obviously delights in exploiting the rhythmic possibilities that the organ offers. Ostinato patterns occur with such frequency that they have become trademarks of his style. Here we can draw parallels with similar techniques of the Hungarian composer Bela Bartók and the ecstatic nature of Messiaen and Alain's music in which a sort of temporal stasis occurs - time stands still even as it moves inexorably forward. Often one or more ostinati provide an unchanging rhythmic and melodic background over or under which other material is heard, producing an almost minimalist effect. One stunning example of the hypnotic potential that Eben's ostinati have can be heard in the second movement, which conveys all the power of a magical incantation.

As in other organ works, a popular dance rhythm, the waltz, as well as jazz improvisation, with its complex cross rhythms and syncopations, can be found in *Faust*. The result is that, even when it refers to the loftiest of spiritual themes, his music remains within our earth-bound grasp.

Brief Descriptive Analysis

Prolog

This movement portrays the bet between God and Satan that sets the cosmic wheel turning. It opens with traditional registrations of contrasting *plena* as the angels, high in the firmament and the keyboards, proclaim the beauty of God's creation. Rapidly articulated triads mix major and minor modes and introduce the Gregorian antiphon *Gloria laus* from the Easter Mass *Dominica in Palmis*. Suddenly the colour changes to dark 16', 8' and 4' and clusters in the lowest register seem to suggest Satan crawling out of

---

[7]Eben, P. Personal communication, September 1985.

the bowels of Hell for his fateful conversation with God. In contrast to the bright, articulate triads of the opening section, a *legato* touch is called for and the language is chromatic.

Eben includes the chant as a divine interjection but the dark quality of this section triumphs. The chant undergoes thematic transformation in that it is no longer in its pure triadic form but altered to include tritones. The ensuing section once again answers with the chant harmonized in block chords and accompanied by a dizzying swirl of semiquavers. The effect of the 8' flute in this passage is a breathtaking curve of sound.

The movement ends with an exciting crescendo from the gentle foundations to full *plenum* with reeds. Thematic material is related to the opening chant in its prominent use of descending seconds and modally mixed triads. Eben reinforces the gradual dynamic crescendo by beginning each new phrase at a higher pitch or octave than the preceding phrase. Just as Goethe allowed Good the final word in his *Prolog*, Eben concludes the movement with ascending phrases that, in their upward surging, could be viewed as a symbol of our innate and inevitable turning toward God.

Mysterium

Eben suggests mysterious, even bizarre, colours in this movement that paints the scene of Faust's first encounter with the forces of Satan, depicted by the left hand changing from Quintadena 8' to Dulzian 16' to Rohrschalmei 8'. A sombre theme, rather serpentine in nature, exploits major and minor seconds as its winds its way through the murky low register of the organ. It is joined by an eerie counter subject which interjects its complicated rhythm, as elusive as the flickering flame of Faust's lone candle. A *stringendo* leads to the *Allegro* in which Faust invokes the evil spirits, a frenzied section which the composer likens to the rite of exorcism.[8] This section includes rapid manual changes and a theme constructed by the most dissonant of intervals: a tritone, second and seventh. Typical of the composer's writing, the theme is fragmented melodically and rhythmically, providing an exciting forward drive. A monumental crescendo leads to the final frenetic statement on full organ, symbolizing the moment at which the spectre proves its power to Faust. Terrified, Faust shrinks in fear while the mysterious opening material closes the movement.

---

[8]*ibid.*

Lied des Leiermannes

Here the drama is taken to the street where a beggar plays the barrel organ and begs for his next meal. A sense of the darkly grotesque surrounds even this ostensibly light-hearted movement. This movement is communicated through the melancholy beggar's song, originally sung on stage and heard here in three stanzas. The shortest of all the movements, it is to be played without rubato, as if the organ grinder is turning the handle methodically from beginning to end.

The *Beggar's Song* is heard first in the pedal, using gap registration of 8' + 2', accompanied by an undulating curve of semiquavers in the right hand, registered 4', 2' with optional 1'. The remaining stanzas place the theme in the manuals, with Regal 8', Flute 4' with optional tremulant, and include interesting hocket-like figurations, as if the melody loses its voice as the hurdy-gurdy runs out of wind.

Osterchöre

The importance of Easter's resurrection and redemption can be seen throughout *Faust*, both in story line and musical material. This movement is a dramatic heavenly interjection than reminds Faust, albeit temporarily, of his own true nature as a child of God. It begins with a trumpet flourish that Eben calls the *Fanfare of Life*. The *Te Deum* is heard in the pedals under jubilant figuration featuring cross-accents and phrasing. A *Song of Resurrection*, original to the stage version, is followed by a Gregorian *Alleluia*, to which it is related. All of these themes, *Te Deum*, *Alleluia* and the *Song of Resurrection*, are characterized by ascending contours, much like the closing section of the *Prolog*. Again the spiritual symbolism is clear.

A turbulent section follows in which the *Fanfare* theme undergoes thematic transformation as it attempts to penetrate the chaos within Faust's own soul. The solidity of the accompanimental ostinato provides an anchor in this section, which includes complicated cross rhythms. The pedal takes over the *Fanfare* while the hands continue the ostinato at different pitch levels, creating a bi-tonal effect. As the climax is approached, motifs from the *Resurrection* theme are interspersed with the ostinato. As in the first movement, the curve from low to high registers and contrasts in organ colour reinforce the powerful drive and direction of this section.

The majestic chorale theme that interrupts the *Fanfare* variant seems to refer to the portion of text in which the choir of angels saves Faust from suicide. Sacred interjection imposes harmonic order, providing an harmonic arch by reinstating the tonal centre of G heard in the opening bars. But Faust is still in chaos; the altered *Fanfare* once again enters to do battle with the chorale. The listener, like Faust, is left with an ambiguous feeling: the protagonist lives but feels no true Easter joy.

Studentenlieder

The fourth movement's collection of drinking songs features some of the most interesting writing in the whole cycle. This is evident from the piece's opening bars, an introduction that displays contrast on three levels: articulation, phrasing and timbre. In this section a staccato tritone figure accompanies a non-legato line in the right hand which features a glissando and ends with a comic falling gesture. It leads to the *Student Song*, a jovial tune that wanders harmonically just as its singers stagger in an alcoholic haze. The contrast of manuals heard in the introduction is enlarged *vis-rvis* clusters that rapidly move from one manual to another. The song is next fashioned as mechanical clock organ music, as delicate and transparent as the preceding clusters were sturdy and dense.

An innocent two-bar interpolation is transformed into an aggressive new theme, marked by sharp rhythms and harmonies based on quartal and tritone structures. It provides an aural separation from the rather trivial, if pleasant, triadic section which precedes it and leads to the next theme, the *Song of the Rats*. Stated in open fifths with a rather martial flavour, it is eventually combined with the *Student Song* in a spectacular conclusion, marked by a final falling glissando and jazz-tinged poly-chord.

Gretchen

Eben reserves his most beautiful writing for the wretched cries of the deserted maiden Gretchen. It begins with fragments of what will later be *Gretchen's Second Song* mysteriously introduced in the pedal and a mirror image figure in the manuals (Copula 8' + 1'). *Gretchen's Theme* enters, a lyrical song with an expressive leap of a major seventh, accompanied by a drone.

The next section introduces *Gretchen's First Song*, a masterpiece of pictorial writing in which the organ imitates the sobs of Gretchen. The composer sought to depict her cries and the catching of breath which accompanies grief. To achieve this effect, three manuals of differing colours are used in a monophonic passage requiring thumbing down technique. The theme becomes freer and lapses into a triplet that foreshadows the musical representation of her famous spinning wheel. *Gretchen's Second Song* enters next, at first alternating with the spinning figure and later accompanied by it. Eventually the spinning wheel figure absorbs the song by delicately defining the melody at the top of each rhythmic/melodic group. The wheel slowly comes to a stop and the first theme enters, this time fragmented in terms of rhythm and register, its disjunct nature reflecting the disorientation and loss felt by the abandoned girl.

Requiem

Petr Eben said that this movement is one of unceasing sadness - the song of one who constantly says: *I am guilty*. An atmosphere of remorse and imploration is conveyed by pitch repetition that Eben likens to a death knell or passing bell. One is also reminded of the similarity between this drone figure and a litany. The words of Jehan Alain, a composer with whom Eben closely identifies, seem to describe accurately the *affekt* of *Requiem*:

> When the Christian soul in distress can no longer find any new words to implore the mercy of God, it repeats the same invocation over and over again in blind faith.[9]

Requiem opens with the tolling of a bell, repeated notes high in the register, out of which emerges a descending chromatic line, the movement's primary theme. In the original stage music the choir sang the text of the *Dies Irae* to this theme. Ensuing phrases introduce the same material, the tolling bell and its chromatic tail, at higher pitch levels; fragmentation and stretto propel the musical line inexorably forward. The stark effect of octaves in contrasting rhythmic and phrase groupings, combined with a *poco a poco stringendo*, makes this section one of unrelenting tension.

As the climactic point is approached, the theme is transmuted into a pedal ostinato, ranges expand in either direction and dynamics increase until reaching the *pesante* and *fortissimo* vertical presentation of the theme. The *subito* decrescendo, reminiscent of the *Finale* of *Nedělní hudba*, reveals the lone voice of the Salicional 8' on which is heard the movement's initial motif. The death knell is repeated like a litany until it fades away - an unanswered prayer.

---

[9]Alain, Jehan: Preface to *Litanies* (1937).

Walpurgisnacht

The apex of *Faust* occurs in this musical depiction of a witches' Black Sabbath. It begins with a dance-like introduction, an innovative section in which Eben uses stereophonic effects that contrast key, timbre, rhythm, articulation, dynamic and phrasing. The composer's use of bi-tonality and echo effects suggests the sonic experience that Faust and Mephistopheles would have had as they stood far off from the witches' revelry and heard two separate sources of music in two different keys.

Just as the witches' *Round Dance* was united with the sacred *Dies Irae* in Berlioz's *Symphonie Fantastique*, Eben allows a sacred theme to be mocked by the witches in *Walpurgisnacht*. The theme is a parody of the Lutheran hymn *Aus tiefer Not*, the German version of *Psalm 130, Out of the depths have I cried to Thee*. The theme appears in various forms throughout the cycle's final two movements, providing a musical and spiritual *Leitmotif*. The solemn chorale is heard as a solo with impish ostinato accompaniment, in bi-tonal manual statements against a double pedal ostinato and fragmented against a tritone pedal tremolo. The profane nature of the thematic transformation is underpinned by the registration that builds from the initial nasal solo of foundations, mutations and krumhorn to a menacing *plenum*. A constant dynamic and rhythmic crescendo leads to an exciting cadenza-like section for manuals and pedal which, in turn, gives way to a gradual decrescendo, most effectively accomplished through a well-planned hand reduction of stops.

The rather forceful opening is succeeded by the fanciful *Song of the Will O'the Wisp*, fashioned as clock organ music. With its quaint timbres of Flutes 8' + 1' and *Allegro grazioso* tempo, it acts as a light bridge to the next section, a strongly rhythmic ostinato of serial construction. Eventually this ostinato becomes the accompaniment to a burlesque witches' dance, set as a trivial and vulgar waltz, a kind of comic *Totentanz*. At first we hear the waltz softly, as though it is at a distance, with the ostinato taking precedence. Soon, however, the demonic waltz breaks free from the ostinato and is stated forcefully in manual chords. Suddenly the pedal breaks in with *Aus tiefer Not* and chorale and witches' dance are juxtaposed in musical and spiritual combat. Though the war is fierce, the sacred theme prevails and the movement concludes with a thundering solo pedal cadenza on the chorale. In Eben's words:

> *The final unison chorale statement on full organ does not leave any doubt that this admittance of one's mistakes, the*

> *confessing of one's faults, is the condition for the salvation in the Epilog.*[10]

Epilog

Eben refers to the inherent arch form of *Faust* when he writes:

> *I think that in some way Prolog and Epilog are connected by contrast of low and high, dark and clear, but in the Epilog in a mood of conciliation, the soul [rises] above the abyss.*[11]

The stability of triads, heard on the soothing timbres of 8' Flutes and Celeste, lends a sense of calm that provides perfect closure to a cycle that has been marked by such overwhelmingly dramatic music. As in the *Prolog*, distantly related triads weave an arched line ultimately centred on C major. *Aus tiefer Not*, the chorale that was parodied by the witches in the previous movement, is now heard as a representation of the saving grace of God's love. As in many of the previous movements, Eben exploits spatial effects to represent heaven and the rising of Faust's soul. Clusters descend gracefully and the chorale gives way to a tranquil ostinato treated canonically.

The only departure from this peaceful mood is the interjection of an angular, twelve-tone passage, the austerity of which recalls the judgement all must face upon death. Yet once again the chorale is heard proclaiming the salvation bestowed upon the sinning Doctor Faust. The final C major chord unites high and low registers - symbol of the peace that has been restored to the living and the dead.

---

[10]Eben, P.: Personal communication, January 1988.

[11]*ibid.*

CONSTRUCTION ON IMPROVISATION: EBEN'S JOB

by Andreas Jacob

The organ works of Petr Eben belong to the few contemporary compositions for this instrument that have acquired a paramount position in the repertory. The reason for this is to be sought in his compositional style which is both clear and understandable, exploiting the sensuous qualities of the organ in full. At the same time, performers notice the seriousness of Eben's approach during the conception of his works, the opulence of sound is never perverted into cajolery of the public. The organist Eben is particularly famous for his improvisations: the experiences gathered when improvising - techniques of playing, characteristic sound-effects appropriate to the instrument - exert an impressive impact on the listener.

Job, written in 1987, is one of the largest solo pieces for organ by Eben. It embodies many aspects of his way of composing and develops an individualistic, expressive musical language. As with many, but far from all of the organ works of Eben, *Job* was created on the basis of improvisations, in this case illustrating excerpts from *The Book of Job*.[1] The texts were chosen in order to reflect the basic stations of Job's story in eight stages. The following titles are given to the movements: *Destiny - Faith - Acceptance of Suffering - Longing for Death - Despair and Resignation - Mystery of Creation - Penitence and Realisation - God's Reward*. Short quotations from *The Book of Job* head each of the movements (*Job 1.11; 1.21; 3.11 & 23; 7.21; 38.1-2; 42.2 & 6; 42.10*) and between them longer passages were inserted that may be spoken by a narrator during the performance (*Job 1.1-3 & 6-21; 2.1-10; 3.1-2, 11-13 & 20-23; 7.16-21;*

---

[1] Eben's latest project in this form concentrates on texts from *The Labyrinth of the World and the Paradise of the Heart* by Jan Ámos Komenský (Comenius): prepared motivic material is elaborated in improvised concert performances and is combined with quotations from chorale texts by Comenius in the *Amsterdam Cantionale* at several points. As compared with a notated version, such improvised early drafts of a work naturally contain more repetitions and spontaneously conceived harmony at the keyboard. The final detailed instructions for registration in works like *Job* result from different experiences with several instruments, making allowances for the inevitable variations of an artistic ideal.

38.1-12, 33 & 35, 40.1-2; 42.1-6, 10, 12-13 & 15-17). Eben's interest in the character of Job from the *Old Testament* is closely connected with his interest in the literary character of Faustus, who was the central figure in his great organ work written seven years earlier. He wrote:

> *After the organ cycle Faust, I felt impelled to return to the same theme - the wager between Satan and God on the fate of a human being - this time an Old Testament subject. Faust relied on his own human strength and failed; Job humbly accepted his misfortune and triumphed.*[2]

Both works centre around the behaviour of the individual in fatal situations. The two cycles are connected by a deeply humanistic approach but quite obviously differ in their musical concept. By the intensive study of the *Book of Job*, Eben was led to higher intensity concerning both the musical gesture and the concentration of the thematic material. This is already to be heard at the very beginning of the work, at the first section of the first movement, *Destiny*:

> *The movement begins Andante with a pedal reed announcement of the motif of Job's Destiny.*[3]

answered by six-four chords in related thirds that is reminiscent of fanfares:

Ex.1 *Job*, 1st. movement: *Destiny*, bars. 1-12[4]

---

[2]Eben, P.: Preface to *Job*, London, United Music Publishers, 1989.

[3]Eben, P. *op.cit.*

[4]Music examples are reproduced by kind permission of United Music Publishers, Ltd. London.

The initial motif consists of a series of intervals enlarging in asymmetric, fan-like movement. During the repetition of the motif, the structural rôle of the intervals of the tritone and the third is stressed by shifting the last notes into the upper third. From this *motif of destiny*, with its dramatic and contrasting bipartite structure, the opening section of the first movement is developed. The pedal enters at different pitches and continues the theme in diverse ways, while the manual takes up the *fanfare motif*, stated in varying intervals of time and space. The movement goes on with a *more turbulent toccata-like middle section*[5] that ties up different repetitive figures, mostly based upon chords of the seventh, in characteristic rhythmic patterns. At last a melody enters in bar 36 that show some affinity with the initial motif through the use of the intervals of tritone and third. This initial motif reappears in rhythmic diminution in the pedal. In general, there is a remarkably high degree of relationship between the motivic material of all the movements, independent of any other musical quotations.[6]

The tendency to melodic extension that is implicit in the initial motif can also be seen in the further treatment of this solo melody. In the following entries, all starting with the same opening of the theme as in bar 36, the range of the melodic line is continuously augmented forming, with increasing clarity, the initial pedal motif in the top part. In the ensuing section, beginning with bar 62, the *motif of destiny* is further developed. As in a mensuration canon, it appears in two parts, in triplets in the top part and as a slower ostinato of the beginning of the pedal motif, the middle part being presented in counterpoint with faster ostinato figures. After the initial motif has been combined with itself in this way, the final section follows which, according the Eben in his *Preface* to the published score, is *spread over the entire sound spectrum of the organ*. Starting points are the rhythmic treatment and the characteristic harmony relying on the triads of the *fanfare motif* - bars 70-78, twice interrupted by bars with ostinato motifs as in the preceding passage - which is finally heard in bars 74 and 75 in different, descending octave positions. The tritone again plays an important rôle in this section, as in bars 72, 76 and 77. The initial motif itself reappears, beginning at bar 79, transposed at four different pitches, in a number of extensions within the intervals of the third and tritone and in

---

[5]Eben, P. *op cit.*

[6]Gans, Christof: *"Jetzt hat mein Auge dich geschaut" (Ijob 42.5). Petr Eben - Hob für Orgel.* Staatsarbeit in Rahmen des 1. Staatsexamens für das Lehramt an Gymnasien, Frankfurt a.M., 1989, chapter *Affinität der Motive*, p.31-37. See especially the synopsis of the motifs, p.37.

rhythmical variants. This motif also is given several octave positions and is harmonised with the characteristic six-four chords or the sixth that are familiar from the first section. The theme has its last entry at bar 90 in the pedal, a third higher than at the beginning, starting on *e*, with the answering *fanfare motif* on the manual spread over three octave positions in descending direction as in the preceding section.

Already in this first movement many elements are to be found which are considered to be essential to Eben's musical language, such as shifting chords in mixture stops, extended continuation of motifs, ostinato figures, characteristic rhythmic patterns [7] and structuring of clearly definable sections. These traits reflect the original genesis of the work in the realm of improvisation, where it was originally conceived and where inevitably considerable elaboration takes place in the final published score. This may be seen, for example, in the rhythmic design of repetitive passages based upon semiquaver figures as in bars 30-35.[8] These six bars at the beginning of the middle section work, with the exception of bar 32, with a toccata-like figure of semiquaver chords generated mainly by the intervals of a third and the tritone or sometimes a fourth. This intervallic structure does not apply only to the vertical pattern but also to the horizontal continuation. At the beginning, in bar 30, four groups of these semiquaver chords are distributed between the two hands: 4 x (2+2). In the next bar six semiquavers are given alternately to the two hands: 3 x (1+1). A *caesura* is introduced at bar 32 by means of a two-part figure of semiquaver sextuplets mainly relying on the intervals of tritone and fourth, which comes to rest on the last note in the bar. This figure is used like an exclamation mark, reappearing in bar 54 slightly changed and restated, marking the end of the passage dominated by the solo melody. The repeated chords begin again at bar 33, now first in the subdivision of 4 x (1+1), then bar 34 as 3 x (2+2). The starting point of this rhythmic process is reached again in bar 35: 4 x (2+2). Now, after the completion of this circle, the melody enters,

---

[7]The strong rhythmic component of Eben's organ works certainly is one of the aspects of his compositional style most attractive to the audience. Janette Fishell comments of the effective and vivid treatment of the rhythmical features: *Whether the effect is one of indomitable repetition or rhapsodic freedom, the composer obviously delights in rhythmically organizing his music in unexpected ways.* Fishell, J.: *The Organ Music of Petr Eben*, Dissertation, Nashville, Tennessee, 1988, p.38.

[8]Traditionally, the tendency of exploiting figuration as a constitutive layer of the music can be demonstrated, probably most obviously in the Baroque era. Cf. Maekelae, Tomi: Von der Idiomatik zur spielerischen Redundanz: Die geheime Logik der Figuren; in *Die Musiktheorie, 3/1998*, pp.217-240.

the accompanying figures being limited to the use of the intervals of a third and the tritone from now on. Passages like the one described may seem playful and figurative at first sight but nonetheless turn out to be determined by a structural process in both rhythm and harmony and may be taken as examples of the compositional concept in major parts of *Job*.

We find another important aspect of Eben's compositional approach is the use of quotations in several movements of *Job*. The Easter lauda *Exsultet* and the *Gloria* (in the 4th. mode) frame the second movement, *Faith*, which is headed *The Lord gave, and the Lord hath taken away; blessed be the name of the Lord*. In the third movement, *Acceptance of Suffering*, with the text *Shall we receive good at the hand of God, and shall we not receive evil also?*, the chorale *Wer nur den lieben Gott laesst walten (If thou but suffer God to guide thee)* is developed. This song reappears in the sixth movement, *Mystery of Creation*, which is also dominated by two other motifs which are often combined with the chorale: a) a sequence of chords, first introduced *pianissimo* and circling around the intervals of a minor second - major third, and b) a "question motif" beginning $a' - eb'' - a'' - f'' - db'' - b$, which is closely related to the thematic material of the other movements not only by the initial tritone. The *Veni Creator Spiritus* is used to characterize Job's repentance and understanding in the second section of the seventh movement, *Penitence and Realisation*, which quotes the verse *I have uttered that which I understood not; wherefore I abhor myself and repent in dust and ashes*. The first section of this movement deals with Job's penitence and here the composer develops a melody of his own with clear reminiscences of the *motif of destiny* at the beginning of the cycle. The eighth and final movement, *God's reward*, is formed by:

> a set of chorale-like variations on a melody by the Bohemian Brothers, Kristus, příklad pokory (Christ, the model of humility) for Christ is truly the personification of the innocent sufferer to the very end.[9]

The eucharist prayer of the *praefatio: Vere dignum et justum est, aequum et salutare* is taken up at the end of the movement and resounds as a conclusion to the work *unisono* on the full organ.

The emblematic use of quotations is a factor with a strongly suggestive effect on the listener, as it is on the performer. It should serve as a

---

[9]Eben, P., *op. cit.*

reminder that chorales function as a basis for improvisation and thereby as a kind of catalyst for the improviser as well as for the composer. This not only explains the existence of quotations in five out of the eight movements but also the powerful undertow which these quotations exert on the movements. The use of quotations, in the context of improvisation, is not so much a drawing upon unchangeable traditional sources as triggering some new and unforseen development.[10]

Using musical forms with a certain historical connotation is a further device that might be understood as a quotation. Thus, Eben chooses for the fourth movement, *Longing for Death*, the form of the *passacaglia*. Here a line descending chromatically through a fifth serves as the ostinato ground bass. The reference to the tradition of the *passus duriusculus* or the lament bass is obvious enough.[11] Through a saraband rhythm, with the typical accent on the second beat, an additional element of ornamental intensification is recalled. The essential despair expressed in the heading of the movement, *Why died I not, from the womb? Wherefore is light given to a man whose way is hid, and whom God hath hedged in?*, gives rise to a conventional formal gradation by Eben in both dynamics and acceleration. In addition, the metre of the movement has to suffer changes after the early variations: bars in 4/4 or 7/8 time break up the original 3/4 time; even bars in 5/4 and 5/8 time are inserted. The piece does not recover from this crisis, even when the 3/4 time is restored. The thematic line appears on the full organ and in a seemingly stable metre but strongly syncopated. The outcome is a return to *pianissimo*, the theme being gradually thinned out and even dissolved. By means of this fourth movement, Eben makes a strong *caesura* within the whole cycle. As in the eighth movement *Finale*, he chooses a variation form to indicate a resting point in the development.

A final reflection on the fifth movement, *Despair and Resignation,* may also serve to study Eben's compositional technique, which finds its exemplary

---

[10]It is for this reason that the best in jazz shows a durability, which was neither planned in its compositional material nor anticipated beforehand at the time of its conception. In contrast to church chorales, it was never consecrated by being included in the liturgical repertory or a hymn book. The *Real Book* is not a canonical compilation in the same sense.

[11]The use of the descending tetrachord in the Baroque era may be called paradigmatic. Cf. Rosand, Ellen, The Descending Tetrachord: An Emblem of Lament, in *The Musical Quarterly, 3/1979, pp.346-359.*

expression here. The text placed at the head of the movement is *Now shall I sleep in the dust, and thou shalt seek me in the morning, but I shall not be.* Eben writes in his preface:

> *This movement is in two parts. The restless first section reflects a despairing Job's rising reproaches against God ("Wherefore dost Thou make me Thy target?"), changing to a plaintive song of submission in the second part.*[12]

This subdivision into two parts is easily perceived. An anguished beginning with the tempo changing between *Larghetto* and *Allegretto* is followed by small semiquaver clusters which rapidly alternate between the hands. The second part begins at bar 60. A new tempo indication, *Molto moderato*, is combined with a continuous ternary metre and a distinct melodic line. In the first section of the movement Eben mainly works with three clearly defined layers of material introduced immediately at the beginning: a) a stationary four-part chord, at first in a high register; b) staccato quavers with a long final note, at first in the pedal, the number of quavers being augmented at each entrance; c) two part groups of semiquavers in chromatic contrary motion.

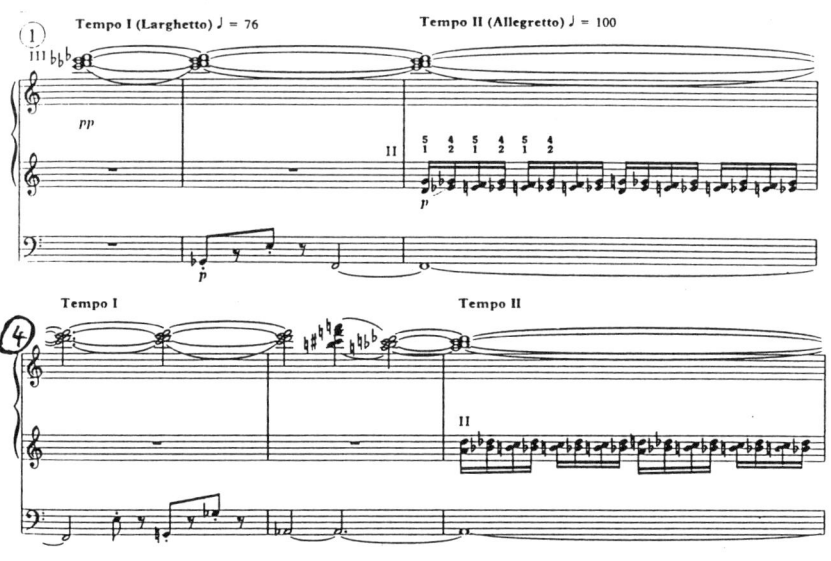

---

[12]Eben, P., *op.cit.*

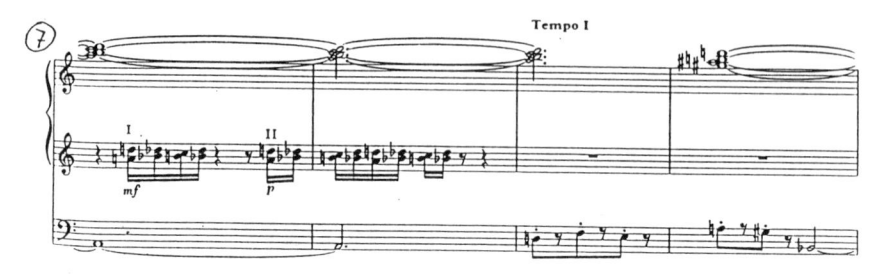

Ex.2 *Job*, **5th. movement:** *Despair and Resignation*, **bars 1-10**

The harmonic organisation of the opening bars is very clear. Chord a) consists of the first three notes, in several layers, of the beginning of the minor scale; the fourth note colours the chord in a specific way. The reference to the minor scale is appropriate, as Eben works with tonal centres. The first chord of Ex.2 evoked d♭ minor with its leading note. Layer (b), at first located in the pedal, brings chromatic additions to chord (a). The groups of notes *e - f - g♭* and *g♭ - g - a♭* are introduced subsequently. At bar 9 the group *d - e - f* (emphasising d minor) is put against the d♭ minor sound of the right hand, the pedal notes *a - g♯ - b♭* of bar 10 allude to the group *g - g♭ - a♭* of bars 4 and 5. The range of (b) is a major seventh. At each entry the number of notes inserted at the beginning increases. This aims at a fan-like melodic extension as in the *motif of destiny* in the first movement. The third layer (c) increases the chromatic range, first in bar 3 from *d* to *g*, later at bars 6 to 8 from *a* to *d*, the "missing" *a♭* is sounded at the same time in the pedal. For obvious reasons, rhythmic activity is to be expected from layer (c) with the fastest note values. After two entries of four crotchets duration each, (c) is thus presented at bars 7 and 8 contracted to one or two crotchets duration, the latter being placed off the beat. This idea of rhythmic contraction is explored further, including entries with durations of, for example, five or three quavers, as in bars 11 and 12. More decisive is the element introduced in bars 11 and 12: a dotted rhythm (dotted quaver + semiquaver) with a strongly declamatory character inserted into the semiquaver groups which have prevailed up to this point. This dotted rhythm is exploited for the musical process from bar 23 onwards. The two hands describe an ascending line with simultaneous contrary motion of the two upper voices - left hand: major second + minor second upwards; right hand: minor third + minor second downwards. At the end of this figure the dotted rhythm appears in the highest part as if it would tear apart the movement - *a' - a♭' - e♭'*.

These elements of "striving upwards" and "wrenching" are further pursued in the following passage from bar 24. The right hand has a melody, strengthened by a 16' stop, (*poco più largamente*) with an upbeat leap upwards towards a dotted quaver. Melodic units are ended by a gesture of "wrenching" in a downwards direction that may also stand separately, as in bar 27. At bar 24 the left hand introduces a counterpoint in scale-like upward motion which reinforces the concluding gesture, emphasizing in a cadential manner the end of each unit with deep-toned *marcato* chords in the left hand and pedal. After the new entrance of layer (c) at bar 31, a recapitulation of the first section begins. Layer (a) appears in the left hand and the deepest possible octave position at bar 32. In addition, the chord of bar 1 is transposed down a fourth from d♭ minor to a♭ minor. This is answered in the right hand by layer (b) at bar 33, which is transposed a tritone. In bar 34 a chord derived from bar 10 and transposed down a second is combined with layer (b) that is derived from bars 4 and 5 and remains in a tritone transposition. Both layers lead to a chord in bar 35 that is to be understood as an inverted form of (a) from bar 10 again transposed a tritone. Now the pedal enters with layer (c) in the form found in bar 11 transposed up a minor second. There follows in order layer (b), derived from bar 9 and still transposed a tritone; layer (a), from bar 10 and transposed down a fourth; layer (c), from bar 11, shortened and transposed up a minor second; and (a), from bar 13 transposed down a fourth. Finally, the different layers are dissolved at bars 41 and 42, (c) is changed in its construction as well as (a). The method of using several possibilities of transposition for an harmonic structure in different voices at the same time is a typical device of Eben's, who thus expresses a critical development of the textual content by musical means. As a further example, this may also be compared with the second movement, starting from bar 17.

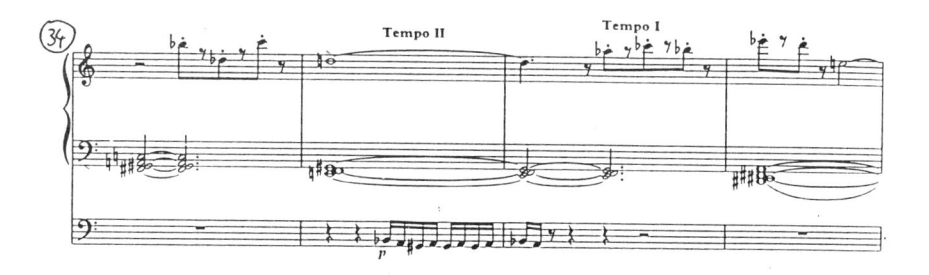

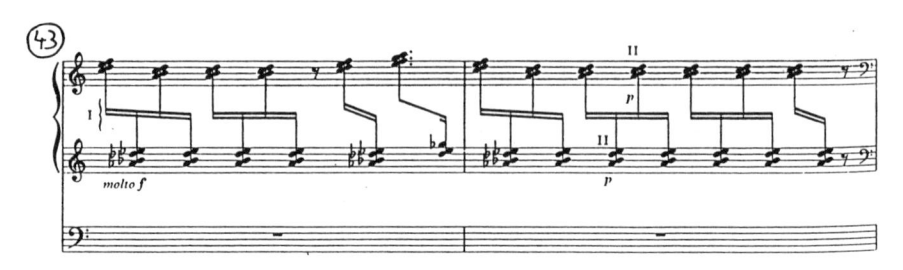

Ex.3 *Job*, 5th. movement: *Despair and Resignation*,
bars 34-37 & bars 43-44

At this point, depicting the desperateness of Job's situation, aggressive chords alternating between the hands come in, bar 43 still involving the characteristic dotted rhythm and later, with the exception of bar 54, as continuous chains of semiquavers. The structure of the chords is visibly influenced by the experience of the improviser. The right hand uses the white keys while the left hand is restricted to the black keys. The number of chord groups is always odd and very irregular. The change from the first manual in *forte* registration to the second in *piano* functions as an echo in some places while in others, such as bars 51 and 52, it serves as a technique for contrast.

This passage is felt like an explosion after the numbness of the first section, mounting up to the declamatory gesture of a group of chords in Lombardic rhythm which is repeated three times, as at bar 54. It describes Job's insurrection against God. This irascible musical gesture is ended, like the first section, with dissolving structures. As a means of giving substance to the transition, layer (c) appears in bar 58 at the end of this section, that layer having taken on a similar function in the opening section. From bar 60 onwards the second main section of contrasting character follows. Both the melodic upper voice and the accompaniment are determined by the minor second as their characteristic interval. The melody itself has a circling, extending character. This tendency towards extension, similar to the first movement, manifests itself in the more far-reaching solo voice from bar 76 onwards. The motivic relationship to other melodic lines, such as those in the first movement, cannot be ignored. The pedal answers with an expressive line that is derived from layer (b) and creates high tension by its wide range. The more closely-knit upper voice from bar 60 re-enters at bar 87 and gradually descends into lower regions.

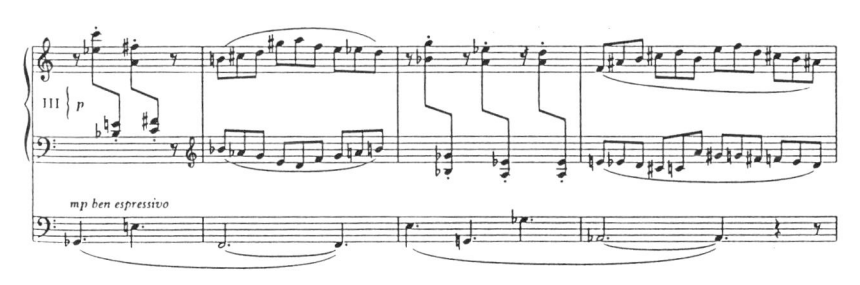

Ex.4 *Job*, 5th. movement: *Despair and Resignation*, bars 60-64 & bars 74-83

Some of Eben's compositional technique may have been clarified by this description of the fifth movement of *Job* and the music examples quoted. The original formulation of the work in improvisation is not denied. At the same time the construction of material and formal procedures indicate a genuinely compositional approach. The clarity of the structure, the delight in the sonority of the instrument and in striking rhythmical patterns, bear witness to his experience as an improviser at the organ, who then enriches his initial ideas with considered reworking. Having reached a certain point, the original content of the improvisation demands adequate formatting of the musical material. The composer is then required to produce a concrete version of the rich diversity of his inspiration. In many ways, Eben's compositional thinking seems related to the attitude that Olivier Messiaen formulated in the preface to his cycle *La Nativité du Seigneur*, when he said:

> *L'émotion, la sincerité, d'abord. Mais transmises à l'auditeur par des moyens sûrs et clairs.*[13]

---

[13]Messiaen, O., Note de l'auteur., in *La Nativité du Seigneur, Fascicule I*, Paris, 1936.

A VOICE FROM THE WHIRLWIND: PERSPECTIVES ON PETR EBEN'S *JOB*

by Michael Bauer

You have heard of Job's patience and have
seen what the Lord finally brought about
               James 5:11

Prologue

It was around the year 1993 when I first encountered Petr Eben's remarkable suite based on the Job story. I can truthfully say that my life as an organist has not been the same since that time. Eben's artistry and the depth of his musico-theological vision have formed me in ways that I could not have anticipated prior to learning this piece.

In the ensuing years I have performed the work on many different occasions, sometimes playing individual movements without narrator, while other performances have featured the entire work with the narrated texts. Several recitals have employed visual images of historic art work created to illustrate Job's life[1], and slides of people from the twentieth century whose lives seem to reflect Job's *sitz im leben*.[2] In addition, I have collaborated on performances of *Job* with members of two dance companies, the University Dance Company at the University of Kansas and the Omega Dance Company from the Cathedral of St. John the Devine in New York. Finally, my wife, Marie Rubis Bauer and I are now culminating this initial phase of activity by recording Eben's complete organ music on the Calcante label.

---

[1] An excellent source to begin a search of the corpus of visual material on Job is Terrien, Samuel L.: *The Iconography of Job through the Centuries: Artists as Biblical Interpreters*, University Park, Pennsylvania, Penn State University Press, 1996.

[2] Many photographers whose work is fitting to this topic were associated with the Farm Securities Administration in the United States during the 1930's. See especially the work of Dorothea Lang, Walker Evans, Ben Shahn, Margaret Bourke-White, Russell Lee, Robert Capa and Arthur Rothstein.

My experience with Eben's organ music has led to several preliminary observations:

1. Audiences invariably sense the integrity and craftsmanship that is infused in each and every piece that flows from Eben's pen. There is a fundamental, universal respect for his command of musical language and his ability to make that language speak in a powerful and compelling fashion.
2. At the end of the twentieth century, a time when many composers are turning back to more traditional tonal materials, Eben writes in an assimilable contemporary harmonic language. Nonetheless, people without any particular musical training seem actually to like his music. In that most rare of all oxymorons, he has succeeded in being both contemporary and popular.

There are three important factors in this regard:

    a. the use of extra-musical ideas to which non-musicians can relate.
    b. employing pre-existing tunes which are familiar to many listeners.
    c. the wonderful quality of lyricism which pervades so much of his music.

One of the most obvious features of Eben's organ music is the consistent use of religious or theological themes throughout many of his works. Eben's stubborn refusal to rend faith from art and begin working in a more secular vein is a testament to the depth of his commitment, particularly in the light of the official atheism with which he was confronted throughout much of his career.

During the last two decades of the twentieth century there has been a renaissance of interest in the relationship between religion and the arts. This movement has spawned books, periodicals, conferences and new religious arts organisations. Eben's development of myth and religious imagery clearly reflects the goals of those who are active in the field. As Wilson Yates says: *the arts are a source in helping identify and understand the religious questions of human existence.*[3] There can be no clearer example of this than *Job*.

---

[3] Yates, W.: *The Arts in Theological Education*, Atlanta, Scholars Press, 1987; p.105.

Furthermore, Eben has connected the literary arts with music, bringing a narrative dimension to his music which enables non-musicians to find their way through a piece, navigating with the map of the text as well as the music. Once again, this is particularly apparent in the case of *Job*. The narrative quality in *Job* suggests the possible use of hermeneutic analysis as one tool in unearthing what the music has to say. John Dixon expands on this approach, saying: *the function of an hermeneutic is to make the narrative present to us so that the work into which the narrative emerges, be it story or painting or symphony, can exert its full force on us.*[4]

This narrative strain is heightened by Eben's choice of pre-existent tunes. The manner in which themes are connected to the text serves to enhance the extra-musical associations available to the listener. Tunes bring to mind not only the texts with which they have traditionally been associated but also the ambience, the evocative power of past liturgical experiences that connect the listener to the faith communities in which he or she has participated.

The tunes themselves are, in turn, part and parcel of the lyrical, pastoral quality in his music. For some casual listeners to Eben's music this may seem like a strange comment. "Lyricism in Eben? All I hear is raw dissonance!" This is simply not my experience. Given the sheer quantity of violence and alienation experienced during the past century, finding a pastoral voice can be a matter of survival. It is particularly important to find a composer who does not give up the life of the mind in order to be pastoral. So much of popular culture, particularly in the church, has divorced the life of the mind from the spirit. Eben does not allow this to happen. In the midst of prophetic, grating harmonies Eben's lyricism is a pastoral element that brings hope and healing to human life. In fact, it is this counterpoint between the prophetic and pastoral dimensions of his music that seems to enliven listeners and performers alike, keeping them searching for hidden meanings, yearning and stretching to reach places they have not reached before.

Studying *Job*

Embarking on a study of Petr Eben's *Job* has been as rewarding in its own way as performing the piece. While there are many ways to analyse a work

---

[4]Dixon, J.W.jr.: *Art and the Theological Imagination,* New York, The Seabury Press, 1978; p.24.

like *Job*, the method that I am pursuing here is what Jon Michael Spencer calls theomusicology. This is his word for *musicology as a theologically informed discipline.*[5] He goes on: *its analysis stands on the presupposition that the religious symbols, myths and canon of the culture being studied are the theomusicologist's authoritative/normative sources.* In regard to the subject here, the text of The Book of Job and the history of its interpretation function as the primary sources for reflecting on Eben's setting of the text for organ and narrator.

It is important to keep in mind that Eben himself provides the exegesis of the text for the listener. There are at least three ways in which it is possible for a composer to function as an interpreter of the Scriptures. First, the composer could be attempting to ask the question: *What really happened in the Biblical account?* In regard to The Book of Job, this involves a foray into the issues of the book's origin and its textual history, setting the work in the context of the culture within which it was written so as to understand what it meant for its own author(s). Surprisingly I believe that Eben engages in this type of exegetical work, if only implicitly, simply by virtue of his selection of texts and the manner in which he has set them.

The second variety of exegesis is to use the Biblical story to further clarify doctrinal points, refining the theological message of the book. As we shall see, in the course of writing music for these texts, Eben does indeed develop a variety of theological points regarding the plight of Job and the problems with which the book deals.

Finally, in the words of Paul Minear, the true function of the scriptural interpretation is to *enhance the modern reader's ability to respond to ancient literature with new appreciations and empathy, to discern overlooked, underground linkages between then and now, to examine current experience through the magnifying glass of archetypal story.*[6]

Clearly Eben has a fund of experience upon which to draw as he relates the plight of Job to modern listeners. To paraphrase Northrop Frye's point about William Blake's paintings of Job, Eben is not simply illustrating the

---

[5]Spencer, J.M.: *Theological Music: Introduction to Theomusicology*, New York, Greenwood Press, 1991; p.3.

[6]Minear, P.S.: *Death Set to Music*; Knoxville, Tennessee, John Knox Press, 1987; p.161.

story, he is recreating it.[7] Through the lens of this work he makes it possible for us to catch a glimpse of the God who speaks from the whirlwind and to identify ourselves in the person of the one to whom God speaks.

As we examine Eben's treatment of Job we search for meanings. It is tempting to simply ask what Eben meant by setting the story as he did. Eben himself has, of course, given us some indication of this in his own words. This, however, ducks the larger question of historical meaning. When a composer releases a work into the world it takes on a life of its own. The work is suddenly an artefact that can be examined for meanings which, however unintended, are there nonetheless. As Bruce Zuckerman points out:

> *one should not fall into the false assumption that meaning is only to be found in the creator's perspective rather than in that of the audience...the meaning of a given work is dynamic because the audience is dynamic.*[8]

In the case of *Job*, we need to keep in mind that there are multiple alternative meanings in part because there are multiple questions and multiple solutions to the questions raised by The Book of Job. In his commentary on Job, Edwin Good says:

> *Not only do I avoid claiming that I have found the truth about Job, I claim that it cannot be found. There is no single correct understanding of The Book of Job.*[9]

Neither Eben's answers nor my own reading of these answers should be canonized as the true meaning of Job. Job 28:12 reads:

> *Wisdom, where can she be found?*
> *Where is the place of discernment?*

---

[7]Frye, N.: Blake's Reading of the Book of Job, in Bloom, Harold, ed.: *The Book of Job*; New York, Chelsea House Publishers, 1988; p.21.

[8]Zuckerman, B.: *Job The Silent*; New York, Oxford University Press, 1991; p.9.

[9]Good, E.M.: *In Turns of Tempest: A Reading of Job;* Stanford, California, Stanford University Press, 1990; p.178.

Norman Habel answers the question by indicating that *wisdom is to be found in the midst of the search*.[10] This may be the best answer of all. Given God's propensity for questioning human wisdom from out of a storm, it is clearly the safest answer.

The Biblical Job
There was a man in the land of Uz whose name was Job...

The Book of Job is one of the most perplexing writings in the Bible. On the surface it is perplexing because of the questions it raises and the answers, or rather the seeming lack of answers, which it presents. Beneath the surface the waters are just as murky. Job may have begun life as a folk tale, sharing many common elements with other ancient near-eastern literature. In its canonical form, the book could have been written by multiple authors. This was a common practice at that time. The consensus among traditional literary and historical critics is that a number of writers contributed to the final product. More recent scholars defend the notion that one person wrote the bulk of the book.

The author may or may not have been a Jew. It is likely that the character of Job himself was not Jewish. This lends a certain universal character to the narrative. Dating the book has proven particularly elusive. Exilic or post-exilic authorship (c.BC 600-300) is the most common suggestion, while the setting for the story itself seems to be in patriarchal times. An exilic time frame for the composition of the narrative can be justified in the light of the suffering that the Jewish people were experiencing and their need to make sense of their plight. Nonetheless, much of the language is archaic and there are potential textual reasons for locating different portions of the work in different eras.

The book itself is organized in three large sections:

1. A prose prologue where Job is tested and presents his initial response of faith.
2. The poetic body of the book, containing three cycles of dialogues between Job and his friends, a poem on wisdom, a concluding monologue by Job, the speeches of Elihu and Job's dialogue with God.

---

[10]Habel, N.C.: In Defense of God the Sage, in Perdue, Leo G. and Gilpin, W. Clark, eds: *The Voice From the Whirlwind*, Nashville, Abingdon Press, 1992; p.30.

3. God's verdict and the restoration of Job's fortunes, presented once again in prose form.

At various times scholars have questioned whether the speeches of Elihu and the poem of wisdom in Chapter 28 are original. This is not the place to go into a detailed analysis of these claims. For our purposes the most important point is to recognize the division between the prose of the prologue and epilogue and the poetic centrepiece, the largest single poem on the Old Testament.

Briefly turning to the Eben setting from a textual standpoint, Eben draws his texts from all three parts of the biblical account:

Movement I (*Destiny*) functions as a sort of overture to the suite, announcing the theme of destiny and giving the listener a clue as to the nature of Job's struggle.

Movements II (*Faith*) and III (*Acceptance and Suffering*) are taken from the prologue. They lay out the two sets of calamities that befell Job and describe his reactions to them.

Movements IV (*Longing for Death*) and V (*Despair and Resignation*) come from the dialogue section of Job. It is interesting to note that Eben has chosen to ignore the dialogues themselves. The three friends, central to most recreations of Job, are entirely absent from Eben's setting. Moreover, to the listener, Job's speeches from the dialogues appear to be monologues, or perhaps are delivered to God. In these movements Job is beaten to the ground and delivered into the depths of despair.

Movements VI (*Mystery of Creation*) and VII (*Penitence and Realisation*) come from the exchange between God and Job at the end of the poetic material. They demonstrate God's power and authority and elicit Job's response.

Movement VIII (*God's Reward*) stands alone as the final denouement of the story. Here God restores Job's standing in the community and grants him even more blessings than he had at the outset of the tale.

The Eben suite actually functions in a quasi-chiastic fashion. Not only can the work be divided as I; II-III; IV-V; VI-VII; VIII, but further connections can be made between the opposing movements in the pyramid:

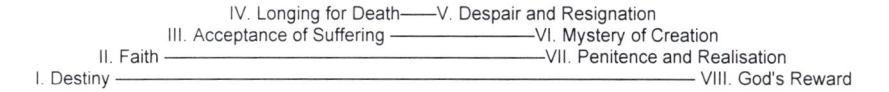

```
            IV. Longing for Death———V. Despair and Resignation
         III. Acceptance of Suffering ————————VI. Mystery of Creation
      II. Faith ————————————————————VII. Penitence and Realisation
I. Destiny ————————————————————————— VIII. God's Reward
```

Movement I (*Destiny*) establishes the conditions wherein Job's fate is determined. The movement works on the assumption that God is in charge of history. Movement VIII (*God's Reward*) can only occur if God is, in fact, in charge of history.

Movement II (*Faith*) presents a picture of Job as, first of all, under attack and then humbled. *The Lord gave and the Lord hath taken away; blessed be the name of the Lord.* Movement VII (*Penitence and Realisation*) similarly ends with Job declaring his own position in humility. *I uttered that which I understood not...wherefore I abhor myself and repent in dust and ashes.* Both declarations are in fact confessions - a confession of faith on the one hand and a confession of sins on the other.

Movement III (*Acceptance of Suffering*) closes the prologue and ends with Job's wife challenging him to curse God. Movement VI (*Mystery of Creation*) opens the concluding dialogue with God and ends with God demanding an answer from Job following his accusation (curse?) of the Almighty. Musically the two movements are further united by the presence in both of *Wer nur den lieben, Gott lasst walten (If Thou but Suffer God to Guide Thee)* throughout Movement III and at bar 24 of Movement VI.

Finally, the two central movements, Movements IV (*Longing for Death*) and V (*Despair and Resignation*), contain a number of obvious textual connections. Death is a particularly prominent theme in both movements. *Why died I not from the womb...* (Movement IV); *I would not live always* (Movement V). The death theme echoes similar statements in the psalms of lament and in Jeremiah, a prophetic figure with whom Job has often been compared. *Cursed be the day I was born! May the day my mother bore me not be blessed!* (Jeremiah 20:14).

The quasi-chiastic order of the movements in Job further heightens the Christological connections that are made explicit in the final movement.

One final note in this brief background account has to do with questions. Perhaps more than any other book in the Bible, Job puts humanity and God in the dock. The fact that much of the book is taken up with questions has the effect of holding the reader's feet to the fire. The search for wisdom - this is, after all, wisdom literature - must continue if human beings are to realize their calling. Some of the questions are actually accusations of either God or Job. Some questions demand an answer, others set dialogue in motion, while still others are rhetorical. This last category applies particularly to God's questioning of Job in the concluding discourse.

One of the interesting features of historic commentary on Job is to see how many different questions emerge from the pens of different writers. Petr

Eben is no different in this regard. He, too, has a series of questions with which he is working as he recreates the classic story. Quite often the answers derived from the book vary, based on the nature of the questions that are asked at the outset.

The overall question in The Book of Job is certainly the problem of evil. Why do bad things happen to good people? How can a good God allow evil to manifest itself in creation? The problem of evil itself takes many different forms under the guidance of different commentators. John T. Wilcox says: *In a broad sense, the issue is whether human individuals get what they merit or deserve in life.*[11] Langdon Gilkey puts it this way: *Does the source of the power of being and of the natural order of existence support, guarantee or further the moral justice of life generally and of history?*[12]

These questions are directed to God and the divine justice. David Daiches compares Job to Milton's *Paradise Lost*, two epics attempting to justify the ways of God. He says: *that God, who is by definition just and right as well as omnipotent, should require justification by a human poet seems somewhat extraordinary.*[13] It is nonetheless the principal theme of both works and implicit within Eben's setting as well.

In the poetic body of The Book of Job there are more or less two sets of answers given to the questions posed by the problem of evil. The two answers are outlined in turn by Job's friends and by Job himself. The three friends present the orthodox line of defence for God. They develop the Deuteronomic view of history, *a view that portrays history as justly ordered, intelligible and predictable.*[14] In such a world the just are rewarded, the wicked are punished and the weak are protected. The wicked may flourish for a while but ultimately they will get what they deserve.

---

[11]Wilcox, J.T.: *The Bitterness of Job: A Philosophical Reading*, Ann Arbor, Michigan, The University of Michigan Press, 1989; p.9.

[12]Gilkey, L.: Power, Order, Justice and Redemption: Theological Comments on Job, in Perdue and Gilpin, *op cit*; p.162.

[13]Daiches, D.: God Under Attack, in Bloom, *op cit,* p.37.

[14]Schreiner, Susan E.: Why do the Wicked Live?: Job and David in Calvin's Sermons on Job, in Perdue and Gilpin, eds. *op cit*, p.133.

By contrast, Job believes that this should be the case but he finds that it is not. His life experience denies what he previously understood to be the truth.

> *Job's main quarrel with the grounding of orthodoxy seems to be, in a broad sense, empirical. Job reports what he himself has suffered and what he claims to know of the weal and woe of others and he claims that the facts are not what the tradition holds them to be. The world, he says, is not like that.*[15]

> *Have you never questioned those who travel?*
> *Have you paid no regard to their accounts -*
> *that the evil man is spared from the day of calamity,*
> *that he is delivered from the day of wrath?*
>
> Job 21: 29-30

Petr Eben's Job
The Lord gave and the Lord hath taken away:
blessed be the name of the Lord

Turning now to an examination of Petr Eben's *Job*, how is the problem of evil approached as it is portrayed in this organ suite? Rather than attacking the issue directly, three related questions may be considered. After their examination, all the information will be assembled in an attempt to determine how Eben's *Job* helps us to further understand the critically important question of evil in human life and human history.

1. The Nature of Suffering.

The first question is "what is the nature of suffering?" This is a question that focuses the attention squarely on Job himself. We learn from his suffering as well as from the connections we make with our own personal experience. Who is the Job of Petr Eben's suite? What picture of suffering emerges as we play and listen to this extraordinary music? Who is the man behind the mask? To answer these questions it is necessary to understand some of the different alternative perspectives on suffering that emerge from the Job literature.

---

[15]Wilcox, J.T.: *op cit*, p.29.

For many in the Judeo-Christian tradition, Job has served as a paradigm, an example to be emulated by people of faith everywhere. This was certainly true in the early church where persecution and suffering were commonplace. In this setting the church could point to Job as one who suffered, was persecuted unjustly, humbly submitted to God and was rewarded in the end. This view of Job is derived from the old adage "the patience of Job" that has its origins in The General Epistle of James, 5:11. Remnants of the Deuteronomic perspective are evident here. The righteous sometimes suffer for a time but God eventually sets the scales in balance and orders the universe according to the dictates of divine justice. Eben himself echoes this notion in the introduction to his organ suite, where he says: *Job humbly accepted his misfortune and triumphed*.[16] Accepting misfortunes becomes the key to redemption.

Clearly the second and third movements of Eben's suite reflect this characterisation of Job. In Movement II (*Faith*), the stage is set with the plainsong *Exultet*. This ancient chant from the Easter vigil service celebrates Christ, the light of the world, as represented by the paschal candle. It is an opening prelude to Job's misfortunes that prefigures the humility of Christ, which Eben will refer to in Movement VIII. Although Eben does not mention the origin of the brief theme upon which the remainder of the movement is based, there is a close relationship between this motif and the opening phrase of the Lutheran chorale *Erhalt uns, Herr*:

Ex.1a Movement II (Faith): Principal motif

Ex.1b Erhalt uns, Herr: Opening phrase

---

[16]Eben, P.: *Job for Organ* (Introductory Notes); London, United Music Publishers, 1989. All music examples from *Job* and quotations by Petr Eben are taken from this source and reproduced with the kind permission of the publishers.

The text normally associated with this chorale clearly expresses the theme of steadfast devotion central to this movement. It further heightens the connection between Job and Christ. The first two stanzas read as follows:

> *Lord, keep us steadfast in Thy Word:*
> *Curb those who fain by craft and sword*
> *Would wrest the Kingdom from Thy Son*
> *And set at naught all He hath done*
>
> *Lord Jesus Christ, Thy pow'r make known,*
> *For Thou art Lord of Lords alone;*
> *Defend Thy Christendom that we*
> *May evermore sing praise to Thee.*[17]

By employing this chorale throughout the movement, Eben is establishing Job as a "man of faith". It brings to mind the Pauline injunction to "pray without ceasing". It is interesting to note that Job himself has often been compared to Abraham as a "man of faith" who was tested by God and finally rewarded in the end.

There are several other programmatic features of this movement. The undercurrents of activity in the opening lines of the movement could, perhaps, be seen as the protagonists plotting Job's suffering:

Ex.2 Movement II (Faith):
Protagonists plotting Job's suffering

Eben himself points out that the scalar passages in the ensuing *Allegro* represent *the resounding strokes of misfortune which descend upon Job's name and family.*

---

[17]Original translation of Martin Luther's hymn, by Catherine Winkworth (1863).

Ex.3 Movement II (Faith): Messengers of disaster

Clearly, the fact that there are four such interjections, mirroring the four messengers of ill will, is not accidental. Following the final messenger, Job falls to the ground and worships for the remainder of the movement, with his prayers becoming more and more intense with time. Finally, in the last four bars, we hear rumblings of the original storm clouds, a reminder that what has happened is real, not a dream or an illusion. Nonetheless, the movement concludes with a quotation from a plainsong *Gloria*, proclaiming that the King of Kings will one day come. Perhaps it is not too much to foresee, in the nativity narrative, the suffering of the cross as the means by which messianic hope is finally fulfilled.

Ex.4 Movement II (Faith): conclusion - Suffering; Gloria

Movement III (*Acceptance of Suffering*) is likewise an excellent example of "the patience of Job". Calamity again strikes Job, this time in the form of an assault on his health:

Ex.5 Movement III (Acceptance of Suffering): Calamity

Job's response is contained in the strains of *Wer nur den lieben, Gott lasst walten (If thou but suffer God to guide thee)* that continues for much of the movement. Interestingly, after the initial onslaught by "the Satan" (Satan is not yet personified as an individual in the text of Job), the movement is set in two large sections. The first chorale section gradually grows more and more anguished in its prayers until Job recalls "the Satan's" afflictions in vivid detail once again. From this point onward Job once again centres his mind and spirit on God in humility and love. Note that Job's plight is set in very human, realistic terms. He is pictured as struggling with the news of his lost possessions and his illness. These things have not been easy for him to accept and Eben pictures Job struggling with them even as he worships Yahweh.

This view of the patient Job squares with the image that is present in the prologue and the concluding dialogues with Yahweh but it has little to do with the Job of the poetic midsection. As Zuckerman points out:

> *there are many ways in which one might characterise Job; one might view him as righteous, forthright, sincere, perhaps a bit prideful; but "patience" is not the most obvious of his personality traits.*[18]

Wilcox paints an alternative picture of Job as a bitter man.[19] The Job who debates the rôle of fate with his three friends certainly challenges God. In many cases he employs legal language to further his cause, at one point calling for an arbiter to decide his case with God. He may even cross the line into blasphemy by claiming that he understands the ways of God. Certainly the Job of the central dialogues is a much more complex and enigmatic dramatic figure than his orthodox counterpart.

This is the Job we encounter in the succeeding two movements. Movement IV (*Longing for Death*) is a giant passacaglia and the affective centrepiece of the drama. The Job of this movement is single-minded, gripped by his dilemma until no other thought can enter his mind. His focus is almost entirely anthropocentric. There is no real argument with God here, simply a determined, heartfelt desire to die. The death wish, while common to Job and Jeremiah, is otherwise unique in ancient Near-Eastern literature. In a brilliant piece of writing, Eben reaches the climax of this *Totentanz*, the climax of Job's anguish and strength, then immediately thins the texture and gradually drops the range four-and-a-half octaves until we find Job lying prostrate on the ground, bereft of any strength or hope.

Movement V (*Despair and Resignation*) shows us a picture of a frantic Job. here his attention is focused on God, not just on himself. Job's complaints are finally expressed in one last outburst of frenetic energy:

---

[18] Zuckerman, B.: *op cit.,* p.13.

[19] Wilcox, J.T.: *op cit.,* p.73.

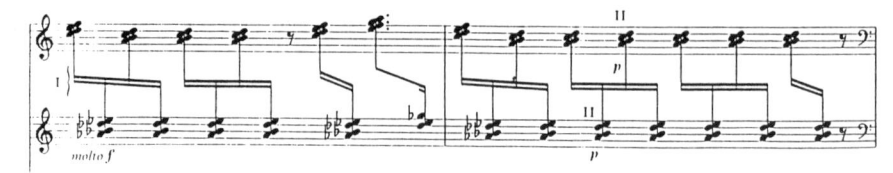

**Ex.6 Movement V (Despair and Resignation):
Climax of Job's Complaints**

Taken as a whole, we experience a counterpoint between the patient Job of the prologue and the rebellious Job of the interior dialogues. This counterpoint itself heightens and extends the dramatic depth of Eben's setting, forcing the listener to account for the many faces of suffering.

2. Is There Meaning and Order in the World?

The underlying issue in regard to suffering may have something to do with its fundamental purpose. Is suffering senseless and absurd, is it merely gratuitous or does it have a rôle to play in the larger divine drama? Another way to put this is to ask whether or not there is meaning and purpose in the world? This question clearly focuses on God rather than on Job. Who is the God who emerges from the pages of The Book of Job and in turn from Eben's setting?

Many people have tried to answer the former question. One approach is to look at the rôle of suffering and redemption. In Judeo-Christian literature the suffering servant and the atoning Son of God are innocent sufferers who serve as vehicles for God's redemptive activity in history. God is redeeming humanity and indeed all creation by participating directly and personally in human suffering. Thus suffering is neither senseless nor absurd. In the mystery of the divine plan it is a necessary precondition to salvation itself.

In a wonderful essay on Job in the sermons of John Calvin, Susan Schreiner unpacks this argument as she describes the work of pre-Reformation commentators on Job.[20] One important early voice was Ambrose. Writing in the fourth century, he presented a Pauline perspective. In the Second Epistle of Paul the Apostle to the Corinthians, Chapter 12, Verse 10, we read:

---

[20]Schreiner, S.E.: *op cit.*, p.129ff.

Therefore I take pleasure in infirmities, in reproaches, in necessities, in persecutions, in distresses for Christ's sake: for when I am weak, then I am strong.

For Ambrose, Job was a spiritual athlete who could not grow stronger without the trials of suffering. This leads him to articulate a neo-platonic answer to the question of suffering. Suffering produces freedom from this world and all its illusions. It liberates human beings from enslavement to the fleeting, false assumptions upon which this human culture is based. By means of a trial of fire human minds and spirits may ascend to heaven and achieve union with the Almighty. Thus, for Ambrose, suffering has salutary effects. It is treasured for its potential to produce spiritual growth. It has meaning.

Eben does not shy away from the implications of Job's trials. He is sensitive to the question of meaning and purpose of suffering. The answer to the question of meaning is uniquely God's answer. Thus it is located particularly in the concluding discourses of God, speaking from the whirlwind.

Movements VI and VII present God's speech, drawn exclusively from the first of two speeches in the biblical account, followed by Job's response. Movement VI (*Mystery of Creation*) is the account of creation that God presents to Job. Contained within this theophany are many rhetorical questions. *Where were you when I laid the foundations of the earth? Who laid the cornerstone thereof; when the morning stars sang together and all the sons of God shouted for joy?* As many commentators have pointed out, in this discourse God is not really answering Job's question. Job has questioned God about why the wicked prosper and the righteous are afflicted. God responds with an extraordinary speech about the creation of the world. This speech does not touch on the merits of Job's case.

The clues to understanding Eben's treatment lie in the opening and closing sections of the movement. The initial phrase clearly evokes a sense of mystery.

Ex.7 Movement VI (Mystery of Creation): Opening phrase

As Wilcox points out, *there are writers in the Rudolf Otto tradition who believe the theophany expresses a peculiar, uncanny, "numinous" awe...*[21] Certainly these opening chords, performed with the swell pedal closed, contain elements of dread, awe, *mysterium tremendum* and fascination. Their numinous quality seems readily apparent but what are we to make of the questioning phrase that rises above them in bar 3?

Ex.8 Movement VI (Mystery of Creation): Questioning phrase

Surely this phrase, which is repeated at the end of the movement, cannot represent God's questions to Job. Throughout the theophany God appears as a majestic figure. Divine power is the content and the context for God's questioning of Job. The questioning phrase, on the other hand, is meek and tentative. Furthermore, the remainder of the opening portion of the movement consists of alternations of the mystery chords followed by the question in canon with itself. The canon is reminiscent of "canon law" as depicted by Bach and the Netherlandish composers. It reminds us of Job's legal case against God.

---

[21]Wilcox, J.T.: *op cit.,* p.135.

Ex.9 Movement VI (Mystery of Creation): Question in canon

Following this we hear the opening strains of *Wer nur den lieben, Gott lasst walten* for the first time since Movement III. What is going on here? Who is really speaking? The answer seems clear enough. In Eben's setting God speaks from the whirlwind but the questioning phrase is Job himself! Even after God has broken the silence and commanded centre stage, we continue to hear the echo of Job's questions, still in search of an answer. This is existential Job, the man who understands his own ignorance and weakness, who, out of sheer moral courage, continues to ask the fundamental questions of life, questions that resonate down the corridors of history to the gates of Buchenwald and the streets of Phnom Penh.

Movement VII (*Penitence and Realisation*) represents Job's final response to Yahweh. Several features of this movement deserve attention. First, we hear an ostinato-like figure in the bass underneath the opening section of the movement.

Ex.10 Movement VII (Penitence and Realisation): Ostinato figure

This ostinato reiterates and intensifies the opening major second from the theme of Job's destiny in Movement I.

Ex.11 Movement I (Destiny): Motive of Job's destiny

Job struggles to respond to God. He argues, perhaps with himself since this is safer, each argument concluding with the same ecstatic figuration found in Movement V (*Despair and Resignation*).

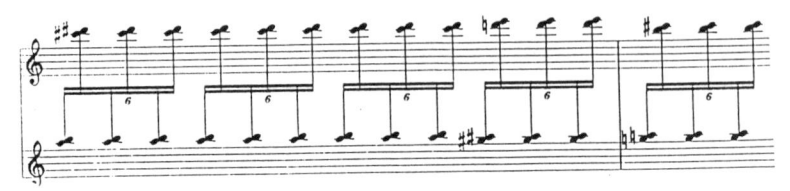

**Ex.12 Movement VII (Penitence and Realisation):
Ecstatic figure**

Finally, with the introduction of *Veni Creator Spiritus*, Job's questions become muted and gentle, until he finally dissolves in the embrace of the Spirit represented by a concluding major triad at the end of the movement. The unanswered question is ultimately resolved in the reality of God's presence, the *substance of things hoped for, the evidence of things not seen.* (The Epistle of Paul the Apostle to the Hebrews, Chapter 11, Verse 1).

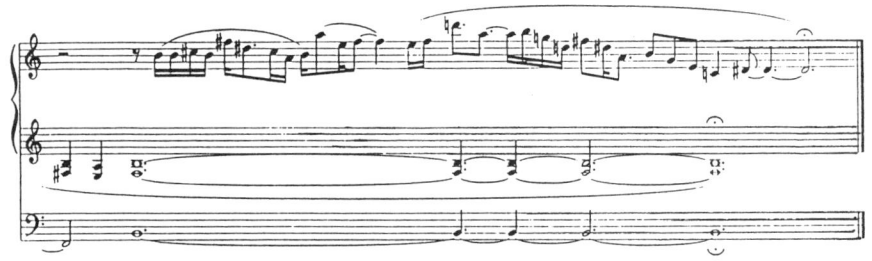

**Ex.13 Movement VII (Penitence and Realisation):
Job's realisation**

Is there meaning and order in the world? In the end Job does not understand how or why this is so but he answers with a quiet yes, an unmistakable benediction to his tortured liturgy.

3. What is the Right Language to Employ in the Divine-Human Relationship?

Kenneth Frieden asks: *What is the right language of relationship to God?*[22] This is the final question in this brief inquiry into the theology of Petr Eben's *Job*. Movement VIII (*God's Reward*) is the focal point of the search. Here,

---

[22]Frieden, K.: Job's Encounters with the Adversary, in Bloom, H. ed. *op cit.,* p.91.

rather than looking at either Job or God, it is necessary to examine the relationship between Job and God.

In this concluding movement, Eben writes a set of variations on the hymn *Kristus, příklad pokory (Christ the model of humility)*. This hymn from the Bohemian Brethren tradition was written by Lucas of Prague. It first appeared in the *Bohemian Hymn Book* of 1501. The composer of the tune is unknown, although it was probably coupled with this text from the beginning. The comparison of Christ and Job is not unique to Eben. James Williams says:

> *The Jesus of the Gospels becomes, for the Christian tradition, the decisive event revealing the reality and meaning of the God of victims...What Job calls for, the Gospels focus on. What Job expresses in a few moments of anguished lucidity, the Gospels illuminate in the story of the Passion. In this sense, I think Christian theology should look firmly and unashamedly at Job as an adumbration of Jesus as the crucified.*[23]

In light of the Job story the concluding stanzas of the hymn text are particularly fascinating. They read:

> *Target of the Devil's rage,*
> *And by his own disowned,*
> *Cursed by strangers and condemned,*
> *Abandoned by his friends,*
> *King of all, he could not find*
> *A place to rest his head;*
> *On that royal head he wore*
> *a crown of thorns instead.*
>
> *For the joy you came to give*
> *You meekly went to die,*
> *Teaching us to bear our cross*
> *To know your kind of joy.*
> *Give us faith to follow you*
> *through cross to faith's reward,*

---

[23] Williams, J.G.: Job and the God of Victims, in Perdue and Gilpin, eds. *op cit.*, p.226.

*Loving as you showed us how,
our humble Servant Lord.*[24]

The hymn serves as a vehicle for the presentation of a powerful climax to the suite. It represents evil transformed by grace, the reconciliation of humanity to God by means of God's participation in human suffering.

One significant characteristic of this setting is its harmonic language. Eben writes in the same prophetic, contemporary style as he has in the earlier movements. This is one of Eben's contributions to the interpretation of the Jobian narrative. At the end, when Job receives his reward, his suffering is still with him. Even though he has acquired new children and doubled his possessions, he will always be the man who was afflicted by God. It is possible to view this as a blessing. Job sees the human condition for what it is. He is living authentically, no longer driven by illusions about the world around him. In the end *the greatest evil was not adversity but rather the acquiescence in the goods of temporality...*[25]

Paul Tillich writes of the relationship between religious style and religious content in art. He says that religious style is *art as an expression of ultimate concern.* Used in this sense, art that expresses a surface view of life, art that is trivial or banal, does not have religious style. Tillich equates religious style with expressionism. He asks: *Is it possible to use these elements of expressionist visual art in dealing with the traditional symbols of Christianity? Sometimes...I am willing to say that it is possible. Sometimes I am not willing to say so.*[26] I believe that Petr Eben's *Job* would help Tillich answer this question in the affirmative. It is religious discourse that begins with reality and does not shirk the hard questions of meaning and existence.

Epilogue
*And the Lord turned the captivity of Job...
and blessed the latter end of Job more than his beginning*

---

[24]Vajda, Jaroslav J.: *So Much to Sing About,* St. Louis, Morning Star Music Publishers, 1991., p.57.

[25]Yaffe, Martin D.: Providence in Medićval Aristotelianism: Moses Maimonides and Thomas Aquinas on The Book of Job, in Perdue and Gilpin, eds., *op cit.,* p.132.

[26]Tillich, P.: Existentialist Aspects of Modern Art, in Dillenberger, John and Dillingberger, Jane, eds., *Paul Tillich on Art and Architecture*, New York, Crossroad, 1987, p.99.

At the end of all this theological argument and positing, how does Petr Eben's *Job* answer the question of evil that exists at the centre of the biblical story? There is, of course, no real answer. At the end of Movement VI the question is still with us. In the final analysis we live our lives with what Frieden calls *linguistic asceticism*.[27]

John Calvin understood this, yet he tried to go beyond mere silence. As Schreiner relates:

> *Calvin struggles with the recurring tension between God's visibility and hiddenness, revelation and silence, knowability and incomprehensibility. Continually he tries to hold these antithetical strains together so that the God of history does not recede into utter inscrutability.*[28]

There are three important lessons that we can learn from Eben in this regard. First of all, we must encounter reality in the language and terms of our own time, open to whatever may come our way. In so doing our language must not be flimsy or shallow. As Tillich says, *we do not have to cover up anything but have to look at the human situation in its depths of estrangement and despair.*[29]

Secondly, we should bear in mind that words are not the only vehicle for human expression. In music and the arts interpretive possibilities are available that expand the limits of theological discourse. This is art doing theology. It is an important and necessary complement to the rational musings of professional theologians.

Finally, it is no accident that the final movement focuses on Christ. God's judgement of Job did not turn out to be the last word on the subject. As Eben demonstrates, mercy and judgement somehow co-exist in the wisdom of God.

---

[27]Frieden, K.: *op cit.*, p.102.

[28]Schreiner, S.E.: *op cit.*, p.135.

[29]Tillich, P.: *op cit.*, p.96.

PETR EBEN'S CHURCH OPERA: *JEREMIAS*

by Ruth Forsbach

Until recently one could read in the introduction to his printed works that they encompassed every genre except opera. And anyone who knows Petr Eben knows how much he wanted to make good this deficiency for as long ago as the 1950's he had found a text which could serve as an ideal libretto for his opera; the long drama *Jeremias* by Stefan Zweig (1881 - 1942), written in exile between 1915 and 1917 and first performed in Zurich at the end of February 1918.

This drama in nine scenes by the Austrian writer is a passionate call for the overcoming of hatred between peoples, against the euphoria of war and the repression of the (vanquished) enemy. The lonely warning prophet Jeremiah whose visions of the fall of Jerusalem lead to his being cursed even by his own mother stands as a symbol for the role of the author himself between nations, a *"voice in the wilderness"*. The concept of humanism and a sense of the supranational unite Petr Eben with Stephan Zweig. Furthermore this drama fascinated Eben because of his personal links with the Jewish people through his father. This chosen people has survived every defeat and every attempt at its annihilation through its will to live and its belief in God. Apart from that Eben was able to draw parallels with the situation in his own country - and it was not least the glowingly lyrical Expressionist language of the author and the numerous choruses which reveal the people as the true partners of the prophet which sustained over several decades his wish to set this drama to music.

Of course for such an immense task Eben needed a commission and the certainty that the opera could be performed. This would never have been possible under the totalitarian system and even after the *"Velvet Revolution"* of 1989 several years passed before he received a commission for a work for which he had been preparing himself inwardly for so many years. Czech Radio commissioned the work and the Prague National Theatre produced it in St Vitus's Cathedral at the Prague Spring in May 1997. As the performance was broadcast live on television many thousands of music-lovers throughout the world were able to see it. I personally had the pleasure of attending the final rehearsal and the performance in Prague. I was also able to observe several phases of the work's creation, including the reading of the much-shortened text and the performance the

Plate 3   Petr Eben with Ruth Forsbach, Remscheid 1994

first four scenes by the composer at the piano in November 1996. In addition, I was able to hear the first two performances in Germany, as an oratorio in Chemnitz on 18th July 1998 and at the Castle Festival in Zwingenberg on 19th September 1998. I therefore hope to be able to give a lively and interesting account of this great work.

1. The Text

Stephan Zweig's drama written during the First World War -it was begun in 1915 and published in 1917 - takes the biblical story of the prophet Jeremiah (c.600 BC) and transfers its timeless problems not only to his own times but also to ours and indeed beyond, all of them determined by power and hatred as triggers of war and destruction. The play is very long. Its nine scenes, lasting over five hours, have frequently lead to cuts and deletions being made in performance. The true partners of the prophet are the Jewish people who, as in a Greek tragedy, act as a Chorus commenting on the action and moving it forward. Apart from Jeremiah there only a few protagonists: the Mother, Baruch, King Zedekiah, and a few minor characters.

It was clear to Petr Eben that far-reaching cuts would need to be made in this extensive original to reduce it to just over an hour which he thought would be a suitable length for a church opera. In three stages he and his wife Šárka filtered the play down to a libretto which concentrates the action into five scenes but retains as far as possible Zweig's language, a feat which I, after repeated readings of the original, did not think possible. Naturally several psychologically important developments fell by the wayside in the process, for example the prophet's despair after the destruction of Jerusalem which almost leads him to turn away from his God. But Eben's comprehensive knowledge of literature and his fine feeling for language enabled him to produce a stringent version of the text, a successful distillation which combines the important elements of the biblical story and the distinctive character of Zweig's language. The introduction of a *"Testo"*, a narrator who gives a brief introductory summary to each scene, a tenor role in the oratorio tradition, is particularly effective. Petr Eben set the work to music in the original German and then pulled of a second feat for the première in Prague by translating this particularly poetic language into Czech which, of course, has quite different emphases. In this too he succeeded admirably demonstrating how a man of broad culture and wide artistic interests, a *"huomo universale"* as I would call him without any reservation, can without any outside help create the best basis for his own work.

A brief summary of the action:

Scene 1: *The Awakening of the Prophet*

Jeremiah is visited by terrible dreams in which he foresees the destruction of Jerusalem. He senses that he is called to be a prophet. Even his own mother does not believe her child's visions and curses him who causes terror in Israel (*Schrecknis wirft über Israel*) for Jerusalem endures for ever (*ewig währet Jerusalem*).

Scene 2: *The Warning*

The people crowd onto the square in front of the King's palace in Jerusalem. They want to shake off the Assyrian yoke and call for war. The desperate warnings of Jeremiah are shouted down and the "strong man", Baruch, wounds him with his sword in order to silence him. However, he has to acknowledge the strength of the prophet's message and becomes the first to believe him.

Scene 3: *The Meeting with the King (The Guards on the Ramparts)*

War has broken out and the Assyrians have already surrounded Jerusalem. King Zedekiah could still achieve peace by submitting to them but he does not heed Jeremiah's words. The people demand that Jeremiah be crucified. The King declines for he is still convinced of Israel's invincibility. Jeremiah lingers in despair: *"O Schmach über mich, dass so dürr war meine .... .wo brachte ich Frieden?". (Ignominy upon me, that my words were so arid where did I bring peace?)*

Scene 4: *The Trials of Jeremiah*

Jeremiah returns to his parental home where his mother lies dying. She recognises her son and embraces him. However, she hears the sounds of war and as she dies she acknowledges the fall of Jerusalem. The enraged crowd comes in search of the prophet who predicted the defeat, takes him captive and throws him in the dung pit: *"Möge er faulen wie seine Worte im Dunkel der Erde". (May he and his words rot in the depths of the earth.)*

Scene 5: *The Eternal Road*

Jerusalem is beaten, the walls razed to the ground, the city occupied by the enemy. All the nobles have been killed, King Zedekiah has been blinded after being forced to watch the murder of his sons. The victor, Nebuchadnezzar, the "King of Midnight" (Der König der Mitternacht) demands that the entire population leave the city when the trumpet sounds[1] three times. In this desperate situation the people recall the prophet, whose words have proved to be true, and fetch him from his prison. He finds words of comfort: *"Unser Gott ist em verborgener Gott und erst in der Tiefe des Leidens werden wir seiner Gewahr, in euch wird er bauen das ewige Jerusalem. Nicht zum Frieden sind wir erwählt unter den Völkern: Weltwanderschaft ist unser Zelt".* (Our God is an invisible God and only in the depths of suffering do we become aware of him, in you he will build the eternal Jerusalem. We have not been chosen among the peoples of the world for a life of peace; we are destined to roam the world.) And so the people go into exile with their blind king, singing as they go, a moral victory for the underdogs: *"Wir wandern den heiligen Weg unserer Leiden - heimwaärts zu Gott, der aller Anfang and Ausgang war."* (We go the holy way of our sufferings - homewards to God who was from the beginning of the world.)

II. The Music

Those who are familiar with Petr Eben's numerous songs know how exactly and sympathetically he follows the inflections of the lyrical language in his melodic lines. Among the little-known and rarely performed works are the *Písně nelaskavé (Loveless Songs)* to texts of, amongst others, the Czech poet J. Seifert for contralto or mezzo-soprano and solo viola. It has to be said that in the only recording I know the viola part is played by the whole viola section of the Czech Philharmonic in order to balance out the drama in the voice-part. Here Petr Eben takes the speech melody of his great model Janacek and projects it further into our time. When I heard this cycle for the first time - on tape; sadly I have never heard it live - it was obvious to me that Petr Eben would have to write an opera sooner or later: such a feeling for drama had to lead him to this form. That his opera was to have a spiritual theme and that it should transcend the merely national with a

---

[1] Or rather, a trombone in keeping with German convention, c.f. Brahms's *German Requiem*

global humanitarian message is as much a part of his creative personality as his acknowledgment of the great musical traditions of his Czech homeland. He found all he reguired of a text in Stefan Zweig's play. In preparing to compose the opera he examined several volumes of Hebrew melodies in order to come as close as possible to the sound of biblical times. As the melodies of Gregorian music also draw upon this biblical tradition they suited well the basic tenor of Eben's religious music. Gregorian chant plays a leading role in his early works; for many years he had to hide the guotations from the critical ears of the Communists but those who had ears to hear recognised the melodies and understood Eben's message. In more recent years he has been able to use them freely and with this public message he reaches the hearts of the people, more easily and more clearly, but perhaps not always more deeply than in totalitarian times!. So - suggestions of Hebrew and Gregorian melody determine the composition of *Jeremias*. In addition there are Eben's typical harmonies, chords spiced with dissonances, ostinato figures, characteristic rhythms. As well as the narrow intervals of the thematic material there are jumps of sevenths and ninths and, of course, tritones which, as the tensest of all intervals, Eben cannot do without. The small instrumental ensemble for which Eben wrote consists of brass (trumpets trombones and horns), Woodwind, strings (with three or four players to a part depending on the circumstances), percussion and positive organ to accompany the recitatives, sometimes Supported by the double bass as a 16-foot instrument. Thus the opera is also suitable for smaller venues and the opportunities for its performance are considerably greater than they would be if a larger orchestra were required.

The music is continuous. Short orchestral preludes or interludes mark the scene changes. Eben uses a something akin to a leitmotiv system to establish connections. Thus, for example, the mother's cry *"Jeremias..."* which is heard three times at widening intervals, or the phrase *"ewig währt Jerusalem"* which is sung to the same sequence of notes, whether by the Mother, the King or the Chorus.

The role of the Chorus is central in this opera: one critic wrote that it is actually a work for baritone (Jeremiah) and chorus. The writing differs very little from Eben's other numerous religious choral works: very precise declamation of the text, frequent parallel lines for soprano and tenor or alto and bass, although there are also some very difficult four or six note chords. Striking and new is also the separation of male and female chorus: as early as the second scene the men sing of their lust for war while the women take up Jeremiah's call for peace. This phenomenon is even more striking in the final scene. In an impressive lament the women sing: *"Gott hat uns gezüchtigt von unsern Sünden. Wir sind verlorem"* (God has punished us for our sins: we are lost) while the men curse the King and the priests. What a feeling of inner peace and trust emanates from the final chorus, which can be repeated ad lib! (A true "exodus" of the Chorus such as Eben visualised as he was composing has not yet been realised.) The solo trombone which summons the exodus of the conquered people must be posted in an elevated position. It is a difficult part but at least it can be played by one of the orchestral trombones and does not require a fourth player; here again, Eben shows himself a practical man as he bears in mind financial considerations attending a performance.

The singing roles are characteristically composed. That of the prophet is central, a dramatic part for baritone, the voice to which Eben entrusted most of his songs. From the first vision to the consolation of the defeated people in the final scene Eben creates a deeply felt personality, in keeping with his own inner feelings. The only more extended arioso section, when in Scene 3 Jeremiah greets the threat of crucifixion as the fulfilment of his longing for death and thus at the same time looks forward to Christ, is a wonderful confession of faith. The mourning after the death of his mother is touching as it reaches its climax with the words *"Gott, es ist hart, dein Bote zu sein"* (God, it is a hard fate to be your messenger). The Mother (lying in the contralto to mezzo register) brings warmth to the opera despite her cursing of her son in the first scene. Her death set against the background of the conflict between love for her child who is *"weltverloren"* (lost to the world) and the recognition of the truth that Jerusalem is lost is a shattering representation of human fallibility and the vulnerability of our relationships. Baruch (a high tenor and a part which is difficult to cast) who experiences the change from warhungry young man to first disciple of the prophet, establishes the link between the People, the King and Jeremiah. (It is he who at the end leads the blind Zedekiah back to his people before the exodus.)

The Narrator (also a high tenor in keeping with oratorio tradition) who gives a brief introduction to each scene, is accompanied only by the organ. Eben deliberately restricts himself to a small positive organ in order to facilitate its closeness to the orchestra which is usually not possible with richer sounding larger instruments. [In his oratorio *Posvátná znamení (Holy Signs)* he gave the organ - preferably two larger instruments - a central role regardless of the distance from the orchestra that this entail.] Even the minor male parts of the warriors have significant thoughts to express. For example, on the ramparts in Scene 2 where the younger one (a tenor) repeats the older man's words *"nicht von Gott kommt der Krieg"* in increasing intervals from fourth to major seventh to minor ninth, or in Scene 3 when one Assyrian soldier has to recognise that *"das ist nicht em Auszug der Geknechteten"* (that is not the exodus of slaves) and the second answers him: *"Ja, sie glauben an das Unsichtbare, das ist ihr Geheimnis"*. (Yes, they believe in the invisible, that's their secret.)

These brief comments on *Jeremias* by Petr Eben can only point to some of the numerous musical levels and beauties of this work. One must hear it as a whole and as often as possible to appreciate it fully. Even at the première in Prague it seemed to me to be a work that "had always been here" but had simply not been available for us to hear until then - surely a good omen for the importance and the future of this church opera!

III. Performances of "Jeremias" to date (August 1999).

1. The first performance in *Katedrála sv. Víta* (St Vitus's Cathedral) in Prague on 25th May 1997 as part of the Prague Spring.

The pressure for the first performance of *Jeremias* to be a success lay heavily on the composer and everybody else involved. It was announced as a central event at the Prague Spring of 1999, was broadcast live on television and relayed by a number of European television stations. St Vitus's Cathedral was of course in every respect a distinguished venue for the first performance but for a variety of reasons Petr Eben would have preferred another Prague church. The huge cathedral is not Without its acoustic problems and the set was also very difficult to erect as a large marble tombstone occupies the centre of the crossing. At the final rehearsal there were problems of co-ordination between chorus, Soloists and orchestra but the performance itself was a great success for everyone involved. The Archbishop of Prague, Cardinal Vlk, introduced the performance and the packed audience followed it with great concentration. It was a success in every respect: the gold-coloured set by A.K.Majewski, the production by Josef Průdek, the outstanding Soloists, with Ivan Kusnjer in the title role, the large Opera Chorus which sang its extensive part froin memory and most convincingly, the ballet of the National Theatre which joined the chorus on the stage and underlined the action with its movements. The performance was conducted by Bohumil Kulínský who had already conducted the first performance of *Posvátná znamení (Holy Signs)* in Salzburg in 1995. This production was also staged at the Litomyšl Festival in the same year and during Holy Week this year (1999) was also given at the National Theatre itself. In the year 2000 it is also to be given with the same forces in Rome, and of course again in Prague.

2. Un-staged first performance in German at the 7th Festival of Central Europe (Bavaria, Bohemia and Saxony) in Chemnitz on 17th July 1998.

It was of course a particular pleasure for Petr Eben that very soon after the first performance much interest was expressed in further performances. He was especially keen to hear the work in German, the language in which it had been composed. The first opportunity was presented by this festival with its emphasis on German-Czech connections. The venue was the great Castle Church in Chemnitz. A abstract blue metal construction by Thomas Thomaschke was set up in the sanctuary which gave scope for various interpretations. The soloists, with the Swede Gunnar Lindberg in the title-role, were excellent, although here they were formally dressed, had their scores in their hands, and stepped forward to sing as in an oratorio. The Chorus was formed by the ars-nova-ensemble of Berlin under of Peter Schwarz: twelve professional singers who stood in a semi-circle behind the soloists and sang the smaller solo passages from there. Petr Eben was astonished at the vocal power of this ensemble which is highly experienced in singing modern music and yielded little to the Opera Chorus. This, then, was a static oratorio version of the church opera but overall it was very convincing. The work, it seems, can be deprived of nearly all its action without losing any of its power of expression.

3. The first German stage production at the Zwingenberg Castle Festival in St Afra's Church in Neckargerach in August 1998.

A middle way between opera and oratorio was found by the third interpretation of *Jeremias*. It was conducted by Guido Rumstadt at the this festival on the River Neckar near Heidelberg which has been taking place for over two decades. The production by Norbert Abel incorporated the sanctuary; piled-up sand-bags and scaffolding formed a very evocative background. The altar-painting was replaced by a war-time photograph of the Church of St Mary Lubeck in flames. Again there were excellent Soloists, in particular the Croatian Josip Lesaja in the title role. He had spent many weeks, as he said, working and thinking himself into the part and this was very clear to see from the way he sang and from the restrained ardour of his movements. Much was only hinted at in this production; for example, the death of the Mother, played by the excellent Annetraud Flitz, who, after she realises that there is to be a war, is lead away by servants.

At the end of the opera the prophet takes the shovel from the workman who throughout the performance has been shovelling sand from the piled-up bags, a symbol of the futility but also the continuity of action, of passing away and continuing life. A pointer to the future of the work was, in my opinion, the involvement of the Chorus. A good church choir from the area had taken on this difficult task but was neither able or willing to sing the work completely from memory. It was therefore placed at the side and was required to master only a limited number of contributions to the action: entrances and exits, standing up, one or two gestures. It was thus a quasi static element while the singers in the sanctuary, of course, sang and acted from memory. This contrast increased the tension and at the same time pointed to an acceptable possibility for future performances in churches by good choirs. The three performances at the festival were very successful and were the subject of detailed press reviews.

In this or a similar form the opera will be given in June 2000 in St Michael's Church, Hamburg on the occasion of the Catholic Assembly, and in Würzburg. In August 1999 it will be performed at the Ossiach Festival in Austria which has a long tradition of performing church operas. It will also soon be heard in England in the place where Britten's church operas were performed. The composer's wish that the opera, which is certainly one of his most important works should not just receive one performance and then be forgotten, has been fulfilled beyond all expectations in the very short time since its composition. May it and the power of its musical and textual message continue to go on its "eternal way".

PERSONAL TRIBUTES TO PETR EBEN

Sieglinde Ahrens

Ubi caritas et amor, Deus ibi est. Congregavit nos in unum Christi amor. Exsultemus et in ipso iucundemur. Timeamus et amemus Deum vivum. Et ex corde diligamus nos sincero...[1]

I first heard this choral work, based on one of the Gregorian antiphons for Maunday Thursday and beginning with a restrained *recitativo* before gradually rising to a five and six voice chorus, on the radio many years ago. Since that time the name Petr Eben has for me been associated with the deep impression of purity, rectitude, warmth and at the same time great strength and solidity, which this chorus left in my memory.

A few years later came my first encounter with the works for organ and an ever-growing fascination with them. My recording of *Nedělní hudba (Sunday Music)*, a work which was little known at the time, was sent to the composer in the summer of 1981 with a request for detailed comments and this lead to an intensive exchange of letters during the course of which we jointly planned further recordings of his organ music and resolved in minute detail all the questions of interpretation which these involved: *Laudes, Okna* for trumpet and organ, *Malá Chorální Partita, Dvě Chorální Fantazie* and finally the first recording of *Krajiny Patmoské (Landscapes of Patmos)* for organ and percussion. Between these there were concerts with *Mutationes*, parts of the *Missa cum populo, Faust, Fantazie pro violu a varhany Rorate Coeli* - a time of many long nights in churches and recording studios!

Our first actual meeting, on the occasion of a lecture recital in Duisburg in 1983, was followed in the succeeding years by several "pilgrimages" to the then still rare concerts or lectures which Eben gave in Germany. How wonderful it is that, since 1989, the master who so much enjoys travelling and making contacts no longer has any barriers to overcome in this respect and that, for him who had long since achieved international fame, the world is now, in the truest sense of the word, open. *Ad multos annos!*

---

[1] *Ubi caritas et amor* is a six-part mixed voice choral work, written in 1964.

Hörður Áskelsson

Petr Eben has a rôle in the development of church music in Iceland.

The history of church music in Iceland is very unusual. For a period of several centuries the only music that was heard in Icelandic churches was hymn-singing and Gregorian chant. On special occasions the only concessions made to art or ornamentation was found by singing in two parts, moving mainly in parallel fifths, a simple sort of organum.

The first organ came to Iceland in 1840, to the Cathedral in Reykjavík. This was an instrument of four stops, built in Denmark. By the end of the nineteenth century most churches had acquired harmoniums and church choirs had been established widely. The first professionally qualified Icelandic organist was Páll Ísólfsson (1893-1974), who studied with Karl Straube in Leipzig. When he returned to Iceland after his years of study in Germany his countrymen had their first opportunity to hear real organ music. After his return, various well-wishers subscribed to fund the purchase of a new three manual organ from Sauer/Walcker of Frankfurt am Oder and people flocked to the Free Church in Reykjavík to hear him play there.

There have been far-reaching changes in the status of church music in the country since then. Many new churches have been built and new good quality pipe organs have been installed in many of them. Church music is flourishing; Icelandic composers have met the call during recent years by writing both for choir and organ, often at the instigation of organists. Perhaps the most significant event in recent years was the inauguration in 1992 of the 72 stop Klais organ in Hallgríms church, a large modern church which dominates the capital city of Reykjavík from its location on a hill-top. This new instrument has had a major impact on Icelandic church music and has led to an increase in numbers both of practitioners and listeners.

At the instigation of the organist of Reykjavík Cathedral, Marteinn Hunger Friðriksson, Petr Eben has been a contributor to the development of church music in the country. In 1994 he was the guest of honour at the short music festival sponsored by the Cathedral, *Cathedral Music Days*, and he was present at the first performance of his motet *Visio pacis* which the Cathedral Choir had commissioned. During the same visit to Iceland and as part of the same festival he performed at a major concert in Hallgríms church, where he improvised magnificently and memorably on the Comenius text *The Labyrinth of the World and the Paradise of the Heart*. That was the first opportunity that I had to meet him and I was delighted both by his music and to be able to make his acquaintance. He presented me with a small volume of organ music, his *Momenti d'organo*, which turned out to be most suitable for use with my organ students in the school of church music associated with the National State church. As a consequence of this, I decided to make the organ music of Petr Eben one of the main areas of emphasis in my teaching during the winter of 1995-6 and my students performed two concerts devoted exclusively to the organ music of Petr Eben, first in Akureyri and then in Hallgríms church in Reykjavík.

One of my outstanding students, Douglas Brotchie, discovered a particular affinity with Eben's music and has placed emphasis on studying and performing it. He featured the last two movements of *Nedělní hudba (Sunday Music)* in his organ diploma concert in 1996 and since then has been systematically exploring Eben's music for organ and obligato instruments. Many of Eben's works for organ have been performed during this period by Icelandic organists and visiting artists, both in recital and during divine service. In 1999 the Icelandic première of *Laudes* was given. Some fourteen organists, as well as other artists (including the composer), have given performances in Iceland between 1993 and 1999 of *Landscapes of Patmos, Okna, Hommage à Dietrich Buxtehude, Nedělní hudba, Job, Momenti d'Organo, Choralfantasie "O Bože veliký", Preludio Festivo No.1, The Labyrinth of the World and the Paradise of the Heart, Visio Pacis, Missa cum populo, Laudes* and *Faust*. His works have been very well received and undoubtedly have been influential on the development of Icelandic church music - a development process which happily is still very active.

On behalf of the church musicians and music-lovers in Iceland, may I convey to Petr Eben our heartfelt appreciation for his wonderful music and add our sincere good wishes and congratulations for his seventieth birthday year. May his music continue to give life and joy.

Gerd Augst

Petr Eben in Mainz

Anyone who has the good fortune to experience Petr Eben today in one of his concerts or lectures is immediately struck by his artistic and personal radiance. Any musician who engages with his musical experiences in their diversity of emotional elements will find a still centre of formal solidity. Anyone who meets Petr Eben personally knows that he is accepted from the very first moment by his immediate friendliness and kindness.

When I consider my own route to Petr Eben, I recall that the early stages were quite difficult. As a young church musician in Überlingen on Lake Constance in the 1960's, I was particularly interested in the organ music of my Bohemian homeland. In a catalogue of scores by Czech and Slovak composers I was impressed by the title *Musica Dominicalis* by Petr Eben, whose name was then unknown to me. I took the piece into my repertoire with great enthusiasm and a few years later I heard the first movement of *Nedělní hudba (Sunday Music)* in a concert series called *Plainsong and Organ Music* on the organ of the Episcopal Institute for Church Music in Mainz, combined appropriately with the unison singing of the plainsong.

While I was working in Mainz, we were visited in 1969, after the tragic suppression of the Prague Spring, by an émigré Czech church musician. Asked about the position of music in his oppressed country, he named Petr Eben as the most important living composer in Czechoslovakia and so we were encouraged to find further organ works from there.

However, a new way to Petr Eben was to take us by surprise. After lengthy and intensive contacts between the parish priest, Msgr. Klaus Mayer, and the artist, St. Stephan's Church in Mainz was to receive its first stained-glass window from Marc Chagall. As the organist there I spent much time thinking about an appropriate musical contribution to the service of dedication.

One day my wife reported on a programme she had heard on the radio. She had found the sound of trumpet and organ fascinating and the back-announcement had said that the piece was *Fenster nach Marc Chagall von Petr Eben (Windows of Marc Chagall by Petr Eben)*.[2] Without having heard the piece and perhaps being even more curious about it for this reason, I wrote at once to the radio station. By a circuitous route I obtained the address of the General Secretary of the Association of Czech Composers and Musicians in Prague. I received no answer to my polite request for help in obtaining the score of *Okna*. Petr Eben was not a loyal party member in his home country. Also, somewhat undiplomatically, I had mentioned that I came from Reichenberg (Liberec).

---

[2] *Okna podle Marca Chagalla* of 1976.

Meanwhile, the first Chagall window was ceremoniously received in Mainz. The musical contributions consisted appropriately of Hebrew and German psalms. To these was added a work commissioned from Theo Brandmüller, who was born in Mainz, which was played by members of the Mainz Philharmonic Orchestra. The solo part was sung by Ursula Mayer-Reinach, the wife of the musicologist Professor Peter Gradenwitz, who features later in this reminiscence. Over a glass of wine after the ceremony, we also met the orchestra's leader, Gerhard Reich, who asked us what thoughts we had about music for any further Chagall windows. My wife recounted her radio experience and we bemoaned our failure to obtain the music by Petr Eben. This name was not unknown to the leader, for he knew friends of the composer in Karlsruhe. A further contact was quickly made and the Gilliar family there was able to give us an address for Petr Eben, who was then spending a year in Manchester as Visiting Professor at the Royal Northern College of Music.

The first letter from Professor Eben arrived on 10th. January 1979. Kindness, poetry, humour and a talent for organisation were all to be found in the letter.

> *Ich bedaure sehr, daß Sie mich so lange suchen mußten (beinahe wie bei den nicht zusammenkommenden Königskindern), und scheinbar war...das Moldauwasser...viel zu tief und verwehrte Herrn..., Ihren Wunsch zu erfüllen.*[3]

The letter cautiously suggested a possible visit to Mainz and most importantly included his agreement to making available the score and trumpet part of *Okna*, which then only existed in a few duplicated copies. The Music Information Centre of the Czech Music Foundation, under its director, Dr. Jan Ledeč, arranged the immediate despatch of the music. Even in those difficult times he maintained generous and friendly contacts with the West. Music unites, as we were to find again and again.

Rehearsals could begin. At the start, work on the organ part was like an expedition with its risks and even more so with its surprising discoveries. For the trumpet part I found in David Tasa, principal trumpet of the

---

[3] *I very much regret that you had to spend so much time looking for me, almost like the separation of the royal children; it would appear that the waters of the Vltava were far too deep and prevented Mr.... from fulfilling your wish.* [The reference to the royal children is an allusion to a German folk-song about two royal children in love but unable to come together because the water which separated them was too deep.]

Frankfurt Opera Orchestra, an ideal and equally enthusiastic partner. While working together we planned the date for the first performance of *Okna* but we were also particularly anxious to invite the composer to our city and if at all possible to hear him at the organ. A programme was quickly agreed with Petr Eben by letter. After our performance of *Okna*, he offered his improvisation on texts from the Book of Job.

But how was he to obtain permission to travel from the Prague authorities, particularly for a concert in a Catholic church? Once more, we had a stroke of luck. The South-West German Radio Symphony Orchestra had programmed Petr Eben's *Vox Clamantis*, for three trumpets and orchestra, for a concert in Mainz. We seized upon this and received an official invitation for the composer from the radio station. And so it all came true and I was able to greet Petr Eben on Mainz station in June 1980. My joy was indescribable and my guest clearly shared it. Within a few days we were able to experience Petr Eben in a variety of circles, speaking excellent German, witty, a lover of art, well-read, humorous and modest. We discussed his problem of appearing in a Christian church with the knowledge of the Prague authorities and I told him that he had been invited to a music school and that, because of the instrument, he was bound to give his organ recital in a church. Petr Eben replied with a wink: *Ja, ja, widerstrebend zwar!*[4]

There was nothing "reluctant" about the great success of his expressive improvisation, so that one could read in the Mainz press that:

> *Eben erwies sich als glänzender Improvisator.... Sein Koncert gehört zu dem Eindrucksvollsten, was die katholische Kirchenmusik in Mainz seit langem vorstellen konnte.*[5]

The radio concert with *Vox Clamantis* was equally successful, as was Eben's talk at the Institute for Church Music, where he gave us a broad insight into his religious compositions. The interpretation of his choral and organ music as lying between tradition and the overcoming of the present became a living statement on faith and Eben showed himself even at this early stage, as he was to do on many later occasions, to be an outstanding teacher and mediator in conversations with teachers and students. Eben

---

[4] *Yes, yes but reluctantly of course!*

[5] *Eben proved himself to be a brilliant improviser.... His concert was one of the most impressive that Catholic church music in Mainz has been able to offer for a long time.*

had also given us many valuable suggestions for the performance of *Okna* - registration, tempi, articulation and so on, but most impressive was the manner of his personal explanations and his unerring, always constructive, judgement.

Petr Eben's first visit to Mainz not only left behind a lasting impression, it also created a considerable circle of admirers and friends, not least among important personalities from the university, the church and from the music scene. Thereafter, as travelling fans, we seized every opportunity to attend Petr Eben's then still rarely permitted appearances in Germany and always heard something new from the overflowing well of his creativity. Workshops and concerts in Bonn (*Faust*), East Berlin and Stuttgart (*Missa cum populo*), Meerbusch, Altenberg and many more could be mentioned.

Okna had its German première in Mainz. After that we were able to perform the work in numerous concerts elsewhere, accompanied by slides of the windows from the Hadassah synagogue in Jerusalem. We took part in the Jerusalem Festival, playing in the Benedictine Abbey of Dormitio on Mount Zion. We heard from Professor Gradewitz in Tel Aviv that, after tough negotiations in Germany and Switzerland, he had managed to get hold of the CD recording on a disc entitled *Homage à Chagall*, where it was coupled with works by Theo Brandmüller and other pieces appertaining to the subject. The wind ensemble of St. Stephan's church in Mainz, conducted by Hans Gerards, also took part in the recording.

At the invitation of the Music Department of the Johannes Gutenberg University and the Episcopal Institute for Church Music in Mainz, Petr Eben paid a second visit to our city in 1990. Such was the success of the lectures and seminars for church music students that at times our plans and timetable were left in complete chaos. A concert of piano improvisations, which was understood and greeted with cheers by experts and others alike, formed a happy conclusion to the visit.

A little flashback, pre-1989. After we had come to know and love Petr Eben in our family circle, we felt the wish to make a return visit to him in Prague. After initial difficulties with the Czech consulate in Bonn, we were granted our first visas. The circumstances and experiences of our journey would fill a book but we are concerned here with the object and focal point of our visit. Petr Eben was waiting for us at Prague Castle. Together with the pleasure of seeing him again in such an historic setting, we had the experience of being expertly guided by him through the exhibition on Bohemian Gothic. He then led us through the city, translating for us as we went until we arrived at his house in Smíchov for refreshments. There we met his dear wife Šárka, whose important rôle at his side we were later to admire many times. He gave us musical presents and she saw to our well-being with typical Bohemian hospitality. A short visit by two of their sons gave us a glimpse into the remarkable lives and professional careers of the *Bratří Ebenové*. On our return journey through Northern Bohemia we came across their first CD of chansons, wittily written, skilfully composed and delightfully performed by the three brothers.

In 1993, after the "Velvet Revolution", we travelled once more through Northern Bohemia. I was interested to see the organs in my home town of Liberec. I knew from Petr Eben that there was one in the council chamber of the town hall. Entrance to the town hall was open to all but in response to my enquiry *varhany?*, the janitor merely shook her head. With the few words of Czech available to me, I gave her to understand that our friend Professor Eben had mentioned this instrument to us. An interpreter was summoned and after a short conversation she opened the door to the chamber with the "Queen of Instruments". Patiently she bore my extensive improvisations born of youthful memories and after her account of the origins of the instrument it became clear to me that, once upon a time, I had received my first organ lessons on this very same instrument. In response to my "thank-you letter", the interpreter wrote: *...Im übrigen muß ich sagen, daß Petr Eben ist ein Schlüssel, der öffnet jede Tür!*[6]

Back to the Eben family. A lively exchange of letters gave us more information about the artistic activities of the youngest son, David. The *Schola Gregoriana Pragensis* had by then become a trade mark for the interpretation of plainsong based upon sound scholarship and vocal refinement. During the course of 1995 this ensemble's travel plans suggested the possibility of a concert in Mainz. Independently of this Petr Eben had also written of plans for a visit to Germany. Our organisation went into top gear. The music department of the university, the Institute of Church Music and the Diocesan Education Centre joined together to form an organisation team and agreed with the Ebens a series of events spread over three days which could take place in the autumn of 1995.

Petr Eben began the series with a lecture on *The Exciting Tension Between Life and Work* and his ideas, conveyed indeed with excitement and supplemented by typical examples of his religious music, demonstrated the

---

[6]*Besides, I must say that Petr Eben is a key which opens every door!*

interplay in which scenic and familiar religious surroundings seemed to be as much a part of the creative process as happiness and suffering in the course of one's own life. In his observations he talked of developments in contemporary music and also of attitudes both right and wrong in a consumer society. To his wish for more gratitude in our times, he added humorously:

> *Denken Sie, wie leicht und Dankbarkeit fallen kann im Vergleich mit anderen Werten wie etwa Nächstenliebe oder Askese!*[7]

Reflecting on this evening, the Director of the Catholic Education Centre, Dr. Walter Seidel, later wrote looking back with great pleasure:

> *Petr Ebens Musik und sein Auftreten, seine Ausstrahlung sind mir unvergeßlich.*[8]

The second evening was provided by David Eben and his choir. In the packed library room of the music department the audience, professors, students and guests heard much of interest about the thousand-year-old tradition of plainsong in Bohemia. Printed examples of various neums contributed to our understanding of the subject and at the end David Eben sang with the entire audience Wenceslas's hymn *Salve pater optime* in honour of the great patron saint of Bohemia.

The climax of the three-day event in Mainz was a concert in the parish church of St. Peter. The first part consisted of Gregorian chants in various forms sung as solos and by the ensemble. The convincing interpretation demonstrated the quality of both the singers' voices and their vocal training, as well as the binding together of all the neumatic details in a great musical form. In the second half we heard Petr Eben's unison *Liturgické zpěvy (Liturgical Songs)* with organ accompaniment interspersed with brilliantly improvised interludes. Beside the plainsong, elements of Czech folk-music were unmistakable in both composition and improvisation and once again the audience received the performance with great enthusiasm.

---

[7] *Just think, how easily gratitude comes to us compared with other values such as love of our neighbour or asceticism!*

[8] *Petr Eben's music, his bearing and the personality he radiates are unforgettable.*

Petr needs people, Šárka Ebenová once said of his ever receptive nature. This applies equally to his composing - never forgetting people, that is how he works.

In my own work as a church musician I have experienced the way Eben's music appeals to young people and musical laymen in our congregations. Thus we performed the *Truvérská mše (Troubadour Mass)* with great pleasure during a study week on church music and the choir of our parish church performed a German translation of the *a capella* Mass both in a concert and during a service. A high point was a multi-lingual service with a visiting Czech choir, at which we sang the *Ehre sei Gott* after the Kyrie *Pane, smiluj se*. The Mainz Youth Choir St. Alban has also taken this work into its repertoire. The degree of enthusiasm which Eben awakens in young people is shown by reactions within our family. One of our daughters wrote a specialist essay about *Nedělní hudba* as part of her school-leavers' examinations, two others use Eben's teaching materials in their own teaching and our youngest received from the composer a manuscript copy of his piano fantasia on *Veni Creator Spiritus* with which she was able to add a real gem to her final college examination.

The next occasion on which we saw Petr Eben in Mainz lay beyond the city's own activities. It came as a complete surprise to us and was of national importance. Together with Professor Bertold Hummel of Würzburg, Professor Eben received the Art and Culture Prize of the German Catholic Church. Within the framework of the 93rd. Catholic Assembly in 1998 and under the motto *Gebt Zeugnis von eurer Hoffnung! (Bear Witness of Your Hope)*, the presentation of the prize took place in the Mainz state chancery. Expert participants greeted the choice of prize-winners exceptionally positively and the speeches made showed that the work, aims and concerns of both composers had been understood and respected both within the church and in the musical world. In his laudatory address, Professor Thomas Daniel Schlee of Linz commented in spirited terms on the prizewinners' artistic skills and their convincing fidelity to their beliefs. The President of the Central Committee of German Catholics, Professor Hans Joachim Meyer, spoke of the composers' part in creating a more humane life and world to live in. In his words of welcome, the Bishop of Mainz and Chairman of the German Bishops' Conference, Professor Karl Lehmann, spoke of the religious dimension of art and culture. Referring to the works of the prizewinners, he said that religious art should resist taking a populist course and appealing to mass tastes but rather should honour God for being different. Turning directly to Petr Eben he said:

> *Heute soll diese Ehrung auch verstanden werden als ein Beitrag zum Verständnis und zur Versöhnung unserer beiden Völker. Dafür sind Sie, verehrter Herr Professor Eben mit Ihrer Musik und Ihrer Lebensgeschichte schon oft und lange eingetreten.*[9]

Bishop Lehmann was so deeply impressed by Petr Eben's speech of thanks that he mentioned it again in his address during the concluding service of the Catholic Assembly:

> *Einer unserer Kunst- und Kulturpreisträger, Herr Professor Petr Eben, hat uns in seiner ergreifenden Dankesrede die Kraft des Glaubens während der Zeit der Unterdrückung in seiner tschechischen Heimat bezeugt. Wir haben in unserer Geschichte genügend überzeugende Vorbilder, die uns ermutigen.*[10]

These words of appreciation from the highest authority shall conclude this contribution on Petr Eben in Mainz. What is not concluded is the continuing and expanding influence of his words in many performances in church and concert hall. Signs of friendship, signs of understanding between peoples will also continue to exert their influence as Petr Eben's letters, above all his wonderful Christmas messages, reach their wide circle of readers. So may Petr Eben's often expressed wish *PAX ET BONUM* echoing from the chorus of his friends and admirers accompany him on his way after the celebration of his seventieth birthday! *AD MULTOS ANNOS!*

---

[9] *The honour conferred on you today should be seen as a contribution to understanding and reconciliation between our two peoples. This is a cause which you, Professor Eben, have long since and often espoused with your music and your life story.*

[10] *In his speech of thanks one of our Art and Culture prizewinners, Professor Petr Eben, has borne moving testimony to the power of faith during the time of oppression in his Czech homeland. We have in our history sufficient convincing models to encourage us.*

Theo Brandmüller

For my friend of many years, Petr Eben.

There are, dear Petr Eben, such things as subcutaneous understandings; that is, we know all about each other and sense that, although we do not meet very often, it is the same and similar things which move each of us and thus also move our audience

The organ inspires the soul". This saying of Thomas Aquinas has been your (and my) motivation for composing all through our lives.

For having given so much to the Queen of all instrumental queens, to the organ, you have my greatest respect as a colleague and friend, and my deepest gratitude.

Your Theo Brandmüller in admiration for all your music!

Irena Chřibková

My memory of my first contact with the music of Petr Eben is quite precise: it was during my third year at the Kroměříž Conservatoire. During one seminar we heard a brand new recording of a new work - *Okna podle Marca Chagalla (Windows after Marc Chagall)* for trumpet and organ. The experience for me was extraordinary and overwhelming. Literally I wished there and then to be sitting at the organ, playing this beautiful composition myself.

From the Conservatoire in Moravia I went on to the Prague Academy, where I played my own interpretation of *Okna* at my final examination. I was guided undoubtedly in my decision partly by Professor Šlechta there and partly from my studies in France with Susan Landale, herself an enthusiastic interpreter of Eben's works.

Petr Eben used to visit the organ department of the Academy, especially at times when he was writing a new work and needed to check the sound of some organ registrations. We were always glad to make an instrument available to him. We knew that he was writing for us. We then attended private hearings of the new works played by the master himself.

My liking for Eben's compositions did not stop with just one of them. As time has gone by I have learned almost everything that he has ever written for the organ. It is music that speaks directly to me through its Biblical themes, its rhythmic drive, invention and broad use of the instrument's sound palette. The fact that Eben is an organist himself is rather important, since he knows all the limitations of the instrument as well as its possibilities, so he is able to write even the most difficult passages in such a way that they can be performed with ease.

My meetings and consultations with the composer tended to take place during the final phase of my study of each of his works. Together we would look for certain colour combinations that would surprise us in the church we were in by sounding different from his original ideas. Yet Petr Eben, by being present where his music is being performed, brings calm and good humour to the situation. He knows how to treasure every interpreter of his music, from conservatoire students to internationally known artists. The joy of performing his music is mutual and is passed on to the public which is ever grateful for the extraordinary gift of Petr Eben's music.

Leopoldas Digrys

The biggest success of a composer's creative work is when his music is performed not only in his native land but also in other countries. Such a composer for us is Petr Eben and his music if often heard here in Lithuania. We can claim that his music is the most popular of the music of the twentieth century that is heard in our country. The three visits of Petr Eben to Lithuania have left the brightest impressions, not only for musicians but also as a very important factor in strengthening the cultural ties between the Czech Republic and our land.

The remarkable sense of goodwill, sincerity, energy and diligence of Petr Eben leaves unforgettable impressions upon all who come into contact with him. His music for organ I have played for over thirty years. This is the most important organ school for myself, which has helped me to mature as an organist. Now I am happy to pass on this experience and love of Petr Eben's music to my students, who now also include his music in their concerts. I am very pleased to have the opportunity to offer my congratulations to Petr Eben, a great composer and outstanding personality, as he enters his eighth decade.

Guy Erismann

Petr Eben is the Czech musician whom I have known best and for the longest time. I first visited him in the seventies, with a friend from Prague, in his flat near the banks of the Vltava. The atmosphere was one of tradition, the Fine Arts, of a leaning towards a certain mysticism wreathed in the Baroque style. The time had come to commission him to write a congregational mass for a Sunday morning during the Avignon Festival. He accepted: it was to be the *Missa cum populo*. In July 1983 he came to Avignon for the première of his new mass, then went on to Cannes for the first French performance of his choral ballet *Kletby a dobrořečení (Curses and Blessings)*, which had received its world première in Den Haag just a month earlier.

Petr Eben has always intrigued me by the very personal way that he integrates the early traditions into his contemporary language. These are not only nineteenth century traditions, the century of the Czech National Revival, of Smetana and Dvořák. Eben delves much deeper into the past, seeking a Czech presence in the Middle Ages and the Renaissance, a living source that would characterize a country still torn apart by its history and its religious conflicts.

As a cultivated Czech, Eben is well aware of the mentality of the Czech peoples, who can reconcile their faith with the quest for historical verity and whose allegiance to Rome does not impede their recognition of the universal humanistic values of Jan Ámos Komenský. If the organ is his favourite instrument, symbolic of the church, he is also a composer of vocal and particularly choral music in the ancestral tradition, from the Bohemian Bretheren to the great oratorios of Dvořák.

The place of Petr Eben in the great outpouring of Czech music after the Second World War is both extended and singular. It is extended like the spectrum of his art which does not sacrifice a modern musical language to a sterile respect for the past and singular because few Czech composers today represent such a total involvement with so many different art forms, variety of genres, themes and the synthesis of tendencies of yesterday and today. In other words, Petr Eben represents his century to the full.

Janette Fishell

Dances of Life and Light: Petr Eben and the Music of the Soul.

I first became aware of Petr Eben's organ works as a young student. The properties that first attracted me to his music, his taste for rhythm, a pervading sense of lyricism and his keen eye for drama, have continued to fascinate and inspire me fifteen years hence. It is with great pleasure that I write these words in tribute to Petr, a friend and constant source of inspiration, in the year of his seventieth birthday.

As a performer I have spent countless hours engaged in meeting the technical demands of his music, yet behind this external, physical struggle to control the notes, rhythms and the console lay a deeper spiritual struggle towards which his music always points. At no time in my life has the Benedictine motto *Laborare est orare (To labour is to pray)* held so much meaning, for the endeavour to understand and perfect his notes has brought with it an awareness that my labour is a prayer and that the human creative spirit must bear witness to greater spiritual truths. When students come to me, keen to study Eben's music, it is always my wish that our work will transcend the technical to fully encounter the *Dance of Life* that pulses beneath the surface of the page.

It is rare when the music we live with as performers, scholars or teachers reaches past both the intellect and senses to touch deeply that part of us that we define as *soul*. If one asks me to say as simply as possible what effect Petr Eben's music has had upon me and my art, then I must say that it is this: through his music I have become aware of a depth of human experience that I otherwise would not have known. Through it I have been able to offer something of this vision to others through concerts, recordings and teaching. Petr's music has not only improved, refined and, to some extent, defined much of my musical development, it has fed my soul. It has constantly challenged me to break from my own "indolence and ingratitude" to see the hand of God behind all events in our lives, those we might see as dark as well as light.

> *Yea, the darkness is no darkness with thee, but the night is as clear as day; the darkness and light to thee are both alike.*
>
> *Psalm 39*

Marteinn Fridrikkson

Who is Petr Eben? This is a question Icelanders were asking ten years ago.

Petr Eben was a name I had heard mentioned when I was a student in Leipzig but I did not know any of his music. Then, later when I was in London several years ago, I happened to see an advertisement for his *Missa Adventus*. I made enquiries in Prague and was sent the music and a recording, because Petr Eben is a person who, although very busy, always has time for his fellow man. He writes letters and he travels, he seeks friends and he finds them. Then he came to Iceland, bringing with him a fantastic choral work and he played his organ improvisations on *The Labyrinth of the World and the Paradise of the Heart*. It was then that we came to know Petr Eben the man, humble but resolute, a man who has something to say to his fellow man, who has a message to impart. He calls upon people to live in a new world, a world of peace and harmony, a world of justice. His music is fascinating, rhythmical, forceful, compelling. It leaves no one untouched.

The same thing can be said for the work that he wrote for the Reykjavik Cathedral Choir: *Visio pacis* of 1994, the text taken from Isaiah and which is the third motet in his *Mundus in periculo*.

Ecce enim ego creo - Behold, I create a new heaven and a new earth.

The music sparkles, rejoicing in beauty and is as vivid as a fairy tale. Yet *Visio pacis* is no fairy tale in Petr Eben's eyes. He means every word. It is a *Credo*, a declaration of faith in the future.

But be ye glad and rejoice forever in that which I create.

The Reykjavik Cathedral Choir is grateful to have received this magnificent choral work. Now Petr Eben is no longer unknown in Iceland. Now his music is frequently performed there. Iceland's organists, choirs, soloists and audiences thank him and send him their best wishes for his seventieth birthday and for the future.

Johannes Geffert

My favourite pieces by Petr Eben.

Who can still remember them? The days of the Cold War in the 1960's in the Federal Republic of Germany. Who in the West in those days believed that on the other side of the Iron Curtain there could be hidden an individual organ culture rich in its own traditions?

And then one day a Czech organist was sitting with us at the family lunch-table who had actually managed to obtain an entry permit and we children thought, with secret horror, of all the possible complications: border controls, secret police etc. In the evening he played some music of Petr Eben at his concert: *Moto ostinato*! What was this? A new music, like nothing we had heard before, free and cheeky, powerful, so pleasingly undogmatic, a musician's music and above all rhythmic!

Rhythm - one of the most important factors in organ-playing: on an instrument which has no scope for dynamic accentuation by touch, on which upper and lower ranges occasionally take different amounts of time to sound in space, many musical nuances must be brought about by subtle timing of the rhythmic impulses. Rhythm - often sorely missed in the *legato* tradition of the performances of the 1950s, in the epic sound-worlds of the German Max Reger school - here it was, clear, demanding and stimulating. *Moto ostinato!*

In Eben's music I have repeatedly sought, found and loved rhythmic subtleties, like the emotional trembling in Gretchen's song from *Faust*, rhythmic developments over more extended passages and dramatic effects achieved by rhythmic precision, as in the *Walpurgisnacht* from *Faust*.

As much other modern organ music developed into a flood of sound without a beat, as novelties of technique and intellectual concepts seemed to push to one side the musicianly idea of simply playing the organ, it was always refreshing and stimulating to hear or to play a piece by Eben.

Does all this mean that Petr Eben is not really a "new" modern composer? On the contrary I would ask: Who can at the end of the millennium still imagine that he is speaking the musical "language of our time" let alone that he is adding to its vocabulary? Is it not imperative rather that a composer should use the sound language that he also uses in a literary, spiritual, intellectual or aesthetic context in his own life?

The idea that, after Auschwitz, one can no longer sing plainsong has been refuted and turned on its head by Eben. He has been imprisoned in a German concentration camp and for that very reason he sings plainsong. No-one who has once experienced him as a human being can imagine any other musical language for him than this, his own. Eben is Eben!

A Czech colleague told me about *Faust*, pointing out that this new work for organ was not intended for the church, a remark which immediately sparked a reaction in me. Organists of my generation had been enthusiastically involved in the attempt to establish the organ as a concert instrument enjoying equal rights in the musical world. In our opinion the freeing of organ music from the narrow confines of church and liturgy was a part of this. I therefore wrote to Petr Eben and indeed received a fair copy of the work. The pages of Part 8 were still a photocopy of his own personal manuscript; in this "original version" the note cluster at the beginning of the pedal solo did not yet exist! I was thus able to give the first performance of the work in the then Federal Republic.

With *Faust* the organ itself, in my opinion, became the object of the drama. Of course, there had always been dramatic organ music - many will think of Bach's *Toccata in d minor* here - but I am thinking rather of the *Sonata* by Reubke which, given a great symphonic organ, really can and must be "produced". *Faust*, however, sets organ against organ. *I use the organ in two different functions: on the one hand in its venerable classical style, on the other in the trivial shape of an orchestrion*, writes Petr Eben in an introductory note.

In so doing, the composer is, of course, as he says, symbolising the tension between good and evil in man, the essential theme of his intended trilogy for organ, *Faust, Job* and *Comenius*. In *Faust*, however, he achieved much more: the suspense of the instrument between spiritual worlds and musical forms of expression. Thus the organ can truly reveal itself as the "Queen of Instruments", as the mistress of, and the meeting point for, centuries of musical history. In *Faust* you can find everything: rhythms primitive and civilised, sounds in (notated) clusters and harmonies, strict forms and improvisatory outbursts, plainsong and jazz. To what richness of tone-painting this tension can inspire the performer! And every good interpreter is grateful to a composer who allows him latitude; Eben's directions are signposts, not chains.

In performances of *Faust* in Germany one can, of course, take for granted a knowledge of Goethe's text and its importance for our culture. To some extent the audience brings its own images to a performance. I personally often think of scenes from the famous Gustav Gründgens film when I hear Eben's music. As this music calls such pictures to life, a performance of Eben's *Faust* can easily become a *Gesamtkunstwerk* with text, music and pictures. At the same time here is music that speaks without pictures and text, as *Job* and *Comenius* do not, in music which draws its own dramaturgy from an idea. Thus the incidental music to Goethe's *Faust*, the work which does not have to be played in church, becomes a spiritual work of art with a central theological message: need and redemption, Faust and Gretchen, Goethe in *Psalm 130*.

However broad in scope *Faust* is as a cycle, however many ideas it might develop and express, it still came into existence spontaneously and through improvisation, as did most of Eben's organ works. I once heard him tell of playing the organ all night for nights on end in a remote Bohemian monastery - hours of improvisation out of which grew the germs of later compositions. And so interpreters of Eben's music can also learn: playfully, in harmony with body and instrument, everything lies well "under the fingers".

Petr Eben, who studied the piano but never wrote major works for the piano, is considered an important composer for the organ in our century. On my desk I have a postcard signed by Eben and Messiaen. There the two are united: Messaien the working-musician intellectual and Eben the intellectual working musician. A motto for Eben's life could be *Moto ostinato*, a symbol of his untiring, restless creativity and for the driving impetus which he likes to hear in the interpretation of his music. And so on his seventieth birthday I wish him a hearty *Moto ostinato* and long may it continue!

Georges Guillard

France regularly produces magnificent, natural born improvisers. But whereas some conscientiously write down their inspirations - even the most banal - on paper, others, on the contrary, refuse the pen which would set in stone that which has been created in the heat of the moment. Deliberately or otherwise, Cochereau, Isoir, Chapuis or Robillard for example, deprive us of masterpieces that we should so like to meditate upon at our leisure after the creative event. Is it idleness? fear of the blank page? conviction that a fleeting moment should remain unique? Who knows?

Thank God Petr Eben is not in that category. I see him as a Pierre Cochereau who would have had the patience to transcribe his improvisations. Perhaps his familiarity with the piano enabled him to overcome such unfortunate inhibitions. Whatever the reason, he sings with the freedom of a bird, plays as naturally as he breathes, his music erupts like a geyser, he rejoices, dances, weeps, bursts out laughing with assurance, without undue reserve but not without refinement and good taste.

His organ music is also - and this is rarer than one might think - that of a craftsman. I mean by this that it bears the hallmark of manual skill: every flourish, leap, stretch, polyphony lies precisely under the fingers, fitting perfectly into the hand. Difficult though it may be, his music is that of the practical musician, which means that it will be played and enjoyed, not merely analyzed.

Our time needs inspiring but also edible nourishment! Cochereau also had this verve, this proud assurance, these sudden fears, this zest for life, this humanity.

Thanks to Eben, the twenty-first century will indeed have its vital source.

Volker Hempfling

As cathedral organist in Altenberg, I was, of course, familiar with the name of the composer Petr Eben. One can hardly not know the wonderful *Nedělní hudba (Sunday Music)* with its artful rhythms. His choral works were, at that time, unfamiliar; I knew of their existence but we all know how difficult it always is to persuade one's choir and later one's audience of the need to perform new choral music. For that, there needs to be an initial spark which I should like to describe briefly.

In 1991 the festival *Europa Cantat* took place in Vittoria-Gasteiz in the Basque country. Here many choirs included little-known works in their programmes. I was keen to hear the Prague University Choir, a very good choir with a wonderful sound. The programme promised a first performance: it was *De Tempore* [11]. I was and still am so enthusiastic about this piece that I immediately wanted to have it for the Kölner Kantorei. We were allowed to give the German première and later, to our great honour, the first performance of the whole triptych.

Petr commented with great pleasure on the recording which we sent him. The enthusiasm of conductor, choir and audience was so great that I wanted to perform more of Petr's music and there was more: the *Pražské Te Deum*. This piece was performed by an *ad hoc* choir as part of the series *Kantate zum Mitsingen* which we were running in Altenberg at this time. The singers were very much in agreement that we should sing something other than Bach for a change and so we rehearsed the *Te Deum* in the presence of the composer. He was delighted with the "mosaic-style" rehearsal: first we took all the easy passages and then gradually progressed until only a few really difficult bars remained. We managed these too, because the motivation to perform the piece was now there.

Since then we have become friends. You, Petr, and your dear wife are delightful people to know, as all your friends and acquaintances confirm. When I include works by you on my courses for choral conductors, which I have done on every course since 1991, I give a short introduction to your music, tell them where you live and so on. At the end I always say: *Petr Eben is the nicest composer I know!*

To celebrate his seventieth birthday, the Kölner Kantorei sang Eben's *Rhythmus de gaudiis* in Bonn, Limburg, Altenberg, Cologne, Washington, Detroit, Princeton, Rutgers, Kingston and New York. Speaking of this work, one of our sopranos said: *At first you think it is difficult and then you sing it as if you have always sung it.* Petr Eben is a composer who writes very singable music and has a very deep understanding of the expressive potential of the human voice.

In the year 2000, the theme of the Kölner Kantorei's programme, which will be given at a number of concerts, is *LUX AETERNA*, the celestial in the music of the twentieth century. The work of Petr Eben which has been

---

[11] This is the third movement of the choral triptych *Verba Sapientiae* of 1991-2, the other two movements being *De circuitu aeterno* and *Laus mulieris*. According to Kateřina Vondrovicová in her listing of Petr Eben's works, the first performance of the whole work was given on 3rd. May 1991 at Cork University as part of the Cork International Choral Festival.

included in the programme is once again *De tempore*: the text and the music end with *In paradisum*....

I am grateful to you, Petr, for your friendship and for your music and I am certain that this will continue to be so in the future. The fine new choral compositions we can expect from you are alone sufficient to ensure this. I and the Kölner Kantorei join together in congratulating you most warmly and wish you continuing creative strength and good health.

Jan Hora

I first came to know Petr Eben at the Prague Conservatoire, where I was a very young organ student in the early 1950's. At the time I was also organist of the Premonstratentian parish church in Prague 6. One day, on the Feast of Christ the King, two Academy students turned up just before the evening Mass - a singer and his accompanist. They were to take over from me for the Introit, Offertory and Communion. Their texts had been set to music by the accompanist himself - Petr Eben. His music, which was an idea that was to grow into his *Liturgical Suite* later, made a deep impression on me in those dark Communist days and I still remember it after all these years. I was struck by its innermost feeling and spontaneous simplicity.

Eben's use of the organ was not accidental; he had been drawn to the instrument from his earliest childhood and was - and is - a brilliant organist himself. It was no accident that he chose to graduate in 1954 with his *Organ Concerto No.1 (Symphonia gregoriana)*. The politics at the time were absolutely against the organ and students like myself never knew whether they would be able at all to complete their studies, since there were omens threatening to do away with the instrument as a subject for study altogether. According to the official atheistic ideology "the sound of the organ brought people to the church and had nought to say to workers on their road to socialism". It was courageous to compose for the organ in that atmosphere. Thus the *Symphonia gregoriana*, apart from its indisputable musical qualities, helped to maintain and strengthen the country's organ tradition at a time when it was being artificially discontinued. Eben did not flinch and he rode out the adverse climate.

When I was preparing myself for the ARD International Competition in Munich in 1957, my professor Jiří Reinberger suggested that I learn Petr Eben's latest work. This later became the first movement *(Fantasia I)* of the

Nedělní hudba (Sunday Music), the other movements not yet having been composed. I copied it out myself and played it at the competition in Munich. It was clear from the favourable reception that the then unknown composer had made a remarkable impression. When the first Prague Spring Festival Competition, scheduled for 1958, put the organ on an equal footing with other instruments in the eyes of the regime, Eben's third movement from the same work, the *Moto ostinato*, was included on the list of compulsory compositions. By that time I was quite familiar with Eben's organ writing and was looking forward to further pieces from him. I was genuinely enthusiastic about his cycle *Laudes* and was able to perform it many times. Similarly, his cycles *Faust* of 1979-80, *Mutationes* of 1980 and other compositions.

In my teaching I am in almost daily contact with Eben's brilliant work, which is to me a source of joy, beauty and ever new discoveries. I am also able to observe the effect that his music has on young people who play it with enthusiasm and a determination to fulfil its expressive and technical demands. Eben's organ works represent the absolute peak of Czech contemporary organ writing and occupy one of the foremost places in the world today. Their international acclaim is underscored by many performances and recordings by the world's best organists. About his cycle *Laudes* Eben himself has written:

> *At a time of rising scepticism and cynicism sweeping the world, I wanted in this music to raise the opposite approach to life: gratitude.*

My own feeling too is one of gratitude - gratitude to Petr Eben for his being among us and for giving the organists among us so many rare musical gems.

Niels Henrik Jessen

It is self-evident that melody and rhythm are essential for most music. Yet when asked to write a tribute to Petr Eben and define my own fascination with his music, these words were among the first to come to mind as being something special to write about.

When talk turns to that of a catchy tune, it normally alludes to genres in which modern serious music is not often included. Eben's music is permeated by fine melodies and I have caught myself many times humming or whistling his themes at unexpected moments. Even though they often use strange intervals and rhythms, they go into your head as would an evergreen tune and, as such, they stay without tiring. If one then starts to talk of a jazzy or fascinating rhythm, the same thing happens. One cannot help but get allusions to rhythmical music, although no one would ever doubt Eben to be a classical composer. When I play his music, I often get this wonderful feeling of "swing". I admit to liking rhythmical music and it is so great letting that liking come out in an organ piece. I believe that very feeling and liking is, in fact, necessary to really understand and appreciate his music.

Francis Poulenc said about himself that he was a mixture of a monk and a rascal. I cannot help but apply that same sentiment to Petr Eben - his biblical quotations and Gregorian inspiration on the one side and his rhythms and humour on the other. The combination of these two poles makes for astonishing and wonderful results. Who else would make "biblical dances", two words that hold his musical universe in a nutshell!

Poles or contrasts are keys to his music but not only in the sense already described. Barrel organ versus traditional mighty church organ in *Faust,* or the contrasts in *Mutationes* both in organ size and the construction of the work, with its use of two instruments, are just two further examples in his organ music. These contrasts are an important part of what makes his music alive, fun to play and a pleasant experience for the audience. They are among my foremost reasons for loving his music and remaining fascinated buy it. As he passes his seventieth birthday, it is my hope that there will still flow much more music from his hand and, as a self-interested organist, I also hope that much of it will be for my instrument.

Andreas Kempin

I first became acquainted with the organ music of Petr Eben in the 1970s through my father who, among other pieces, regularly played parts of *Nedělní hudba (Sunday Music)* during services. It was also this music, together with above all that of J.S. Bach, which awoke in me the wish to become a church musician and to perform this colourful, rhythmically interesting and immediately appealing music myself. I then met Petr Eben himself for the first time in Mainz, when he improvised on readings from the *Book of Job*, on 11th. May 1980.

In July of the same year my parents an I visited Petr Eben in Prague, where he impressed us with his knowledge of history as he showed us round Prague Castle. What horrified me and gave me great cause for concern was the way he looked over his shoulder again and again during conversations on the street. In the political situation, which was so difficult for him, the unspoken question: *Is anyone listening to dangerous things not meant for their ears?* was all too clear for us to hear. On the return journey from Prague my father was killed in a road accident. Petr Eben telephoned and wrote to us in the most moving terms to express his sympathy and concern for us. At this time a deep bond grew between us which makes itself felt whenever we meet again.

In the October of the same year, I myself played the first movement of *Nedělní hudba* in public for the first time. Later, during my organ studies, I worked at Eben's compositions time and again. The first time I was able to organise an entire organ recital of his works with spoken introductions to them was not only important for me personally but I also made the acquaintance of his charming and devoted wife. Apart from that, Petr Eben brought more scores along with him which would lead to further collaborations.

His extremely friendly and yet very definite way of discussing the interpretation of his works became very important to me. Where the realisation of his works presents technical difficulties, he can be very generous but in matters of rhythmic precision or registration he is very precise in his directions. If an amateur choir has difficulties with the harmonies or the intonation of his work, he encourages, praises and helps in his kind and discrete manner without, however, ever seeking to ingratiate himself - and he never relaxes his standards.

The fact that even in the year of his seventieth birthday he found time to come to a concert in the priory church of Essen-Werder and that we were thus also able to hear for the first time the *Schola Gregoriana Pragensis*, under the direction of his son David, was a source of great pleasure.

I owe to Petr many happy hours spent in the study and performance of his works. What riches he has presented to musicians of our time, it is as yet impossible to fully assess. I personally still have many treasures to discover. Much respected and much loved Petr Eben, thank you for your fatherly friendship, for the time that you make available to your many admirers throughout the world and for your music, in which you and your Christian faith are present for all to hear.

Kamila Klugarová

It is a long time since I first entered the Brno Conservatoire as an organ scholar. A colleague a few years older than me was studying for his final examination and the work he chose to play was Petr Eben's *Nedělní hudba (Sunday Music)*. While I was still struggling with pedal scales, he was allowed to play music that I found enormously appealing. He had no idea that I listened behind the door while he was practising! I had to wait to experience the complete *Nedělní hudba* until my own finals at the Academy but already at the Conservatoire my imagination was caught by Eben's *Moto ostinato*. My postgradual studies would have been unthinkable without Eben's music and so his *Laudes* came into my repertoire.

Then came D-day. It was sometime towards the end of 1980 when Petr Eben asked me, in his typically modest way, whether I would be willing to undertake the first performance of his cycle *Faust* in its entirety, Jan Hora having given the first performance of just part of it in Prague in March 1980. I still remember how faint I felt, stammering out that surely such confidence in me was somewhat misplaced. After that came the first ever recording of Eben's *Organ Concerto No.2* with the Czech Philharmonic Orchestra conducted by Libor Pešek, as well as subsequently the Czech premières of his cycles *Job* of 1987 and *Biblické tance (Biblical Dances)* of 1990-91, recordings of his pieces for solo organ and opportunities to share my knowledge and experience with students at the Janáček Academy in Brno, as well as with participants at master classes. I do not know what still awaits me, nor what may pass me by, but I shall never forget that day when I felt faint and stammered out my reply to the composer.

Yet I was looking forward to 24th. March 1981 but also I was a little apprehensive. It was the day of the world première of Petr Eben's complete *Faust* at the Brno Beseda. Three weeks later came the Prague première of the whole work on 13th. April at the Rudolfinum, recorded live by the then Czechoslovak Radio. If this recording has not been destroyed, it is the only evidence of what I am to relate here, except for the testimony of the composer himself, of course. Soon there were negotiations about recording the work on disc but regrettably just four parts of it, since Eben at that time was not among the composers who could rate a whole LP record to himself, as far as the authorities were concerned. He telephoned me and, in his typically nice way, spent the first five minutes apologising. He then asked me if I would be willing to learn the somewhat revised version of the eighth and longest part of the cycle, the *Valpuržina noc*

(Walpurgis Night) by the date earmarked for the recording. Now Petr Eben is not known for revising his works once set down and this was an exception. As I was to learn later, he had been persuaded to do so by his gentle and delightful wife, Šárka. I agreed, of course, waiting for the music to arrive by the post. How many pages were new? It was not important. In fact, I am proud that the pedal solo near the end was written partly for me. All I knew then was how many brilliant ideas Eben had simply laid aside. I still say that the balls of crumpled paper that had ended up in his waste-paper basket would be enough for many a composer to write a whole symphony.

Before 1989 our required duties as artists included regular tours in the then Soviet Union. What each one of us used to experience there would fill a voluminous book of memoirs and that is certainly true also in my case. But there were other valued moments, rare though they were. One of these compulsory visits came my way in June 1982, a year after I had had the honour the give the first performance of the complete *Faust* cycle. It was blindingly clear that *Faust* could not be absent from my programmes. What reconciled me to the tour was the fact that it was to be short, just five concerts, that I was to be spared the rigours of the Russian winter (I had once suffered and survived minus 45 degrees Celsius in Irkutsk) and that once again I was able to see Leningrad (now St. Petersburg again), a place of remarkable architecture, of the famous Hermitage, of the atmosphere of Peter the Great, which I liked to breathe. Moreover, ever since visiting Finland, I enjoyed the "white nights".

The concert took place in the Glinka Hall. The console of the organ, an electrical instrument by our own Czech firm of Rieger-Klos of Krnov, was placed in such a way that many people in the audience could watch my face. This did not make me particularly happy. The second part of the programme was devoted to *Faust*, for I had never been an advocate of the idea that every recital must end with a full organ *tutti* - but of course that is how the penultimate part of the cycle, the *Walpurgis Night*, ends. It has happened on several occasions that the audience begins to clap at this point. That night, however, there was another surprise in store for me. I had just finished the seventh part of the cycle, *Requiem*, when my intuition told me that there was a change in the atmosphere in the hall and I heard a rustle. I looked up and what I saw was quite incredible. The whole audience had stood up and remained standing for a minute, perhaps even two. It was at that moment that I fully understood not only the motto of this movement: *And on your threshold - whose blood?* but also the timeless words of the composer himself:

The Requiem is...a painful pang of conscience burdened by crime.

Susan Landale

March 1977, a cold, misty afternoon in the centre of Prague. In front of the church of Sv. Jakub near the Old Town Square, a group of three people wave to a man standing alone, carrying a briefcase and obviously waiting for them. However, they do not attempt to approach one another - that is forbidden and would be severely reprimanded by the Communist authorities. The youngest of the group, a dark-haired woman carrying a music case, smiles at her friends and walks a few metres across the church front towards the lone man who is waiting. He smiles at her, they shake hands...Petr Eben and I have met for the first time.

This first of many, many visits to Prague is engraved indelibly in my memory. Preparing what was perhaps the first L.P. recording in Western Europe of Eben's *Nedělní hudba,* I was deeply conscious of my complete lack of background and my inadequacy in assuming a critical approach to the music. At the same time the recording project in Berlin seemed to me sufficiently important to try and fill these gaps as best as I could. No one in France knew anything about the music of Petr Eben. A visit to its source was imperative. I shall never be able to express sufficiently my gratitude to my friends Ken and Lydie Pearson, at that time with the British Council in Prague, who made this visit possible. On that day none of us could have imagined what was to follow in the wake of this first meeting.

As it was, something I was only to discover more than two years later, my own apprehension and misgivings in feelings of *I'll never be able to play it properly; he must be expecting a Russian-style piano technique; I must be out of my mind to expect him to listen,* were more than matched by Petr Eben's own puzzlement over this decidedly bizarre occasion: *a female organist (hardly to be taken seriously) from Scotland (must be very economical with her practise time) living in France (no doubt charmingly superficial in her attitude to her work)*...altogether a pretty uncompromising picture on both sides before we had even started!

The rest is now history but looking back on that day I never cease to be amazed by all that has happened since. The discovery of music that was totally new to me, incredibly rich, exciting, profound, full of colour and magnificently written for the organ and virtually unknown in our western countries, completely overwhelmed me. Added to that, the extraordinary kindness, spontaneity and generosity of its creator brought new warmth to my heart. Sitting in the study on the top floor of the then Eben home in the Smíchov district of Prague while he introduced me to the score of *Okna* only a short time before its first performance, I was stunned by the depth of his artistry and the simplicity with which he explained his faith and his inspiration. Many things were to change as a result. My crusade for his music, which started on that day, has brought me joy and enrichment far beyond anything that I could have imagined. The scores studied with him, the fun, the arguments, the concerts, recitals, masterclasses and lectures given, the articles written, the friends made, the countries visited and - perhaps the most important of all - the awakening to the goodness, the truth, the praise of which we are all capable...Yes, Petr Eben is indeed a worker of miracles.

Šárka Ebenová, his wonderful wife, never failing companion, accomplice and guardian angel, whose unbounded hospitality and bubbling humour has illuminated so many of my stays in Prague, has taught me also how the warmth of the family foyer can triumph over the disastrous and oppressive conditions of daily life in Czechoslovakia before the Velvet Revolution in 1989.

It is with a deep sense of gratitude and humility that I write these lines as a tribute to one of the truly great musicians and humanists of our time, who has given so much to music and who has kindled a spark in the hearts of so many. His flame is one that nothing will extinguish. Thank you Petr for lighting our paths in the *Labyrinth of the World and the Paradise of the Heart*.

Lothar Mohn

I should like to be even more modest than the composer himself in my congratulations on his seventieth birthday. The meetings with him here in Hanover, first on the occasion of the *Biblické tance (Biblical Dances)* and then in 1999 for a performance of his *Organ Concerto No.1 (Symphonia gregoriana)*, were decisive moments in my musical life.

Performances of Petr Eben's works are becoming more frequent in this part of Germany. Thus there was a concert in May 1999 with the title *Hommage* à *Petr Eben*, which included *Faust, De circiuto aeterno, The Song of Ruth, Salve regina,* the *Moto ostinato* from *Nedělní hudba* and the *Pražské Te Deum*. On the very day I wrote this, I heard the cycle *Závoj a slzy (Veils and Tears)*. It is good that so many musicians are taking up our friend's music and I am convinced that this is not only the case this year when we celebrate so significant a birthday.

Petr Eben's musical language has an unmistakable, appealing and unerring style. He is not a composer who sits in an ivory tower but one who seeks contact with his audience and they are grateful to him for his clear and yet moving language. The wonderful thing is that his compositional well still continues to gush forth as it always has.

A small incident by way of conclusion. In connection with the performance of Eben's *Organ Concerto No.1* which I conducted earlier in the year, I heard from the principal horn of the orchestra in Hanover that he had seen the poster advertising the concert and was determined to be there as a member of the audience. He had played the work a few years earlier and still remembered it as an extremely fine piece, even though as a professional musician he came into contact with new pieces on an almost daily basis. Two days before the performance my own first horn withdrew. I contacted this professional principal and he completely revised his plans for the weekend just to be able to play in this work. Can there be greater praise from a pro?

I thank Petr for everything and wish him good health, time and an inexhaustible compositional well!

Karel Paukert

My first memories of Petr Eben go back to my student years at the Prague Conservatoire. At that time he was a student of Pavel Bořkovec at the Prague Academy of Musical Arts. We younger students regarded him as a rôle model. In my own mind he was a prophet. We often saw him on Sunday mornings with his breviary, as he was rushing to Mass in another part of the city other than that he resided in, possibly for fear of being prosecuted for his religious beliefs. Beyond a greeting, I did not find the courage to address him - until one day.

But I have to preface that encounter by describing an experience - the première of his first organ cycle, *Nedělní hudba (Sunday Music)* given complete on 26th. October 1959 - an event that I will never forget. The Dvořák Hall in the House of Artists (Rudolfinum) was packed for the concert of the Guild of Composers (Svaz skladatelů) in which the organist Milan Šlechta gave a stunning performance of Eben's work. Communist Party officials and the upper echelon of the oppressive ruling class gathered for this special concert of "socialist creativity". Many of us bystanders, in silent opposition, awaited a miracle. And a miracle it was. The official programme notes spoke of the struggle of the working class and Sunday as a day of well-deserved rest. Curiously, the original title of the work in Latin, *Musica dominicalis*, did not raise their suspicion. These programme notes certainly did not lead us to expect the glorious quotation from the Gregorian chant *Salve regina* in the Finale. It was a real food for the soul for many of us impoverished and spiritually oppressed. I have been a fan of Petr Eben ever since.

Back then to my first encounter with Petr Eben. The Theatre of Jiří Wolker in Prague, which catered primarily for children and young people, was getting ready for an exchange trip abroad with the youth theatre in Dresden. I was the oboist of the theatre's small orchestra and my excitement was tremendous. My first trip abroad! Never mind that Dresden was only just across the Czech border in Eastern Germany. I was determined to be a sort of cultural messenger on Eben's behalf. It did not take very long to conceive of a grand plan to carry his music as a gift to the organist Herbert Collum, whom I planned to visit during that trip. My German was atrocious but I dared to plan a visit to this famous organist of the Kreuzkirche. I telephoned to Petr Eben and he kindly invited me over to his flat in Smíchov. I explained what I intended to do and he kindly suggested that I take the score of *Nedělní hudba (Sunday Music)*, just off the press. He sat down and began to write a long paragraph in the score, which turned out to be a dedication to Herbert Collum, all in German and without consulting a dictionary. That impressed me very much.

When I came to America, of course I played Eben and my students did too. I came to know him better when he came to Cleveland in October 1984, as I had organized concerts of his music and was privileged to spend most of the waking hours in his company for several days. An extensive interview conducted with him by the music critic Wilma Salisbury, filling nearly an entire page of Cleveland's *Plain Dealer*, made him known overnight not only to the citizens of Cleveland but also to others across the country as word was disseminated. His concerts at the Museum and at St. John's Roman

Catholic Cathedral in Cleveland were a stunning success. His improvisations for the students of my organ class were astonishing. He improvised on demand à la Brahms, Debussy and the styles of many other composers. In the concert on the following day his improvisations included that on *Good King Wenceslas* as only he could. A few years later, when he sent me a printed copy of *A Festive Voluntary (Variations on Good King Wenceslas)*, I realised that the Cleveland improvisation was a precursor to this new opus. It was a distinct honour for me to give the first American performances of his *Landscapes of Patmos* and *Momenti per organo*.

I treasure his Christmas letters, written to all his friends around the world in German, whatever their nationality, couched in a literary style worthy of great writers. He keeps astonishing me with the breadth of his interests and I am eagerly expecting further fruits of his creative genius.

Christian Praestholm

On 22nd. January 1997 a concert including religious music from the Czech Republic took place in the *Basilique Sainte Clotilde* in Paris. The second half of this concert was dedicated to music by Petr Eben. The occasion marked the composer's sixty-eighth birthday and he was invited to Paris to be present at this celebratory concert.

At that time I was a student of Susan Landale at the *Conservatoire National de Région de Rueil-Malmaison* in Paris and had just finished working on Petr Eben's first work for organ solo, the *Musica dominicalis (Nedělní hudba)*. It had become a tradition at the Conservatoire that every year an organ student would perform the whole of a major work and in November 1996 Susan Landale had the idea for me to play this work on such an occasion. She placed this recital for the morning of the day of the birthday concert and persuaded Petr Eben to come so that the organ class could have the chance to meet him. Even though he was very busy composing and had the deadline for his church opera *Jeremias* looming, it was not difficult to persuade him to come to Paris for a few days and to spare time for us students. First he told us about his life, his music, composing techniques, sources of inspiration and related topics, then there was a short presentation and analysis of the *Musica dominicalis* before I finally played the work.

Musica dominicalis was a work that I wanted to play for a very long time as part of my début concert at the conclusion of seven years of organ studies at the Royal Academy of Music in Aarhus, Denmark and it was the only piece that had remained constant as part of the ever changing shape of the final programme! Back in 1991 my first piano teacher at the Royal Academy of Music gave me the score and it did not take long before I was captivated by its inventiveness, imaginative textures, thrilling rhythms and powerful energy. Eben's idiomatic writing for the organ shows a composer that knows his instrument intimately and that always makes it a pleasure to work on one of his organ pieces.

Because of Susan Landale's personal relationship with Petr Eben and her great experience with his music, it made it too tempting not to study that particular piece with her, even though my début concert was not going to take place for another eighteen months. It has truly been a great experience for me to have had the opportunity to meet and talk to Petr Eben. Since then I have played several of his other organ works and I must say that, perhaps apart from *Laudes*, the *Musica dominicalis* remains my personal favourite, a piece I have played several times and hope to perform many more times in the future.

Peter Schwarz

Laudatio

(Given on 24th February 1999 at a concert to celebrate Petr Eben's 70th birthday in the Lesser Hall of the Konzerthaus in Berlin.)

The astronomical clock on the Old Town Hall in Prague is depicted on the cover of the score of Petr Eben's *Pražské Te Deum (Prague Te Deum)*. This symbolises in compelling fashion both objective time and the subjective changes which take place within it. In addition, it projects earthly time into a universe whose infinity dissolves our human limits. In the autumn of 1989 the clock on the Old Town Sqyare experienced with the people of this country, whose name was shortened to the cold and unfriendly CSSR, the so-called "Wende" (turning point). Petr Eben rightly calls this exciting political transformation a revolution.

As is well known the brave attempt to establish "Socialism with a human face" in August 1968 had been brutally repressed and stifled by the military.

In this fateful year Petr Eben's *Sunday Music* for solo organ, composed in 1958, appeared in print, a musical sign of hope and a pointer to the liturgical place of Sunday in our increasingly profane world. The opening theme of the first fantasy of this *Sunday Music* sounds to my ears like an "overcast" quotation of the old Pentecostal antiphon *Veni sancte spiritus*. I feel the *Prague Te Deum* of 1989 for mixed choir, four brass, timpani and percussion is an answer to this.

Petr Eben writes in his introduction to the work: "In the last forty years we really had no cause as the Czechoslovak nation to sing a *Te Deum* in our country. What I wrote in 1950 was a bitter *Missa Adventus et Quadragesimae*, an Advent and Shrovetide Mass, which expressed our feelings so well, those of mankind struggling for its freedom and its faith, and of the church battling for its existence. When at last freedom was restored to us so suddenly in 1989, the Gregorian motive of the *Te Deum* with its joyously rising line poured from my soul and, despite all the turbulence which the revolutionary period brought with it, I still managed to compose the *Te Deum* around New Year 1990 as a song of thanksgiving for everything that had happened."

Petr Eben is a practicing Catholic, as was Olivier Messiaen, so it is not surprising that the organ, essentially a large, enhanced wind instrument, makes a decisive sound in his musical thinking. It proclaims a spiritual language to the world. Its long, unending breath bears the voice of the gospel with its promise of a new world which is still closed to us in our earthly life.

Petr Eben's organ music occupies this spiritual-liturgical position: the *Sunday Music*, *Laudes*, *Job*. Even in the two organ concertos and *Mutationes* of 1980, Gregorian fragments are audible. The organ undergoes a remarkable change in the incidental music to Goethe's *Faust* which was written in 1976 for the Vienna Burgtheater. In the early 1980's came a version of this music for organ solo. In the nine central scenes the organ sometimes loses its grave dignity and sobriety to become a barrel organ or the accompaniment to a street-singer. But the Cantus firmus of the *De profundis* steps in the way of this temptation - impressively so in the wildly squeaking, whistling, roaring Witches' Sabbath.

The human voice is, alongside the organ, a living instrument to which Petr Eben entrusts above all in his choral works, either in the liturgical sphere or in the realm of folk music, for instance in the alternately gruesome and beautiful *Songs of Love and Death*, written in 1958, examples of delightful Bohemian folk-songs far removed from the world of counterpoint.

There are two aspects of Petr Eben's musical life which must not be forgotten: his pedagogic and pragmatic gifts and his relatively recent turn towards opera, in particular to church opera.

The teacher-pragmatist: witness not only the Czech version of Carl Orff's *Schulwerk* or the easily understood and grasped pieces written particularly for children and young people but also the easily accessible liturgical songs which became necessary after the second Vatican Council. These never give any hint of being "Gebrauchsmusik" (utility music) but the reveal the professional composer who has his ear on the heart, his finger on the pulse of humanity.

The opera composer: Reading Stephan Zweig's lengthy play *Jeremias* as long ago as the 1960's sowed in Petr Eben's mind the seeds of a plan to set this work as an opera in German, but not until the summer of 1996 did the composer actually enter and begin to work in this new and exciting field. The opera's dramatic kernel is the conflict between Jeremiah (bass-baritone) and the people (the chorus). A Narrator (tenor) tells the story. There is no biblical evidence for the part of the Mother of Jeremiah; she is a literary invention of Stephan zweig's. The action is accompanied by a chamber orchestra with a few woodwind and brass, strings and organ.

Vox Clamantis is a key work of the composer, teacher and performer, Petr Eben, whom we honour today. The work (the call of the voice in the wilderness) for three trumpets and orchestra was written in 1969, at a time, that is, when the shadow of dictatorship had again descended like a blight onthe lands of Bohemia and Moravia. This call gives life and breath again and again to Petr Eben's music, whether in quiet, reserved tones or in piercing clarity and brightness. All this resides in the last instance in a spiritualliturgical frame in which Christian and Jewish thought, ancient traditions and many other sensitive impulses have their place and their life.

Wolfgang Seiber

Petr Eben   Homo Sui Juris

1. The Man

The musician Petr Eben is something quite out of the ordinary. As a complete person with a sensitive soul and a kind heart he demonstrates, thanks to his immense energy, great diversity. His compositional, improvisatory, philosophical, theological, and social sensitivity, ability and knowledge are bewildering. The Aguarian Petr Eben, convivial and always welcoming, creates trust in his fellow beings for in totalitarian times trust was strange, dead, and came into its own only in the products of the spirit and the soul, that is of Art. In the search for beauty, and the purpose of human existence, Petr Eben demonstrates his admiration for our nature and this admiration leads to his trust in God.

2. Meeting in Prague

Petr Eben is an exciting person. His eyes sparkle, his lean figure moves nimbly towards us visitors from Switzerland. Petr Eben is interested and welcoming with his excellent, expressive German, his experience of life, his trust and unwavering convictions, his piety, his philosophical foundation and his great wealth of religious and liturgical music. In no time at all backgrounds are established and circumstances explained.

3. His Wife

The Petr Eben Company is an harmonious operation, sometimes a bold enterprise, as his wife Šárka points out, so varied are the areas covered and thus the activities of this musician. He composes and improvises, gives historical and pedagogical lectures, introduces performances of his music, is a piano and organ accompanist, and is always on hand to advise editors and students. A teacher by training and a passionate connoisseur of German literature, resolves logistical and psychological problems, stands by her husband in all his undertakings, orders his working life, "takes part". This estimable couple is a "firm" of nearly fifty years standing, with lofty values of human respect, and is an example to all of us in the world of music and to our children of a life full of love, culture and actions with flair.

4. His Music

Petr Eben's longing for sources and origins ("the first word spoken by a child, the first lines written by a poet, the first compositions of a young man in love") in music, namely Gregorian chant and folk-song radiates from everything hge writes. Just as his personal appearance - without a sterile wall, without narcissistic laurel wreath - strikes one as expressive and matter-of-fact, so Petr Eben's music appears many-faceted with jazz elements, for example, with a tarantella or a chorale-like passage standing out and contrasted, with Janáček-like spirals of repetitions, with no concerns about the sacred and the secular coming into contact. With exciting modulations, in sequences or repetitions, Petr Eben is able to present his compositions and improvisations as a rich mixture of colour and texture, and with a liveliness which stems from a remarkable conciseness: always vital and exciting, easily understood by the ordinary music-lover but appealing equally to the intellectual.

5. The Lucerne Idea

Meetings with colleagues from other countries, cultural stimuli, impulses in general, act as a driving force upon our capacity for work, our imagination and our convictions. Church music in particular needs to be stimulated by powerful forces and not only by that of pop music; this is why the Lucerne Academy of Music regularly initiates meetings of composers. In the field of organ music these actually take place in Lucerne, the centre of Swiss church music, with, for example, a visit by Naji Hakim from Paris. Petr Eben, with Olivier Messiaen, the only contemporary composer to write great music for organ, celebrated his 70th birthday in January 1999. Lucerne joined in the celebrations and honoured the composer during the week from 1st to 9th June 1999. Our guest from Prague gave lectures, accompanied songs at the piano in the subtlest manner, acted as narrator in programmatic works, and improvised at one of the international Court Organ concerts. Lucerne musicians played works by Eben - *Krajiny Patmoské (Landscapes of Patmos)*, *Missa* for unison voices, the *Pražské Te Deum (Prague Te Deum)*, the *Marienvesper*, *Okna*, the *Secret Songs*, the *Cello Sonata* - for solo voice, choir, trumpet, violoncello, percussion and speaker and performed his organ works on the five-manual court organ (1650 - 1977).

Peter Stadtmüller

Meetings with Petr Eben

I had known the name Petr Eben for a long time. If I remember correctly I had heard it first from an organ student at the Stuttgart Music Academy who came from the Sudetenland. That must have been in about 1965. At that time I did not know any of his works nor did I have any scores. Where could one have bought them? Communism reigned in the East and had partitioned itself off from the West. Over the years one heard occasionally of an impressive work for organ in several movements, the *Sunday Music*, but that had been published in Prague and was therefore not obtainable. Not at least through the normal channels. Finally in 1980 Universal in Vienna published the little partita *O Jesu, all mein Leben bist du*, a piece which fascinated me from the very first moment and which I enjoy playing to this day.

In the same year, 1980, I finally met Petr Eben himself. He had come to Mainz for a performance of his orchestral piece *Vox clamantis in deserto* by the South-West-German Radio Symphony Orchestra of Baden-Baden, and the Episcopal Institute for Church Music took the opportunity to invite him to give a lecture about his works to its students. In the evening there was a most impressive concert in the Church of St Antony including the *Chagall Windows* with David Tasa (trumpet) and Gerd Augst (organ), and in the second half an organ improvisation by Petr Eben. What a fantastic musician and improviser this Petr Eben was! And yet at the same time he was an extremely charming and modest man of engaging sincerity and deep piety.

That was the first impression I formed of him and in the course of the succeeding years when we met again - which was sadly relatively seldom - and gradually came into closer contact, this impression became ever deeper and stronger.

We met again in Berlin in 1985 at a meeting of church musicians from both halves of Germany at which the *Missa cum populo* (minus the *Credo*) received its first performance at a service in St Hedwig's Cathedral. It was impressive to see how the composer assisted at the choir rehearsals for the Mass. It is not particularly easy to sing and given the lack of rehearsal time there were plenty of problems. Apart from that the parts were in manuscript and correspondingly difficult to read. At this gathering we had our first conversations, the subject-matter of which naturally included professional matters such as questions of interpretation and the like.

And since then we have exchanged letters which now amount to a considerable pile. Highlights of these are Eben's Christmas letters, always with handwritten personal sentences at the end, with reports of astonishing levels of activity, full of acute observations on contemporary events, but also of reflections on and gratitude for everything he has experienced, letters which reveal a man who, inspite of all the evil in the world and inspite of everything he has himself endured, has remained an optimist and knows that he is in God's protective care.

Since this meeting in Berlin Eben has sent me most of his works for organ, always with a warm dedication, and there have been tapes, records and more recently CDs of many works for organ and other pieces. Even our daughters, flautist and oboist respectively, have received pieces for their instruments and were of course tremendously proud to do so. I received a printer's draft of *Hommage à Dietrich Buxtehude* before the work was published; I was fascinated and immediately set to work to study it. I have played the work in public but prefer to do so from the printed score which was published by Schott shortly afterwards. The first occasion was in April 1988 in the inaugural concert for the newly restored organ in the Music Faculty of the Johannes Gutenberg University in Mainz. This was probably one of the first - if not the first - performance after the première given by Martin Haselböck and was received with great enthusiasm. Since then I have played the piece many times, twice on the radio (for Südwestfunk Mainz and Sender Freies Berlin) and 36 times at concerts, most recently at a Lecture Demonstration on the Fisk organ at the Old West Church in Boston, Massachusetts. No other new work has featured so frequently in my programmes.

We met again at the Stuttgart Bach Festival in 1987 where Petr Eben gave a thrilling concert of improvisations on texts from the *Book of Job*, and in the Music Faculty of Mainz University in January 1990 when he gave a highly entertaining evening of improvisations and lead a workshop on selected organ works played by our students. I shall never forget the way he began the improvisation evening with the words: *"This is the first time that I can appear in public without fear of political repression."* A weight had been lifted from his shoulders and the audience sensed this. For me and my family it was a particular pleasure to have Petr Eben as a guest in our house and I believe he felt at home with us.

There were two further occasions when were able to meet him in Mainz. Firstly, in 1995 there was a lecture on life and work at the Education Centre of the Diocese of Mainz and a choral concert with his son David's Schola Gregoriana Pragensis and organ improvisations, and finally in 1998 there was a video presentation of his church opera *Jeremia*s and a brilliant performance of *Job* by Professors Gerhard Gnann and Hans-Jürgen Kaiser with an introduction by the composer.

Since 1988 I have regularly performed the *Song of Ruth* and several cycles of the liturgical songs both in Germany and the United States with my friend Dr Vernon Wicker from Seattle. After one performance at Kempen on the Lower Rhine it suddenly occurred to us that we should ask the composer to write a piece for us, that is for baritone and organ, on texts by Thomas von Kempen, for the anniversary celebrations of both the writer and the town in 1994. To our great pleasure Eben agreed and wrote *De Nomine Caeciliae* of which we gave the first performance in St Mary's Church in Kempen on December 12th 1994 - although the printed score of the work makes no mention of this. Since then this piece forms another regular item in our repertory and is scheduled to have several performances in this the year of Eben's 70th birthday.

Unfortunately I have not actually met Petr Eben very frequently but for me he was always present over the years through his works Organ students of mine and of other teachers in the Music Department have played a great number of them; even the last movement of *Krajiny Patmoské (Landscapes of Patmos)*came up once in the examinations - with percussion. And I myself have studied a large number of them and played many in public. There have been few programmes in recent years without a piece by Petr Eben. We have corresponded over innumerable points of detail with questions about the actual notes, about suspected and actual misprints, articulation and phrasing, choice of manual, about tempi and registration and - occasionally - about matters of technique and the "playability" of certain passages. Much of the music is not exactly straightforward. It is a reassuring to hear from the composer that in the last resort his metronome marks are not to be taken too seriously.

I have always been fascinated by Petr Eben's inventiveness, his powerful rhythmic originality, his wit, his formal variety, the richness of his harmonies and his precise conceptions of timbre.

In my forty-five years as performer and teacher I have not felt so close to any other contemporary composer and no other composer has been so frequently represented in my recital programmes as Petr Eben. To have him as a friend is my great good fortune, an honour and a cause for deep gratitude.

Alena Veselá

I had the good fortune, many years ago, to meet Petr Eben at a time he was writing his first cycle for solo organ *Nedělní hudba (Musica dominicalis) (Sunday Music)* of 1957-59. The third section, *Moto ostinato*, was one of the Czech works prescribed for the Prague Spring Festival Competition and it was causing a great stir. Of the six pieces to choose from, most competitors picked the Eben work. I would say that it marked a milestone in the appreciation of his music.

The organ became Eben's favourite instrument and his organ output is very large. Personally, I consider that his *Laudes* of 1964 for solo organ, *Okna (Windows)* after Marc Chagall of 1976 for trumpet and organ, and *Krajiny Patmoské (Landscapes of Patmos)* of 1984 for organ and percussion to be the most beautiful organ works of this century.

I am one of the great admirers of Petr Eben's work and consider myself fortunate to be able to count myself among his friends. As I studied more of his compositions my deep regard for him grew and grew. His works are seldom missing from my concert programmes in different parts of the world and there is good reason for that: the inclusion of Eben on the programme is a sure guarantee of success, so enthusiastically is he appreciated everywhere.

We can be proud of having a composer of such calibre in our country. His work is a rare gift which we are glad to offer to our keenly receptive public. As I have found, there is a great deal of interest in Eben's work among young organists in various countries throughout Europe, as well as across America, where I have held classes in the interpretation of his music. Thus today we can say truthfully that his work has become known everywhere.

Petr Eben is a good and kind man. He shines with these attributes. On the occasion of his seventieth birthday, I wish him much health and creative elan - much human happiness also.

DISCOGRAPHY OF RECORDINGS OF WORKS BY PETR EBEN

By Peter Herbert

Kateřina Vondrovicová's book on Petr Eben included, in an alphabetical list of the works, the recordings known to her. [i] This first substantial Eben discography was an invaluable starting point for the creation of the current work. Johannes Landgren had also commenced his own own listing of Eben recordings and most generously made this available. [ii] The number of further recordings discovered and the number of those issued in recent years has been so great as to result in a discography several times larger than originally anticipated. The work remains very much in progress, even with regard to older recordings. At its current stage of development, it is certainly incomplete. However, it is intended that work should continue so that it can be placed on a proper, scientific footing. [iii]

The aim has been to include recordings in all sorts of recording format and in which a work or works by Petr Eben appear. In addition, recordings in which Petr Eben appears as performer have also been included in Section 2, even where he is not performing one of his own works. It has proved difficult to obtain information about several such recordings, especially those on which Eben improvised on piano as an accompaniment to poetry readings, for example.

The discography is in two sections, with the second having four parts.

Section 1 is an alphabetical list of works (using largely English titles) with a key to recording label and number.

Section 2 (a) is a listing by label of all recordings about which there is reasonable confidence in the details shown. The listing includes label, number, format, year of recording (or year of publication if the recording date is unknown) and details of the works by Petr Eben with available performer information and title of the recording if known. Footnotes include

---

[i] Kateřina Vondrovicová: "Petr Eben", Panton 1995.
[ii] Personal communication.
[iii] It is hoped that this discography will have an extended life at the Göteborg Organ Art Center (GOART) on their Internet web pages currently residing at http://www.hum.gu.se/goart/w-1.htm

details of works by other composers that also appear on each recording. Section 2 (b) is a list of recordings of uncertain status, about which there is too little information to be confident in including them in the main listing. Section 2 (c) is a list of library archive recordings which are only available on loan. In Section 2 (d) is a short list of spurious recordings which are mentioned only to help others avoid them. Though all four parts of section 2 are similar in appearance, only the recordings in section 2 (a) are included in the alphabetical key in Section 1.

The great detail shown in Section 2 was felt to be necessary and important because it demonstrates in tyhe most direct manner the musical context in which the Eben works are to be found in recordings.

It is no surprise that *Nedělní hudba (Sunday Music)*, in particular the third movement, *Moto ostinato* and *Okna podle Marca Chagalla (Windows after Marc Chagall)* are easily the most recorded works of Petr Eben. Strong representation is also shown for various other works, such as *Laudes*, *Hommage à Dietrich Buxtehude* and *Pražské Te Deum (Prague Te Deum)*. Perhaps most surprising is the great range and depth of works recorded. In this respect, the proliferation of semi-private recordings by choirs both inside and outside the Czech Republic and by individual organists has contributed a remarkable number of entries and testifies to the ever-increasing popularity of both vocal and organ works by Petr Eben.

The author is conscious of the probability of error and omission and welcomes new and additional information about any recordings included and of any not included. Apologies are also extended to the reader for the size of the fonts used, the sheer volume of recordings necessitating economy of scale.

It would have been impossible to achieve the present degree of completeness without the aid of a great number of people. Principal amongst these was Petr Eben himself, who, without knowing the precise purpose of the author's enquiries, took a great deal of time to provide information. The author also most gratefully ackowledges the assistance of numerous persons with deep gratitude and regrets any omissions. [i]

---

[i] Thanks are owed to, inter alia, the following: Carmen van den Akker (EMJ Neerpelt), Ellie Bakx, Jana and Pavel Bílek (Široký dvůr), Zdeněk Bruderhans, Tomáš Draštich (Jeřabinka), Homer Edwards (Calcante), Robert L. Edwards, Jana Gonda (Supraphon), Byron Gorman, Sonja Greiner (Europa Cantat), Hyperion records, Jiří Jirák, Brian Johnson (Herald), Nigel Judson (Red Hedgehog), Arvo Kartul (Tartu University), Ambros Koch, Matthias Koll (Bonner Kammerchor), Pavel Konečný (Oktáva), Patrick Lambert, Johannes

1. Alphabetical Listing of Recorded Works

In this section, no attempt is made to indicate whole or part works. For this it is necessary to refer to the listing in Section 2. Recordings without catalogue number, or for which a number is currently unknown, are indicated by the tilde sign (~). The titles of works in this table are largely only in English. Where appropriate, Czech titles are shown in Section 2 (a).

About Swallows and Maidens	Chandos: CHAN 9257; Martech-Corp: ~; Panton: 11 0358
Ancient Cosmetics	Brain Music: BOCD 4916
Anno Domini – Vorübergang des Herrn	Erzbistum Paderborn: 2021379-4360
Antiphons and Psalms	Campanula: Campanula 1; Supraphon: 11 1205-4; 0 29 9889
Apologia Sokratus	Supraphon: 0 19 0558; 1 19 0558; 0 12 0880; 1 12 0880
Arrangements of Folk Songs	Supraphon: DV 5194; DV 5195
Autumn is Already Ripening	Český rozhlas: CR 0066-2; Panton: 08 0204; 88 0204
Biblical Dances	Bayer: BR 150 009; B.Hulsroj: 220199; Gothic Records: G49106; Hyperion: CDA 67195; IFO Musikproduktion: IFO CD 000 45; Opus 3: CD 9302; Organum: OGM 599035; Pro Organo: CD 7023; Regent Records: REGCD 114; Signum: SIG X79-00
Bilance	Supraphon: 1 12 0613
Bitter Earth	Opus 3: CD 1992; Panton: 81 0898-1
Brass Quintet	Český rozhlas: CR 0053-2; Supraphon: 1 19 0946
Campanae gloriosae	IFO Organ Document: CD 030
Cantica Comeniana	Azymuth: AZ 1027; AZ CD 01027; Lunarion: LN 0008-1; LN 0008-2; LN 0008-4; VUS Pardubice: VUS 001-2
Cantico delle creature	Arti Audio: AA 0810; Azymuth: AZ 1027; AZ CD 01027; Lunarion: LN 0008-1; LN 0008-2; LN 0008-4; Melisma Musik: ME 7122-2; Opus 3: CD 9102; Panton: 81 0827-1
Carol Singers from Těšín District	Český rozhlas: CR 0066-2
Catonis moralia	Hungaroton: HCD 31840; Ljubliana: LD 0384; Neerpelt: 6851 173; Supraphon: 1 12 2315
Chamber Music: on Seifert's Collection of Poems "Maminka"	Supraphon: DV 15046
Christmas Songs	Musica Intima: MI-001
A Collection of Foreign National Songs	Weikert Tonnstudio: TW993032; TW993102

Landgren, i. A. C. Lang (Musica Sacra International), Gayle Martin, Graham Melville-Mason, Cynthia Morris (Cork Festival), Laura Sandham, Yumi Sato (Brain Music), Radek Šipka (Svatopluk), Judith Cook Tucker (World Music Press), William Van Pelt (Organ Historical Society), Gudrun Schröfel (Mädchencor Hannover), Ken Taniyama, Mgr. Anna Urbancová (Žatecký příležitostní sbor), Wolfgang G. Haas-Musikverlag, Eisuke Yamamoto.

Concerto for Organ & Orchestra No 1	Motette-Ursina: 40151
Concerto for Organ & Orchestra No 2	Panton: 8110 0391; 81 0391; 81 1141-2
Concerto for Piano and Orchestra	Panton: 81 9018-2; Supraphon: 0 89 9988; DV 5988; SUA 18 594; SUAST 58 594; SV 8161
Curious Songs	Český rozhlas: CR 0066-2; Supraphon: 1117 3200; 1119 4623
Curses and Blessings	Panton: 81 0740-1; Supraphon: SU 3384-2
Day's Experiences, A	Český rozhlas: CR 0066-2
De nomine Caeciliae	Signum: SIG X79-00
De sancto Adalberto	Supraphon: SU 3288-2
Desire of Ancient Things	Azymuth: AZ 1027; AZ CD 01027; Opus 3: CD 9102; Panton: 81 0794-1
Die Frage nach dem Geist	Bass Line Records: BassLine 1
Differences and Opposites	Supraphon: ~
Dissatisfied Prince The	Supraphon: DM 15181
Dobrý a upřimný jest Pán	Svatopluk: L1 34519226
Duetti per due trombe	De Plein Vent: DPV CD 9571; Panton: 11 0410
Duettini	Nibiru: NIBIRU: 0139-2
Elce pelce kotrmelce	Supraphon: 1 29 9844; 11 3997-1
Epitaph	Supraphon: DV 6113; SV 8233
Faust	Bayer: BR 150 016; B.Hulsroj: 220199; Etcetera: KTC 1115; Hyperion: CDA 67195; Image Records: ~; Lyrinx: LYR 031/33; Mitra: 16 167; Panton: 8110 0295; Pro Organo: CD 7023
Festive Voluntary On Good King Wenceslas, A	Calcante:CD 012; Pro Organo: CD 7023
Four Choruses on Latin Texts	Ars Musici: AM 12052; Àzuoliukas: JAD C 082; Azymuth: AZ 1027; AZ CD 01027; BMG Ariola: 74321 18148 2; Campanula: Campanula 1; DSV DSV-001; Jade Records: JACD 91015; JACD; 57942; Lunarion: LN 0008-1; LN 0008-2; LN 0008-4; Mediason: MEDD 112; Opus 3: CD 9302; Panton: 81 0794-2; 81 0827-2; Ventus: DSV 001
From Life to Life	Bon Art Music: / Fanton: ~; Lunarion: LN 0008-1; LN 0008-2; LN 0008-4
Greek Dictionary	Balkanton: BXA 11728; Brain Music: BOCD-4506; BOCD-4612; OSBR-15026; Nibiru: NIBIRU: 0139-2; Panton: 8111 0416; 81 0312-1; Styltón: RS0548200; Supraphon: 1 19 2408; 1112 2455; Thorofon: CTH 2107
Green Twig is Sprouting, The	Český rozhlas: CR 0066-2; Formánek ~; Panton: 01 0110, 11 0567; Supraphon: 4784-M; 4786-M; 1 19 1192; DM 5638; DM 5703; DM 5912; DM 5913; DV 5638; World Music Press: T26; T27; T29
Hommage à Dietrich Buxtehude	Amabile: AM 0022-2; Ambiente: ACD 9502; B.Hulsroj: 220199; Etcetera: KTC 1115; Hyperion: CDA 67194; NCRV: NCRV 9090; Priory: PRCD 618; PRCD 643; René Gailly: CD87 108; Supraphon: 11 0564-2; 11 0564-2; Victoria: VCD 19080

Hours of the Night	Panton: 8110 0037; 81 0037
House at Pooh Corner, The	B&M Music: 0096-2
In Honour of Charles V	Univerzita Karlova z Praze: ~
In the Grass	Český rozhlas: CR 0066-2; Supraphon: 04 205/06; DM 5911; DM 5912
Jan Palach Organ Improvisation	AR(i)STON ~; Melantrich: Z1 0001-1
Job	B.Hulsroj: 220199; Cadenza: CAD 800 903; Calcante:CD 027; Hyperion: CDA 67194; Melisma Musik: OPUS 7087-2; Multisonic: 31 0095-2; Panton: 81 0924-2; Pro Organo: CD 7023; Supraphon: SU 0181-2; SU 3177-2; Victoria VCD 19080
Labyrinth of the World and the Paradise of the Heart,The	Clarton: CQ 0022-2; HaasClassicCologne: HCC 2000 001
Landscapes of Patmos	Balance Music: BAL 94121; Multisonic: 31 0097-2; Opus 3: CD 9301; Panton: 81 0827-1; Revilo: F 670 384
Laudes	B.Hulsroj: 220199; Chamade: CHCD 5620; Delta Records: DRS 86-637; Lyrinx: LYR 031/33; Melodiya: 33CM-04409-10; Multisonic: 31 0097-2; Opus 3: CD 9102; Priory: PRCD 485; Revilo: F 670 384; Supraphon: 0 11 0470; 1 11 0470; 11 0564-1; 11 0564-2; Teldec: 66 23 410-01; Victoria: VCD 19080
Leopold the See-Through Crumb-Picker.	Weston Woods: ~
Letters to Milena (Kafka) Piano Improvisations	Supraphon: 0 18 0630
Little Sorrows	Signum: SIG X47-00
Liturgical Songs	Antiphona: AA 0040 2231; Amabile: AM 0020-2; CDA WN 101995; Rottenburger Dom: 280696; Signum: SIG X79-00; Supraphon: 1119 9749
Love and Death	Azymuth: AZ 1027; AZ CD 01027; Capitol: SP 20307; Newton Choral Society: AFU-3030; Panton: 81 0755-1; Supraphon: DV 5755; SP20307; SUA 1?; VUSUK VUS UK 1997
Loveless Songs	Signum: SIG X81-00; Supraphon: 0 89 9988; DV 6194; SU 3011-2; SUA 18 751; SUA ST 58 751; SV 8308
March of the Castle Guard	Clarton: CQ 0019
Mare nigrum	Dreamlife Corporation: DMCD 1-4; Pehy/Atypus: AY 0011 2
Missa adventus et quadragesimae	MBC: MBC-9603101; Priory: pr 125; Supraphon: 11 1428-1; 11 1438-2; 11 1438-4; Ultravox: UCD 005; Wuppertale Kurrende: WKK 0011
Missa cum populo	Křik: KK 102-2; Panton: 81 0801-1; 81 1141-2
Momenti di organo	B.Hulsroj: 220199; Signum: SIG X79-00
Most Secret Songs, The	Signum: SIG X47-00; Supraphon: SU 3011-2
Mundus in Periculo	DKR: DKR 03
Music: for Oboe Bassoon and Piano	Supraphon: 1 19 1054

Mutationes	Amabile: AM 0022-2; B.Hulsroj: 220199; Lyrinx: LYR 31/33; Priory: PRCD 289; Supraphon: 10 3375-1; 1111 3375
National Songs for Mixed Chorus	Svatopluk: L1 34519226
Nic ať tě neděsí	Svatopluk: L1 34519226
Nursery Songs	Signum: SIG X81-00
Oči všech se upirají k Tobě	Schóla z Ostrožské Lhoty: ~; Svatopluk: L1 34519226
Old Testament Fresco	Panton: 81 1398-2131
Old Time Love Incantation, An	Azymuth: AZ 1027; AZ CD 01027; Canticum: CANT 011; N.Arizona Univ. Chorale: NACM 09; Panton: 8112 –426; Supraphon: 0 89 9988; DV 5995; SUA 1888 506
One Hundred Folk Songs	Supraphon: DM 5911; DM 5912; DM 5913
Opponents The	Panton: 81 0949-1
Ordo modalis	Nibiru: NIBIRU: 0139-2; Supraphon: 0 11 0429; 1 11 0429; 0 18 0753; 1 18 0753; 11 0480-1
Orff's School I. II.	Supraphon: 0 42 0107; 1 43 0107; 1 19 1194
Piano Goes into the World, the	Panton: ~
Piano Improvisations	Supraphon: 1 18 1528
Piano Sonata in D♭	Capitol: SP 20039
Piano trio	Panton: 81 0850-1
Pictures of Hope 5 Part Motet	IFO Musikproduktion: IFO CD 00 5000
Pragensia	Panton: 11 0563; Supraphon: 1 19 1397; 1 12 1607
Prague Nocturne	Panton: 81 0827-1
Prague Te Deum	Arco Diva: GZ L 40507; ECM New Series: 837 1539; Křik: KK 102-2; Opus 3: CD 9302; Orfeus: OR 0010-2131; Supraphon: 11 1438-2; 11 1438-2; 11 1438-4; 11 2224-2
Proprium festivum monasteriense	Antiphona: AA 0039 2231
Quintetto per stromenti a fiato	Supraphon: 0 41 0119; 1 41 0119; SUA 10 892; SUA ST 50 892
Religious Songs for Folk Singer	Supraphon: 0 29 9891
Rhythmus de gaudiis Paradisi	Corkfest Records: 96
Risonanza	Nibiru: NIBIRU: 0139-2
Roundabouts and Stars	Supraphon: DM 10189; DV 10208
Six Love Songs	Elly Bakx: 97-07-171; Nibiru: NIBIRU: 0139-2; Signum: SIG X47-00; Supraphon: 04 109; DM 6157; SU 3011-2; SV 8275
Six Songs on the Poetry of Rainer Maria Rilke	Signum: SIG X47-00; Supraphon: 1112 2455; SU 3011-2
Small Chorale Partita	B.Hulsroj: 220199; Delta Records: DRS 86-637; Motette-Ursina: 20241; Multisonic: 31 0098-2; Psallite: 60041; Revilo: F 670 384
Sonata for Flute and Marimba "Wood and Wind"	Arbitrium: ARBITRIUM 1116; Supraphon: 1119 2766
Sonata for Oboe and Piano	AMC: AMC 04; Chinese disc: M360
Sonata semplice	Panton: 01 0719; 81 1398-2131; Wheldrake Sound Recordings WSR 96001

Song of Ruth	Bonton 71 0057-2; Opus 3: CD 1991; Signum: SIG X79-00; Supraphon: 11 1438-2; 11 1438-2; 11 1438-2
Songs from Těšín Region	Signum: SIG X82-00; Supraphon: SU 3011-2
Songs to Lute	Nibiru: NIBIRU: 0139-2; Signum: SIG X82-00; Supraphon: 1 12 1484
Spiritus mundum adunans	Kammerchor des Instituts für Musikpädagogik der Universität Leipzig: VKJK 00298; Křik: KK 102-2; Melisma Musik: ME 7122-2
Spring Ditties	Český rozhlas: CR 0066-2; Panton: 8111 0416; Signum: SIG X81-00; Supraphon: DM 10155; DV 10137
S touhou	Svatopluk: L1 34519226
String Quartet. "Labyrinth of the World & the Paradise of the Heart"	Supraphon: 10 3377-1
Suita balladica	Integral Classic: INT 221107; Multisonic: 31 0065-2; Supraphon: 0 18 0753; 1 18 0753; DV 5522; SUA 10073
Suita liturgica	Supraphon: SU 3373-2
Sunday Music	AGK: 12 216; Amabile: AM 0010-2; AM 0022-2; American Guild of Organists: AGO 109-112-4; Audite: 51 004; B.Hulsroj: 220199; BWE Classics: BWE 0221; Capitol: SP 30834; Cathedral: CRMS 854; Centaur: CRC 2042; Christophorus: SCGLX 73 884; Connell Digital Classics: CONNELL 1; Crystal Records: S182; CTS: 801 207; 810 621; Dordt College: E-552; Edit: 41 0055-2; European Guild of Organists: EGO 007; Gayle H. Martin: 001; Gothic Records: G 49110; Herald: HAVPCD 238; Hyperion: CDA 66978; JAV Recordings: JAV 107; JAV 109; JAV 112; Lyrinx: LYR 031/33; MCB/Michael Woodward: MW 934; Melodiya: 33D-030347-48; C10 30491 002; Mixtur: MXT 2005B; Motette-Ursina: 40151; Multisonic: 31 0098-2; Musica Organum: MO 20.4009; Organum: OGM599035; OX Records: OX CD-41; OX CASS-41; Pallas: 120; Pro Organo: CD 7023; St. David's Church: SDS 100; ~; Supraphon: 0 89 9988; 10 0564-1; 11 0564-1; DM 5715; SUF 20 098; Teldec: 66 22 038-01; Vista: VPS 1062; Wedum Gård: WGRCD0497; York Ambisonic: YORKCD108; YORKMC108
Tabulatura nova	Bravo Pardubice: BP 0001-2; Panton: 8111 0174; 81 0174; Supraphon:1119 2938
Ten Chorale Preludes	Bonton: 71 0081-2; Vista: VPS 1062
Ten Poetic Duets	Amabile: ZR 0002
Three Quiet Songs	Supraphon: 1112 2455
Tres iubilationes	Opus: 3 CD 9302

Trouvère Mass	Amabile: ZR 0002-2; Azymuth: AZ 1027; AZ CD 01027; Bohemia Music: BM 0025-2; BM 0025-4; Opus: 91 2409-2
Tune of the Castle Guard	Clarton: CQ 0019-2
Two Chorale Fantasias	Bonton: 71 0081-2; Delta Records: DRS 86-637; Melodiya: C10 30491 002; Multisonic: 31 0097-2; Panton: 8110; 0044; 8111 0044; 81 0044; Priory: PRC 232; Revilo: F 670 384
Two Festive Preludes	Calcante: CD 027; Multisonic: 31 0003-1; 31 0003-2; Opus 3: CD 9301
Two Invocations for Trombone & Organ	BIS: BIS CD 488; Classico: CLASSCD122; Opus 3: CD 9301; Supraphon: 11 1438-1; 11 1438-2; 11 1438-4
Two Songs from the Amsterdam Cancional of J.A. Komenský	Musik Centrum Pardubice: MC 017
Ubi caritas et amor	Azymuth: AZ 1027; AZ CD 01027; Brain Music: BOCD-4712; Opus 3: CD 9301; Panton: 81 0794-1; Supraphon: 0 12 0880; 1 12 0880
Veils and Tears	Gutingi: gut 226
Verba sapientiae	Antiphona: AZ 1027; AZ CD 01027; Bonner Kammerchor: 11163; Brain Music: BOCD-4615; Hope College: CD 1193-02; Lunarion: LN 0008-1; LN 0008-2; LN 0008-4; Musica Sacra International: ~
Verses About Love	Supraphon: DV 15190
Versetti	Calcante: CD 027
Vesperae in festo nativitatis	Lunarion: LN 0008-1; LN 0008-2; LN 0008-4; Rottenberger Dom: 280696; St. Olaf Records: OM230; Supraphon: 11 1438-1; 11 1438-2; 11 1438-4; Vergera: 14013-SL
Vox clamantis	Panton: 01 0277; 11 0277; 01 0300; 11 0300; 81 1141-2
War a Misfortune	Panton: 8112 0306
Wind Quintet	Supraphon: 0 28 0306
Windows after Marc Chagall	ABAKUS: LC 6461; Amati: SRR 9104; Arnold: AVL 96263; BIS: BIS CD 565; EMI: CDC5 55086-2; CD-EMX 2290; Fermate: FER 2008; Gallo: GALLO CD-604; GALLO 47-604; G.face 24 Bit Recording: PRCG-1001; Gothic Records: G 49067; ICM Diessenhofen: MKH 40289; Lyrinx: LYR 031/33; Mitra: 16 205; Multisonic: 31 0098-2; 31 0347-2; Opus 3: CD 9102; Panton: 11 0672; Pro Organo: CD 7026; RCA: 09026 61186-2; Revilo: F 670 384; Simax: PSC1088; Soli Dei veritas: 74321470182; 74321470202; Suisa: MKH 40289; Supraphon: 10 3019-1; 1111 3019; T.O.G.: ~
Winnie the Pooh	B&M Music: 0063-2
World of Children, The	Supraphon: 0 29 0446

2. Alphabetical Listing of Recording Labels

45	45rpm 7 inch Record.		LP	Long-Playing Record.
78	78 rpm 10 inch Record.		MC	Musicassette.
CD	Compact Disc.		RT	Reel to Reel Tape.
EP	Extended Play 7 inch Record.		VC	Video Cassette.

Where information as to recording number is absent, a question mark (?) is used. Where recordings apparently have no number whatsoever, this is indicated by "No Number". Where known, the record title is shown in a san-serif typeface between quotation marks. For recordings where Petr Eben appears as performer, his name is included in **bold type**.

ABAKUS
LC 6461   LP   **Windows after Marc Chagall.** *Okna podle Marca Chagalla.* Albrecht Eichberger (trumpet); Joachim Dorfmüller (organ).

AGK
12 216   CD   1996   **Sunday Music.** *Nedělní hudba.* Stephan Wehr (organ). "Orgelkonzert in Niederaltaich". [i]

Amabile
AM 0006-2   CD   1993   **De Angelis.** Children's Choir JITRO; Michal Chrobák (piano); Jiří Skopal (conductor). "Czech Children's Choir Jitro". [ii]

AM 0010-2   CD   1994   **Sunday Music.** *Nedělní hudba.* No. 3, *Moto ostinato.* Václav Uhlíř (organ). "Czech Organ Music". [iii]

AM 0020-2   CD   1999   (1) **Liturgical Songs.** *Liturgické zpěvy.* (selection).
(2) **Four Choruses on Latin Texts.** *Čtyři sbory na latinské texty.* No. 1, *Mater cantans filio;* No. 3, *De spiritu sancto.* Children's Choir JITRO; Jiří Skopal (conductor). "Closing the Century". [iv]

AM 0022-2   CD   1999   (1) **Hommage à Dietrich Buxtehude.**

---

[i] Johann Sebastian Bach: *Toccata and Fugue in F, BWV540;* Felix Mendelssohn-Bartholdy: *Sonata in d minor Op.65-6 "Vater unser im Himmelreich".*

[ii] Otmar Mácha: *Oh, Mountain, Oh!;* Zdeněk Lukáš: *Echo; The Small Wreath;* Miroslav Raichl: *Merry Minizoo;* Zoltán Kodály: *Ave Maria;* Henk Badings: *Kyrie Eleison;* Irving Berlin: *Give me your Tired, your Poor;* Samuel A. Ward & Julian Harvey: *America the beautiful;* Oscar Peterson: *Hymn to Freedom;* Walter Hawkins: *I'm Goin up a Yonder.*

[iii] Bohuslav Černohorský: *Toccata in C major; Fugue in g minor; Fugue in D major;* Jan Zach: *Prelude and Fugue in c minor;* Josef Seger: *Fugue in c minor; Fugue in F major;* František Xaver Brixi: *Toccata and Fugue in a minor; Pastorella in C major;* Jan Křtitel Kuchař: *Fantasia in g minor;* Leoš Janáček: *Adagios 1 & 2; Glagolitic Mass - Postlude;* Bohuslav Martinů: *Vigilie.*

[iv] Jan Jirásek: *Te Laudamus;* Bohuslav Martinů: *Špalíček – Carrying out Death;* Ilja Hurník: *Voda, Voěnka;* Otmar Mácha: *Lašské helekačky;* Miroslav Raichl: *Veselé minizoo;* arr. Miroslav Raichl: *Czech Folksongs - A když vy mě má panenko, Koukal na ni přes bednění, Ty bysterské zvony;* Slovak folksong – *Tancuj, tancuj, vykrúcaj.*

ZR 0002-2		CD	1999 1999 1994	(2) **Mutationes.** (3) **Sunday Music.** *Nedělní hudba.* František Vaníček (organ). (1) **Ten Poetic Duets.** *Deset poetických duet.* 3 songs. (2) **Trouvère Mass.** *Truvérská mše.* Iuventus Cantans; Vlastislav Novák (conductor). [i]

amadeus-chor

P 06081 CD 1997 **Cantico delle creature.** Der amadeus-chor; Julian C. Tölle (conductor). [ii]

Amati

SRR 9104 CD 1998 **Windows after Marc Chagall.** *Okna podle Marca Chagalla.* Gunther Beetz (trumpet); Georg Schäeffner (organ). "Concertos for Trumpet". [iii]

Ambiente

ACD 9502 CD 1995 **Hommage à Dietrich Buxtehude.** Michael Vetter (organ). [iv]

AMC

AMC 04 CD 1998 **Sonata for Oboe and Piano.** *Sonata pro hoboj a klavír.* Jan Adamus (oboe); Květa Novotná (piano). [v]

American Guild of Organists

AGO 109-112-4 MC   **Sunday Music.** *Nedělní hudba.* No. 3, *Moto Ostinato.* Clay Christiansen (organ). "Celebrating the Completion of the Renovation of the Salt Lake Tabernacle Organ". [vi]

Antiphona

AA 0011-2231 CD 1991/3 **The Green Twig is Sprouting.** *Zelená se snítka.* No. 11, Kdyby tu nic nebylo; No. 14, Na našem sádku. Dětský a mládežnický pěvecký sbor Jizerka; Michal Chrobák, Jiří Pašek (piano); Jaroslav Jirásko, Gabriela Hlubučková (violin); Alena Bradloá,

---

[i] Bohuslav Martinů: *Petrklíč;* Benjamin Britten: *Missa Brevis in D.*
[ii] Private promotional issue. Josef Rheinberger: *Abendlied;* Wie lieblich sind deine Wohnungen; Jörg Duda: *Ave Maria;* Heinrich Schütz: *So fahr ich hin;* Heinrich Kaminski: *Psalm 130;* Giuseppe Verdi: *Pater Noster;* Zoltán Kodály: *Jesus und die Krämer;* Sergej Rachmaninov: *Ave Maria;* Francis Poulenc: *Gloria – Laudamus te, Dominus Deus, Angus Dei, Domine fili unigenite.*
[iii] Johann Molter: *Trumpet Concerto no.1 in D;* Johann Hertel: *Trumpet Concerto no. 1 in E flat;* Giuseppe Torelli: *Sonata à 5 con tromba in D*
[iv] Dietrich Buxtehude: *Prelude in C 1347; Nun bitten wir den Heiligen geist 209; Prelude in G 148;* Georg Böhm: *Partita Freu dich sehr, o meine Seele;* Egil Hovland: *Suite for Organ no. 2 Op.79*
[v] Georg Telemann: *Partita No.4;* Robert Schumann: *Three Romances Op.94;* Antonio Pasculli: *Concerto for Oboe and Piano "La Favorita";* Emil Viklický: *Ignác v koridoru*
[vi] Franz Liszt: *Fantasy & Fugue on "Ad Nos ad Salutarem Undam";* Edwin (Henry) Lemare: *Toccata & Fugue in C;* Camille Saint-Saëns: *Prelude & Fugue in B;* Edward Elgar: *Imperial March;* Sergey Rachmaninov: *Prelude in G minor;* Cook: *Fanfare;* Frederick Delius: *On hearing the first cuckoo in spring;* Henri Mulet: *Tu Es Petra;* Percy Whitlock: *Sortie;* Dietrich Buxtehude: *Prelude & Fugue in D;* Dmitry Kabalevsky: *Variations;* Johann Sebastian Bach: *Alla Breve;* Jehan Alain: *2nd Fantasie;* Leo Sowerby: *Fanfare.* 4 cassette set (Eben work on tape 4, side B).

AA 0016 2231	CD	1994	Václav Brádlov (conductors). "Dětský a mládežnický pěvecký sbor Jizerka Semily". [i] **Verba sapientiae.** Brněnský akademický sbor; Jaroslav Kyzlink (director). "Czech Choral Music". [ii]
AA 0039 2231	CD	1996	(1) **Verba sapientiae.** No. 3, *De tempore* (2) **Proprium festivum Monasteriense.** [iii]
AA 0040 2231	CD	1997	**Liturgical Songs.** *Liturgické zpěvy.* (selection). Children's Choir JITRO; Jiří Skopal (director). "Modern Czech Church Music". [iv]

Arbitrium

| Arbitrium 1116 | CD | | | **Sonata for Flute and Marimba "Wood and Wind"**. *Sonáta pro flétnu a marimbu.* Zdenek Bruderhans, A.Aungles, E. Kariks, C. Webb, M. Elphinstone (flutes); A. Grigg (marimba), E. Bruderhansová (piano). "...At North Terrace". [v] |

ARCODIVA

| GZ L 40507 | CD | 2000 | **Prague Te Deum.** *Pražské Te Deum.* Czech Philharmonic Chorus; Lubomír Mátl (chorus master); Prague Trumpeters; Josef Svejkovský (director). "Pražské jaro 2000". [vi] |

AR(i)STON

| No number | LP | 1969 | **Organ Improvisation (Jan Palach).** Antonie Hegerlíková, Radovan Lukavský, Jan Tříska, Václav Voska (actors); Miloš Beran, Václav Bláha, Jiří Brda, Karel Havránek (Speakers); |

---

i   Henry Purcell: *Blow up the Trumpet;* Domenico Gallo: *Domine ad adjuvandum;* Wolfgang Amadeus Mozart: *Ave verum corpus;* Karel Blažej Kopřiva: *Salve regina;* José M. Gomar: *Ave Maria;* André Caplet: *Sanctus;* Benjamin Britten: *Bulalow;* Deo *gracias;* Randall Thompson: *Alleluja;* Zdeněk Lukáš: *Quam pulchra es; Věneček; Poselství hudby;* Antonín Dvořák: *Šípek; Prsten;* Miroslav Raichl: *Zářící kočár;* Otmar Mácha: *Hymnus;* arr. Miroslav Raichl: *A když vy mě; Přeštický panenky;* arr. Milan Uherek: *Teče voda, teče;* arr. Blanka Kulínská: *Plzeňská věž;* arr. Walter Hawkins: *I'm goin' up a Yonder*

ii   Kryštof Harant: *Missa quinis vocibus super dolorosi martyrů;* Jan Zelenka: *Caligaverunt oculi mei; Tenebrae factae sunt;* Jan Novák: *Missa Philadelphiae*

iii   Orlando de Lassus: *Carmina chromatico;* Adrian Willaert: *O bone mio fa;* Kryštof Harant: *Sonatas;* Henry Purcell: *Burial Sentences;* Robert de Pearsall: *Lay a Garland;* Felix Mendelssohn: *Warum Toben die Heiden;* Lulius Lucink: *Kyrie, Gloria, Agnus Dei;* Jan Novák: *Dic per omnes.*

iv   Petr Řezníček: *Salve Regina;* Ilja Hurník: *Missa Vinea crucis.*

v   Joseph Boismortier: *Concerto in a for five flutes;* Antonín Rejcha: *3 Romances;* Georg Telemann: *Sonata in E for two flutes;* Zdeněk Klusák: *1-4-3-2-5-6-7-10-9-8-11; Invenzionetta;* Wolfgang Amadeus Mozart: *Andante in C;* Christoph Willibald Gluck: *Dance of blessed spirits;* Maurice Ravel: *Habanera;* Nicolò Paganini: *Moto Perpetuo.*

vi   CD issued with the programme for the Prague Spring 2000. Karel Husa: *Music for Prague 1968 – Introduction and Fanfare;* Luboš Fišer: *Fifteen Prints after Dürer's Apocalypse;* Jaroslav Rybář: *Four Fantasias after Klee – 3rd & 4th movements;* Svatopluk Havelka: *Percussionata – Synthesis;* Miloslav Ištvan: *Seven Movements for Symphony Orchestra – part;* Viktor Kalabis: *Concerto for Orchestra – Adagio. Con moto calma;*n Sylvie Bodorová: *Terezín Ghetto Requiem – Dies irae, Libera me;* Otmar Mácha: *Variations and Theme on the Death of Jan Rychlík.*

			Petr Eben (organ). "Kde končí svět na paměť Jana Palacha". [i]
Arnold			
AVL96263	CD	1996	**Windows after Marc Chagall.** *Okna podle Marca Chagalla.* Robert Edwards (organ); Craig Parker (trumpet). [ii]
Ars Musici			
AM 12052	CD	1997	**Four Choruses on Latin Texts.** *Čtyři sbory na latinské texty.* No. 4, *Salve Regina.* Freiburger Domkapelle; Raimund Hug (Conductor). "Marienlob durch die Jahrhunderte". [iii]
Arti Audio			
AA 0810	CD	1990	**Cantico delle creature.** Noorus Mixed Choir; Ene Üleoja (conductor). "Segakoor NOORUS, Tallinn". [iv]
Audite			
51 004	LP	1976	**Sunday Music.** *Nedělní hudba.* No. 3, *Moto ostinato;* No. 4, *Finale.* Matthias Janz (organ). [v]
Àzuoliukas			
JAD C 082	CD		**Four Choruses on Latin Texts.** *Čtyři sbory na latinské texty.* No. 4, *Salve regina.* Bernardas Vasiliauskas (organ); The Àzuoliukas Boys' Choir; Vytautas Miskinis (conductor). "Terra et coeli". [vi]
Azymuth			
AZ 1027	LP		(1) **Four Choruses on Latin Texts.** *Čtyři sbory na latinské texty.* No. 4, *Salve regina.*

---

i   Texts by Karel Toman, Jiří Orten, Gabriela Mistralová, Vladimír Holan, Jakub Deml, Miroslav Holub, František Halas, Alois Jirásek, Fráňa Šrámek
ii Private recording, not on general release. Johann Sebastian Bach: *O Mensch, bwein' dei' Sünde gross BWV 622;* Prelude and Fugue in E flat BWV 552; Camille Saint-Saëns: *Fantasie in E flat;* Louis Vierne: *Arabesque;* César Franck: *Chorale in b minor*
iii Anon: *Ave Maria, Dei Genitrix; O praeclara virginum Maria;* Jacobus Florius: *Regina coeli;* Alard du Gaucquier: *Magnificat im 1. Ton;* Tomás de Victoria: *Quam pulchri sunt gressus tui;* Philipp Zindelin: *Maria fein, dein Gnad mich b'schein;* Hieronymous Bildstein: *Ave virgo gloriosa;* Michael Praetorius: *Sie ist mir lieb die werte Magd;* Johann Stadlmayr: *Magnificat über Leggiadre Ninfe;* Johannes Brahms: *Marienlieder Op. 22: Nr. 1 Der englische Gruß;* Joseph Rheinberger: *Salve Regina;* Edvard Grieg: *Ave maris stella EG 150;* Max Reger: *Geistliche Gesänge op. 138: No. 4 Unser lieben Frauen Traum;* Christopher D. Wiggins: *Ave Maria;* Peter Planyavsky: *Deutsches Magnificat*
iv Zoltán Kodaly: *Adventi Enek;* Lajos Bardos: *Libera me;* Mikolajus Čiurlionis: *Sanctus;* Konstantin Türnpu: *Valvur (guard);* Urmas Sisask: *Ave Maria; O Salutaris Hostia; Stabat Mater Dolorosa; Dona Nobis Pacem;* Kuldar Sink: *Kyrie Eleison; Agnus Dei;* Mart Siimer: *Homme (tomorrow);* Anti Marguste: *See on Eesti (This is Estonia);* Veljo Tormis: *Inkerin illat (Ingrian Evenings)*
v   Max Reger: *Fantasie und Fuge über B-A-C-H Op.46*
vi Algirdas Martinaitis: *Visions of Semaitija;* SergeiTaneyev: *Nocturne;* Nicolai Rimsky-Korsakov: *Ne veter, veya s vysoty;* Bernard Andrès: *Le temps Chemine;* Charles Villiers Stanford: *The blue bird;* Jimmy van Heusen: *Here's that rainy day;* Alessandro Scarlatti: *Exultate Deo;* MauriceDuruflé: *Notre Père;* Javier Busto: *Ave Maria;* Jurijus Kalcas: *Salve Regina;* Trond Kverno: *Ave maris stella;* Gabriel Fauré: *Cantique.*

AZ CD 01027 CD

(2) **Cantico delle creature**. Canticorum Jubilo (1, 3-8)
(3) **An Old Time Love Incantation**. *Starodávné čarování milému*.
(4) **Desire of Ancient Things**. *Dech dávno zašlých dnů*.
(5) **Ubi caritas et amor**.
(6) **Love and Death**. *Láska a smrt*.
(7) **Cantica Comeniana**.
(8) **Trouvère Mass**. *Truvérská mše*. The Prague Madrigalists (1-3); Czech Philharmonic Choir (6); Canticorum Jubilo (4, 5, 7); Vocal and instrumental ensemble (8); Miroslav Venhoda (1-3; Oliver Dohnányi (4, 5, 7) Josef Veselka (6) Jaroslav Krček (8) (conductors).
Programme as Azymuth AZ 1027

Bakx, Elly
97-07-171 CD 1997 **Six Love Songs**. *Šestero piesní milostných*. No. 1, *Noci milá;* No. 2, *Du bist mîn;* No. 3, *Unter den Linden;* No. 4, *Non mi mandar messagi;* No. 5, *Summer is come*. Elly Bakx (soprano); Corrine Kaczmarek (piano). "Summer is Come". [i]

Balance Music
BAL 94121 CD 1995 **Landscapes of Patmos**. *Krajiny patmoské*. Ruth Spitzenberger (organ); Reinhard Toriser (percussion). "Orgel und Schlagwerk". [ii]

Balkanton
BXA 11728 LP **The Greek Dictionary**. *Řecký slovník*. Chamber Capella Polyfonia; Ivelin Dimitrov (choirmaster).

B&M Music
0063-2 CD 1996 **Winnie The Pooh**. *Medvídek Pú*. Marek Eben (Narrator and Singer). "Medvídek Pú"
0096-2 CD 1997 **The House at Pooh Corner**. *Zátiší Medvíka Pú*. Marek Eben (Narrator and Singer). "Zátiší Medvídka Pú"

Bass Line Records
BassLine 1 CD 1998 **Die Frage nach dem Geist**. Regensburger Domspatzen; Roland Büchner (conductor). "Pueri Cantores". [iii]

---

i Produced as part of a training project. The songs were recorded for use in a film and the CD is at present available for sale privately.
ii Harald Genzmer: *Concerto for Organ and Percussion;* Johann Sebastian Bach: *Concerto after Vivaldi in a minor for organ BWV 593; Violin Concerto in a minor BWV 1041 for marimbaphone and organ;* Matthias Schmitt: *Rêve Curieux*.
iii Heinrich Schütz: *Jauchzet dem Herrn alle Welt; Die Himmel erzählen die Ehre Gottes; SWV 368;* Hans Leo Hassler: *Cantate Domine;* Knut Nystedt: *Peace I leave with you;* Michael Praetorius: *Audite silete;* Max Reger: *Pange Lingua op. 61b, Nr. 2; Die Nacht ist kommen; Er ist's;* György Deak-Bardos: *Eli, Eli;* Heino Schubert: *Psalmenkantate II;* Thomas Gabriel: *Ave Maria;* Felix Mendelssohn: *Herr, nun lässest du deinen Diener;* Ein

Bayer Records

BR 150 009	CD	1994	**Biblical Dances.** *Biblické tance.* No. 4, *The Wedding at Cana.* "Die Orgel tanzt". Rainer Selle (organ). [i]
BR 150 016	CD	1994	**Faust.** No. 5, *Students' Songs.* Nicol Matt (Organ). "C-dur et Walpurgisnacht". [ii]

B. Hulsroj (Denmark)

220199   CD   1999

(1) **Sunday Music.** *Nedělní hudba.* No. 3. *Moto ostinato.*
(2) **Laudes.** No. 2, *Lento*
(3) **Small Chorale Partita.** *Malá chorální partita.*
(4) **Faust.** No. 4, *Gretchen.*
(5) **Mutationes.** No.1, *Impetuoso.* No. 2, *Allegretto.*
(6) **Job.** *Hiob.* 4th Movement.
(7) **Hommage à Dietrich Buxtehude.**
(8) **Momenti di organo.** No.6, *Adagio.*
(9) **Biblical Dances.** *Biblické tance.* No. 4, *The Wedding at Cana.* Niels H. Jessen (organ).

BIS

BIS CD 488	CD	1991	**Two Invocations for Trombone and Organ.** *Dvě invokace pro trombón a varhany.* Gunnar Idenstam. Christian Lindberg (trombone). "The Sacred Trombone". [iii]
BIS CD 565	CD	1992	**Windows after Marc Chagall.** *Okna podle Marca Chagalla.* Anthony Plog (Trumpet), Hans-Ola Ericsson (Organ). "20th Century Music for Trumpet and Organ". [iv]

Tag sagt es dem anderen; Lerchengesang; Heinz Martin Lonquich: *Ave Maria;* Otmar Faulstich: *Ehre sei Gott in der Höhe;* Gerthold Hummel: *Atme in mir, Heiliger Geist;* Gottfried August Homilius: *Domine ad adjuvandum me;* Anon: *Aver verum corpus;* Ruggiero Giovanelli: *Jesu summe benignitas;* Berthold Hummel: *Dankhymnus;* Orlando di Lasso: *Domine labia mea;* Joseph Rheinberger: *Abendlied;* Giovanni Gabrieli: *Jubilate Deo;* Kurt Hessenberg: *Als Jesus von seiner Mutter ging;* Frank Leenen: *Te Deum;* Edvard Grieg: *Mein Jesus macht mich frei;* Thomas Morley: *Fire,fire;* Hans Lang: *Muß i denn zum Städele naus;* Javier Busto: *Salve Regina;* Grzegorz Gerwazy Gorczycki: *Tota Pulchra es Maria;* Mikolaj Zielenski: *Laetentur caeli;* Anon (Spanish 14c.): *O virgo splendes;* Leland B. Sateren: *III. Sermon aus "The Day of Pentecost".* 2 CD set (Eben work on CD 1)

i   Camille Saint-Saëns: *Danse Macabre;* Louis Vierne: *Organ Symphony nos.1 – 6;* Jehan Alain: *Litanies for Organ;* Funnell: *Introduction and Allegro;* Peter Planyavsky: *Toccata alla Rumba;* Robert Elmore: *Rhythmic Suite – Rhumba;* Wilscher: *Toccata alla Rhumba;* Maurice Ravel: *Bolero*

ii   Eric Satie: *Choral;* Modest Mussorgsky: *Night on the Bare Mountain;* Eric Satie: *Commedia Dell'arte;* Goethe: *Auerbachs Keller In Leipzig (Faust);* Eric Satie: *Der Tango, Der Klo-Fall, Messe Des Pauvres: Kyrie, Dixit Domine, Priere Des Orgues;* Leoš Janáček: *Glagolitic Mass – Organ Solo;* Eric Satie: *Die Rennen, Blinde Kuh;* Berthold Brecht: *Leben Des Galilei;* Vinko Globokar: *Toucher;* Eric Satie: *Der Flirt;* Camille Saint-Saëns: *Danse Macabre;* Eric Satie: *Choral*

iii   Franz Liszt: *Hosannah from Cantico del sol S677; Cujus animam from Stabat Mater S679;* Gardner Read: *Invocation Op.135; De Profundis Op.71;* Anders Hillborg: *U-Tangia-Na;* Alfred Schnittke: *Schäll und Häll;* Jan Sandström: *Lacrimae, lacrimae*

iv   Plog: *Four Themes on Paintings of Edvard Münch;* Alan Hovhaness: *Prayer of St. Gregory;* Vincent Persichetti: *The Hollow Men;* André Jolivet: *Arioso barocco;* Lowry: *Suburban Measures.*

BMG Ariola
74321 18148 2   CD   **Four Choruses on Latin Texts.** *Čtyři sbory na latinské texty.* De Angelis. Prague Children's Chorus; Čestmír Stašek (conductor).

Bohemia Music
BM 0025-2   CD   **Trouvère Mass.** *Truvérská mše.* Radost Praha; Vladislav Souček, Zdena Součková (Choirmasters); Marek Špelina, A Rypan (recorders); Jan Nedvěd (guitar); Přemysl Vacek (theorbo); J. Dvořák (bass). [i]
BM 0035-4   MC   Programme as Bohemia Music BM 0025-2

Bon Art Music / Fanton
No number   CD   1997   **From Life to Life.** Kvintus. "Životem k životou – From Life to Life". [ii]

Bonner Kammerchor
11163   CD   1996   **Verba sapientiae.** No. 1, *De circuitu aeterno.* Bonner Kammerchor Collegium Cantorum; Peter Henn (conductor). "Bonner Kammerchor Live '96". [iii]

Bonton
71 0057-2   CD   1991   **Song of Ruth.** *Píseň Ruth.* Virginie Walterová (mezzo soprano); **Petr Eben** (organ). [iv]
71 0081-2   CD   1991   (1) **Ten Chorale Preludes.** *Deset chorálnich předeher.* No. 5, *Když se Kristus narodil;* No. 7, *Nastala noc;* No. 10, *Chral pokojně Boha zpěvem.*
(2) **Two Chorale Fantasias.** *Dvě chorální fantazie.* No. 2, *Chorální fantazie na Svatý Václave.* Věra Heřmanová (organ). "Czech Organ Music of the 20th Century". [i]

---

[i] Benjamin Britten: *A Ceremony of Carols;* Léo Delibes: *Messe Brève*
[ii] Niel van der Watt: *Pula;* arr. Johann va der Sandt: *Bhombela;* arr. H. Villa Lobos: *Estrela e luanova;* arr. Uve Urban: *Linstead Market;* arr. Oskar Merikanto: *Tuulan tei;* Anthony Tammer: *Što mi je milo;* arr. Milan Uherek: *Chodila Maryška;* arr.Jindřich Jindřich: *Hančička;* Václav Felix: *Hu vokýnka;* arr. Oldřich Halma: *Mikulecká dědina;* arr. Robert Loyd: *Good Morning, Mr.Zip;* arr. Frank Churchill: *Heigh-ho;* Kahn Gus: *Toot, Toot, Tootsie Good Bye;* arr. Kirby Shaw: *Java Jive;* arr. Robert Sund: *Goodnight, sweetheart;* arr. Jeff Guillen: *Goin' To Set An' Rest Awhile;* z Taize: *Bless The Lord My Soul;* arr. William Stickles: *Give Me That Old Time Religion;* arr. Ralf Groesler: *Go, tell it to the;* arr. William Stickles: *Amen;* Randall Thompson: *Alleuia;* David MacIntyre: *Ave Maria;* arr. William Stickles: *Sometimes I Feel Like a Motherless Child;* arr. Jueregn Lissewski; *Didn't it rain;* arr. Mark Hayes: *Walking in the spirit*
[iii] Hugo Wolf: *Sechs geistliche Lieder - Einklang;* Paul Hindemith: *Puisque tout passe; En Hiver;* Felix Mendelsohn: *Die Nachtigall Op.59; Warum toben die Heiden; Richte mich Gott Mein Gott, warum hast du mich verlassen Op.78;* Max Reger: *Ich hab die Nacht geträumet; Der Mond ist aufgegangen;* Hugo Alfvén: *Zum Tanze da geht ein Mädel;* Michael Dücker: *Gitarren spielt auf;* Heinrich Schütz: *Geistliche Chormusik 1648 - Die Himmel erzählen;* Anton Bruckner: *Ave maria; Christus factus est; Virga jesse floruit*
[iv] Antonín Dvořák: *Biblical Songs; Ave Maria; Hymnus ad laudes in festo ss. Trinitatis; Ave maris stella;* Zdeněk Lukáš: *Proverbs.*

Brain Music

BOCD-4506	CD	1995	**The Greek Dictionary.** *Řecký slovník.* No. 1, *Megalofrosyne; Charmone – syntychia.* "48th All Japan Chorus Contest in Takamatsu". Asako Kamiya (piano); Nagara High School Chorus Club, Gifu Prefectural; Tomio Sawajima (director). [ii]
BOCD-4612	CD	1996	**The Greek Dictionary.** *Řecký slovník.* No. 1, *Megalofrosyne;* No. 2, *Kalokagathia;* No. 7, *Amfisbetesis;* No. 8, *Algadon;* No. 9, *Charmone – syntychia.* Yoshiko Ogasawara (piano); Female Chorus Fiore; Junko Matsuda (director). "49th All Japan Chorus Contest in Utsunomiya". [iii]
BOCD-4615	CD	1996	**Verba sapientiae.** No. 3, *De tempore.* Toyonaka Mixed Chorus; Keiichi Suga (conductor). "1996 49th All Japan Chorus Contest". [iv]
BOCD-4712	CD	1998	**Ubi caritas et amor.** Toyonaka Mixed Chorus; Keiichi Suga (conductor). "1997 50th All Japan Chorus Contest in Tokyo". [v]
BOCD-4916	CD	1999	**Ancient Cosmetics.** *Odvěka kosmetica.* No. 4, *De pulchritudine sempiterna.* Mulberry Choir; Taeko Kuwabara (conductor). [vi]
OSBR-15016	CD	1999	**The Greek Dictionary.** *Řecký slovník.* No. 1, *Megalofrosyne; Charmone – syntychia.* Nagara High School Chorus Club, Gifu Prefectural; Tomio Sawajima (director). [vii]

---

i Bedřich Wiedermann: *Toccata and Fugue in f minor;* Klement Slavický: *A Variation Fantasia;* Vladimír Werner: *Sequentiae per organo;* Silvie Bodorová: *Musica per organo;* Jan Jirásek: *Ad unum;* Miloslav Kabeláč: *Fantasia*

ii Jacob Arcadelt: *Tempo verr' ancor;* Lajos Bardos: *Himnusz a Naphoz;* Akira Nishimura: *Ukiyoni; Aru Shouzou;* Benjamin Britten: *Missa brevis – Kyrie, Gloria, Agnus Dei;* Florent Schmitt: *On dist que; Prince et bergere; La mode commode;* Teruaki Suzuki: *Mori e - Chikyuu Saijiki '90;* Béla Bartók: *Bolyongas;* Jozsef Karai: *Ejszaka*

iii Tokuhide Niima: *Tobu;* R. Murray Schafer: *Sun;* Giaches de Wert: *Lasso, quand' io creadea di viver schiolto;* Johannes Sebastian Bach: *Singet dem Herren ein neues Lied;* Takatomi Nobunaga: *Shun-Shu Sanshu;* Akira Miyoshi: *Chiyuu eno Ballade - Watashi ga Utau Wake; Shinmoku no Na;* Giuseppe verdi: *Quattro pezzi sacri - Laudi alla Virgine Maria;* Hendrik Andriessen: *Missa Simplex – Credo; Agnus Dei;* Takashi Fujii: *Kaze ga Fuki, Kaze ga Fuki;* Waldemar Bloch: *Kyrie; Credo; Benedictus*

iv Giaches de Wert: *Lasso, quand' io credea di viver sciolto;* Francis Poulenc: *Sept Chansons – Blanche neige; Tous les droits; Belle at ressemblante; Marie;* Felix Mendelssohn: *Trauergesang;* R. Murray Schafer: *Gamelan; Fire;* Richard Strauss: *Der Abend;* Akira Miyoshi: *Tatakanohibi; Kakode;* Takatomi Nobunaga: *Syunsyusansyu;* Hidea Kobayashi: *Yasashiki Uta Kara – 1. Sawayakanagogatsuni, 2. Mata Rakuyourin de*

v Zoltán Kodály: *Esti dal;* Arne Mellnäs: *Aglepta;* Sebastián de Vivanco: *Sicut lilium inter spinas; Cantate Domino canticum novum;* Carl Orff: *Ave Maria;* Akira Miyoshi: *Sunadokei;* Traditiional Japanese: *Donguri no Koma;* Javier Busto: *Missa brevis "Pro pace" – Kyrie; Gloria;* Akira Miyoshi: *Ahaha; Furusato no Hoshi;* R. Murray Schafer: *Seventeen Haiku – nos. 3, 5, 7, 8, 14, 16*

vi Josquin Desprez: *Ave verum corpus;* Milko Kolarov: *Spring;* Otmar Mácha: *Hojaja, hojaja;* Masahiko Hasebe: *Darumasangakoronda;* Ryan Cayabyab: *Mass - Gloria;* Zoltán Kodály: *Akik midig elkésnek; Norvég lényok;* Francisco Guerrero: *Alma redemptoris mater;* Francis Poulenc: *O Magnum Mysterium; Videntes steliam; Hodie Christus natus est;* Kou Matsushita: *Ki;* Akira Miyoshi: *Koukyoushi Umi Kara 2, 3;* Zdeněk Lukáš: *Ave verum corpus;* Veněček Josef Zajíček: *Baba Yaga*

vii Zoltán Kodály: *Köszöntése; Quattro madrigali – Chi vuol veder;* Lajos Bardos: *Bécr a Rónán; Ave Maria; Ave maris Stella; Himnusz a Naphoz; Vejnemojnab mazsikal;* Béla Bartók: *Leanykerö;* Miklós Kocsár: *Ó havas ardö námaságo;* György Orbán: *Audi Voces; Lauda Sion;* Costanzo Festa: *Madonna la Prendo Ardire;* Jacob Arcadelt: *Tempo Verr' Ancor;* Giammateo Assola: *Deus, canticum novum cantabo;* Makiko Kinoshita: *Natume*

Bravo Pardubice
BP 0001-2   CD   1998   Tabulatura Nova. Petr Saidl (guitar). [i]

BWE Classics (Bonneville Worldwide Entertainment)
BWE 0221   CD   Sunday Music. *Nedělní hudba*. No. 3, *Moto ostinato*. Clay Christiansen (organ). "How Sweet the Sound" [ii]

Cadenza
CAD 800 903   CD   1999   (1) **Job.** *Hiob.* Gerhard Gnann (narrator); Hans-Jürgen Kaiser (organ).
(2) Commentary on the composition, Job, by **Petr Eben**

Calcante Recordings
CD027   CD   (1) **Two Festival Preludes.** Dvě slavnostní preludia.
(2) **Versetti.**
(3) **A Festive Voluntary**: Variations on "Good King Wenceslas".
(4) **Job.** Marie Rubis Bauer (organ) (1-3); Michael Bauer (organ) (4). "Eben, Complete Works for Organ, Vol.1".

Campanula
Campanula 1   CD   1998   (1) **Antiphons and Psalms.** *Antifony a Žalmy*. No. *Veselte se, nebesa*.
(2) **Four Choruses on Latin Texts.** *Čtyři sbory na latinské texty*. No. 3, *De angelis*, No. 4, *Salve Regina*. Campanula Jihlava Mixed Chorus; Pavel Jirák (conductor). "Musica spiritualis". [iii]

Canticum
CANT 011   LP   197?   **An Old-Time Love Incantation.** *Starodávné čarování milému*. Moravští madrigalisté Kroměříz. Jiří Šafařík (conductor). "Europäische a-capella-Chormusik". [iv]

---

na Uta; Nanio Sagashini; Japanese children's and folk song: *Kagome, kagome; Karasu Kanemon Kanzaburō; Kariboshi Kiriuta; Gujōbushi; Obaba*

[i] Astor Piazolla: *Milonga del Angel; Chorao da Saudade;* Agustin Barrios: *Julia Florida;* Roland Dyens: *Tango en Skai;* W. Muthspiel: *Drei Tonspiele;* John Duarte: *Susa Cosa*

[ii] William Mathias: *processional;* Thomas Arne: *Flute Solo;* Johann Sebastian Bach: *Prelude and Fugue in B BWV544;* Max Reger: *Benedictus Op.59;* Alfred Hollins: *A Trumpet Minuet;* Frank Bridge: *Adagio in E;* Charles Callahan: *Aria;* Charles-Marie Widor: *Adagio from Symphony No.6;* arr. George Shearing: *Amazing Grace;* Richard Wagner: *Prelude to "Die Meistersinger"*

[iii] Dietrich Buxtehude: *Prelude and fugue in a sharp minor;* Marian hymn of 1565: *Fit porta Christi pervia;* Hymn of 1600: *Exultet caelum laudibus;* Prachatice kancionál: *Vstoupil jest Kristus na nebe;* Giovanni Croce: *O vos omnes;* Wolfgang Amadeus Mozart: *Ave verum Corpus;* Petr Tchaikovsky: *Svjatyj Bože;* Jan Novák: *Ego dilecto meo;* Camille Saint-Saëns: *Requiem Op. 54 -Hostias et preces;* Benjamin Britten: *A Boy was Born;* Attila Reményi: *Le Christ est monté pres de Dieu;* Zdeněk Lukáš: *Liturgické písně - Rozsvěť v srdcích našich; Pater noster;* František Tůma: *Stabat Mater.*

[iv] Iša Krejčí: *Madrigaly na slova K.H. Máchy;* William Byrd: *This sweet and merry month of May;* Jacquet of Mantua: *O Jesu Christe;* Tomás Luis de Victoria: *Officium Hebdomadae Sanctae; Caligaverunt oculi mei;* Bohuslav Martinů: *Six Czech Madrigals*

Capitol

SP 20039	LP		**Piano Sonata in D♭.** *Sonata in Des pro klavír.* **Petr Eben** (piano).
SP 20307	LP		**Love and Death.** *Láska a smrt.* Žilina Mixed Choir; I. Kállay (choirmaster).
SP 30834	LP		**Sunday Music.** *Nedělní hudba.* No. 1, *Fantasia.* R. Bürgomeister (organ).

Cathedral

CRMS 854	LP		**Sunday Music.** *Nedělní hudba.* No. 4, *Finale.* Jiří Ropek (organ).[i]

CDA

WN 101995	CD	1995	**Liturgical Songs.** *Liturgické zpěvy* (selection). "Venite populi".[ii]

Centaur

CRC 2042	CD	1988	**Sunday Music.** *Nedělní hudba.* Haig Mardirosian (organ). [iii]

Český rozhlas

CR 0053-2	CD	1991	**Brass Quintet, Variations on a Chorale Theme.** *Žesťovy kvintet, Variace na chorál..* Prague Brass Quintet. "Contemporary Czech Music for Wind Instruments". [iv]
CR 0066-2	CD	1998	(1) **In the Grass.** *V trávě.* (2) **The Green Twig is Sprouting.** *Zelená se snítka.* (3) **Curious Songs.** *Zvědavé písničky).* (4) **The Autumn is Already Ripening.** *Už zraje podzim.* (5) **A Day's Experiences.** *Co se za den zažije.* (6) **Spring Ditties.** *Jarní popěvky..* (7) **Carol Singers from the Těšín District.** *Koledníci z Těšínska.* Czech Radio Prague Children's Chorus (1, 2, 3); Bambini di Praga (4); Blanka Kulinská (1, 4), Bohumil Kulinský (1, 2, 4) (directors). Czech Wind Quintet (2); Viktor Kalabis (2) (piano); Pavel Jurkovič (3) (tenor); Prague Children's Chorus (5, 7); Čestmír Stašek (3, 5, 7) (director); **Petr Eben** (3, 5, 7) (piano) Severáček Children's Chorus (6); Milena Uherková, Milan Uherek (6) (directors). "Petr Eben To Children".

---

[i] Jan Křtitel Kuchař: *Fantasy in g minor;* Josef Seger: *Prelude and Fugue in D; Toccata in E;* Bohuslav Černohorský: *Toccata in C; Fugue in A minor;* Bedřich Wiedermann: *Toccata and Fugue in d minor*

[ii] Josef Rheinberger: *Venite populi;* Johannes Brahms: *Two Choral Preludes;* Felix Mendelssohn: *Prelude and Fugue;* Robert Schumann: *Two Canons;* Albert de Klerk: *Missa Duo Seraphim;* Max Reger: *Toccata and Fugue.*

[iii] Jean Langlais: *Suit Brève; Three Characteristic Pieces*

[iv] Alois Piňos: *Serenade for BBB;* Jan Kapr: *Brno Allegro;* Pavel Blatný: *Two Movements for Brass Instruments;* Evžen Zámečník: *High Jinks;* Zdeněk Šesták: *Sonata Sinfonia;* Miloslav Ištvan: *Shakespeare Variations*

Chamade
CHCD 5620   CD   Laudes. No. 4, *Gravimente – Vivace fermo*. Thierry Escaich (organ). "Orgues d'Île de France 1". [i]

Chandos
CHAN 9257   CD   1994   About Swallows and Maidens. *O vlaštovkách a dívkách*. Nos. 1, 2. 3, 7 & 9. Prague Chamber Choir; Josef Pancik (choirmaster); Marián Lapšanský & Daniel Buranovský (pianos). [ii]

Chinese disc, Peking
M 360   LP   Sonata for Oboe and Piano. *Sonáta pro hoboj a klavír*. Vítězslav Hanus (oboe); Hanusová (piano).

Christophorus
SCGLX 73 884   LP   197?   Sunday Music. *Nedělní hudba*. No. 3, *Moto ostinato*. Rudolf Walter (organ). "Bohemian Organ Masters". [iii]

Clarton
CQ 0019-2   CD   1996   (1) **Tune of the Castle Guard.** *Znělka Hradní stráže*.
                                               (2) **March of the Castle Guard.** *Pochod Hradní stráže*. Fanfare Orchestra of the Castle Guard; Jan Šivec (conductor). "Prague Castle Trumpeters". [iv]
CQ 0022-2   CD   1996   The Labyrinth of the World and the Paradise of the Heart. *Labyrint světa a ráj srdce*. Marek Eben (narrator); **Petr Eben** (organ).

Classico
CLASSCD122   CD   1995   Two Invocations for Trombone and Organ. *Dvě invokace pro trombón a varhany*. No.1. *Moderato*. The Civil Servant Duo of 1984: Niels-Ole Bo Johansen (trombone); Ulrik Spang-Hanssen (organ). [v]

---

i   Albert Alain: *Toccata;* Jehan Alain: *Deuils, Variations on a theme of Clement Janequin, Litanies;* Thierry Escaich: *Symphonie Improvisée sur le nom "ALAIN"; 5 Verses on "Victimae Paschali"*

ii   Antonín Dvořák: *Moravian Duets Op.32;* Josef Suk: *Ten Songs for female voice and piano four hands*: Bedřich Smetana: *Three-part choruses for female voices*

iii   Jiří Ignac Linek: *5 Pieces from the Coronation Intradas for Maria Theresia;* Jan Zach: *Prelude & Fugue in c minor;* Jan Křtitel Kuchař: *Fantasia in g minor;* Bohuslav Černohorský: *Fugue in a minor;* Josef Seger: *Pastorella in D; Motet;* Musil: *Sonata solemnis;* Leoš Janáček: *Postlude from the Glagolitic Mass*

iv   Bells of St. Vitus Cathedral; Bedřich Smetana: *Fanfares from Libuše;* Michal Kocáb: *Flag of the President of the Republic;* Karel Bělohoubek: *March of the Castle Guard;* Antonín Dvořák: *Armida – "Christ's Flag";* *Hussite Overture ex.;* Jarmil Burghauser: *Intrada Sancit Adalberti;* Jan Fischer: *Marches I & II;* John Dowland: *Leggiero; Lento;* Johannes Eccard: *Leggiero;* Michael Praetorius: *Moderato;* Mortaro: *Canzon "La Malvezza";* Lande: *Fanfare;* Johann Pezelius: *Intradas I, II & III;* ohann Sebastian Bach: *Sarabande;* Anon: *Fanfares I – IV;* Jarmil Burghauser: *Intrada Resurrectionis; Canonisation of St. Agnes of Bohemia; St. Wenceslas Chorale; Intrada Pentacostes;* Johann Störl: *Sonata no. 5;* Josef Svejkovský: *Fanfare of the Bohemian Estates;* Josef Suk: *Praga, excerpt*

v   Gustav Holst: *Duo Concertante;* Edward Elgar: *Sonata No. 2 (Severn Suite for Brass Band);* Alexandre Guilmant: *Morceau symphonique;* Franz Liszt: *Hosannah from Cantico del sol;* Joseph Guy Ropartz: *Piece*

Connell Digital Masterworks

| CONNELL 1 | CD | 1991 | Sunday Music. *Nedělní hudba*. No. 3. *Moto ostinato*. Stephen M. Distad (organ). "Organ Potpourri". [i] |

Corkfest Records

| 96 | CD | 1996 | Rhythmus de gaudiis Paradisi. Cantique; Blánaid Murphy (director). [ii] |

Crystal Records

| S182 | LP | 1981 | Sunday Music. *Nedělní hudba*. William Osborne (organ). [iii] |

CTS

| 801 207 | LP | | Sunday Music. *Nedělní hudba*. Sieglinde Ahrens (organ). |
| 810 621 | LP | | Sunday Music. *Nedělní hudba*. Sieglinde Ahrens (organ). |

De Plein Vent

| DPV CD 9571 | CD | 1995 | Duetti per due trombe. Guy Touvron, Frank Pulcini (trumpets). "Sonnez trompettes". [iv] |

Delta Records

DRS 86-637	LP	1980???	(1) **Two Chorale Fantasias**. *Dvě chorální fantazie*.
			(2) **Small Chorale Partita**. *Malá chorální partita*.
			(3) **Laudes**. Kathryn Ulviden Moen (organ). "Czech Organ Music". [v]

DKR

| DKR 03 | CD | | Mundus in Periculo. No. 3. *Visio Pacis*. Dómkórinn i Rejkjavik; Marteinn H. Fridriksson (conductor). [i] |

---

    in E flat for Trombone and Organ; Ralph Vaughan Williams: *Toccata "St. David's Day" and "The White Rock" from Two Organ Preludes on Welsh Folksongs;* Giaochino Rossini: *Cujus animam from "Stabat Mater", transcribed.* Franz Liszt

i   George Frederick Händel: *Allegro maestoso from Water music suite;* Charles-Marie Widor: *Andante sostenuto from Symphonie gothique;* Eugene Gigout: *Toccata in B minor;* Samuel Barber arr. William Strickland: *Adagio for strings;* Joseph Mouret: *Rondeau;* Charles-Marie Widor: *Toccata from the Fifth symphony;* Johann Sebastian Bach: *Wake, awake, for night is flying;* John Philip Sousa arr. Thomas Murray: *Stars and stripes;* Johann Packelbel: *Canon in D;* Franz Liszt: *Introduction and fugue on Ad nos, ad salutarem*

ii   Harry Warren: *Chatanooga Choo Choo;* J. Gawlas: *Na Istebnym Zakazali;* Michael McGlynn: *Geantraí;* Hugo Alfvén: *Zum Tanze;* D. Coombes: *Bobby Shaftoe;* Hoagy Carmichael: *Georgia on my Mind;* Lajos Bardos: *Cantémus;* P. Kostiainen: *Jaakobin Pojat;* Veljo Tormis: *Distributing the Dowry Chest;* Ó Laoghaire: *Éirigí Suas;* Wolfgang Mozart: *At the Fair;* Hjálmar Ragnarsson: *Grafskrift;* John Rutter: *It was a Lover and his Lass;* David H. Cox: *Song of the Paving Stones;* György Orbán: *Lauda Sion;* T. Widdicombe: *Little David Play on Yo' Harp;* Tomás de Victoria: *Ave Maria;* Michael Holohan: *No Sanctuary;* Michael Neaum: *Water of Tyne;* D. Hood: *When the Saints*

iii Sigfrid Karg-Elert: *Three Impressions Op.72*

iv Eric Satie: *Carillon;* Johannes Sebastian Bach: *Six Etudes;* Nicolai Rimsky-Korsakov: *Two Duets;* Edgar Cosma: *Duetti per due trombe;* Gilles Herbillon: *Création;* Igor Stravinsky: *Fanfare for a New Theatre;* Michel Corrette: *Sonnez Trompettes.*

v   Miloslav Kabeláč: *Fantasia;* Jan Hanuš: *Contemplazioni. Lugubre in memorium 16.1.1969; Suita lirica – Vivace assai;* Luboš Sluka: *Via del silenzio;* Miloš Sokola: *Passacaglia quasi toccata na téma BACH;* Jan Zach: *Fugue in a minor;* Jan Křtitel Vaňhal: *Fugue in B;*

Dordt College, Iowa
E-552   LP   1979   Sunday Music. *Nedělní hudba*. No. 3. *Moto ostinato*. Joan Ringerwolle (organ). "Dordt College Dedicatory Organ Recital". [ii]

Dreamlife Corporation
DMCD 1-4   CD   1996   Mare Nigrum. Nos. 1 & 2, *Danza, Canto*. Luise Walker (guitar). "Essence". [iii]

DSV
DSV-001   CD   Four Choruses on Latin Texts. *Čtyři sbory na latinské texty.* De Angelis.

ECM New Series
837 1539   CD   1993   Prague Te Deum. *Pražské Te Deum*. Prague Chamber Chorus; Josef Pančík (conductor); Marta Beňačková (soprano); Walter Coppola (tenor); Josef Kšica (organ); Dagmar Masková (soprano); Peter Mikuláš (bass). [iv]

Edit
41 0055-2   CD   Sunday Music. *Nedělní hudba*. No. 1, *Fantasia*. Kamila Klugarová (organ). [v]

EMI
CDC5 55086-2   CD   1993   Windows after Marc Chagall. *Okna podle Marca Chagalla.* John Wallace (trumpet); Simon Wright (organ). "Virtuosi". [vi]

---

i   Jón Porstednsson: *Lofich Gud;* Matthias Jochumsson: *Lofsöngur;* Davidssalmar Vertu Gael; Hallgrimur Pétursson: *Vist Ertu;* David Stefansson: *Márienvers;* Thomas Aquinas: *Adoro te.*
ii Charles-Marie Widor: *Organ Symphony No. 6 – Allegro moderato;* A. van Noordt: *Psalm 116;* Helmut Walcha: *O Mensch, bewein dein Sünde gross;* Johann Pachelbel: *Von Himmel hoch;* Jan Sweelinck: *Fantasia auf die Manier enies Echo;* Franz Liszt: *Prelude and Fugue on the Theme BACH*
iii **CD1.** Václav Matiegka: *Sonata in e minor Op.31/4;* Fernando Sor: *Le Carme, capriccio Op.50;* Carcassi: *Le Songe de Rousseau, Air Varié;* Walker: *Regenerate (Triplets);* Miguel Llobet: *from "16 folksongs Settings";* Bayard: *Yellow Bird;* Maximo Pujol: *Sonatine pour guitare;* **CD2.** Mauro Giuliani: *Concert in A-major for Guitar and Orchestra, Op.30;* Lind: *Study for arpeggio;* Fernando Sor: *Fantasy Op.16 (Theme and variations);* Enrique Granados: *Valses poeticos;* Walker: *Variations on a Catalonian Song;* **CD3.** Salvador Bacarisse: *Romance for Guitar and Orchestra;* Carosa: *Pieces for lute;* Kramskoj: *Study in D-major;* Fernando Sor: *Variation with a theme from "Die Zauberflöte";* *Etude Op.35, No.13&17;* Mauro Giuliani: *Handel Variations;* Francisco Tárrega: *Capriccio Arabe; Jota Arragonesa;* Nicolo Paganini: *Romance from Sonata in A-major for Guitar;* Mario Castelnuovo-Tedesco: *Concerto for Guitar and Orchestra;* **CD4.** Isaac Albéniz: *Granada Serenata;* Llobet: *La Filadora;* Heitor Villa-Lobos: *Prelude No.3;* Fryderyk Chopin: *Nocturne Op.9;* Franz Schubert: *Ave Maria; Moment Musical;* Santorsola: *Concertino for Guitar & Orchestra;* Joaquin Rodrigo: *Concerto de Aranfuez for Guitar and Orchestra*
iv Leoš Janáček: *Our Father;* Antonín Dvořák: *Mass in D*
v   Charles-Marie Widor: *Organ Symphony No.5 in f minor – Toccata;* Max Reger: *Introduction and Passcaglia in d minor;* Paul Hindemith: *Sonatas for Organ – No.3;* Bedřich Wiedermann: *Toccata and Fugue in f minor;* Johann Sebastian Bach: *Six Trio Sonatas BWV525-30 – No.4 in e minor; Leipzig Chorales BWV651-68 – Schmücke dich, o lieb Seele;* Jehan Alain: *Le Jardin Suspendu*
vi Girolamo Fantini: *Sonatas for Trumpet and Basso Continuo – nos.1, 2 & 8;* Giuseppe Tartini: *Trumpet Concerto in D;* Jean Françaix: *Sonatine for Trumpet and Piano in C;* George Enescu: *Legende;* Jean-Baptiste

CD-EMX2290   CD   1993   Programme as EMI CDC5 55086-2

Erzbistum Paderborn
2021379-4360   CD   1999   **Anno Domini – Vorübergang des Herrn.** Oratorio. Jutta Potthof (soprano); Jochen Kupfer (baritone); Domkantorei & Domchor Paderborn; Choralschola der Benediktinerabtei Königsmünster; P. Michael Hermes (director); Wolfgang Kühnhold (speaker); Theodor Holthoff (musical director).

Etcetera
KTC 1115   CD   1991   (1) **Faust.**
(2) **Hommage à Dietrich Buxtehude.** Niels Henrik Jessen (organ).

European Guild of Organists
EGO 007   CD   **Sunday Music.** *Nedělní hudba.* No. 4, *Finale.* Zygmunt Strep (organ). "Orgelmusik aus vier jahrhunderten". [i]

Fermate
Fer 20008   CD   1993   **Windows after Marc Chagall.** *Okna podle Marca Chagalla.* Bernhard Kratzer (Trumpet); Martin Sander (organ). "Trompete und Orgel im 20. Jahrhundert". [ii]

Formánek
No number   CD   **The Green Twig is Sprouting.** *Zelená se snítka.* No. 7, *Jarní slunce.* Children's Mixed Chorus Formánek; Kamil Trávníček (conductor); Martina Reichlová (piano). "Formánek a jeho hosté". [iii]

Gallo
GALLO CD-604 CD   1990   **Windows after Marc Chagall.** *Okna podle Marca Chagalla.* David Tasa (trumpet); Gert Augst (organ). [iv]
GALLO 47-604 MC   1990   Programme as Gallo GALLO CD-604

    Arban: *Fantasy and Variations on Auber's "Actéon";* Alexandr Goedicke: *Concert Etude Op.49;* Carl Höhne: *Slavonic Fantasy*

[i]   Joseph Jongen: *Sonate Eroica, Op.94;* Mikolaj z Krakowa: *7 Danses from the Tablature of Jan Z Lublina;* Johann Sebastian Bach: *Prelude and Fugue in e minor BWV548;* Malling: *Aus dem Leben Christi*

[ii]   Henri Tomasi: *Semaine Sainte à Cuzco;* Jean Langlais: *Seven Chorales;* Hans Schilling: *Canzona on "Christ ist erstanden";* Sigfrid Karg-Elert: *Canzone and Toccata Op.85 no.1;* Fr. Sebastian Wolff: Fantasia and Fugue in D

[iii]   Zdeněk Lukáš: *Sluníčko;* Miroslav Raichl: *Zakukala kukalenka; U souseda dobrá voda;* Věroslav.Neumann: *U nás v kapele;* E. Stašek: *Den jako malovaný;* Valachian folksong: *Tráva neroste;* Silesian folksongs: *Panimamo; Kočka leze dírou;* Folk songs from Těrchov: *Od Mijavy cesta; Z tej mijavskej brány; V Bošáci je pekný dom; Hej, idem, idem; Ide kračum, ide; Ej horou horou / Ouce, moje ouce; Dze śe kuri, tam śe kuri; Dobri večar frajirečka moja*

[iv]   Wladimir Vogel: *Evocation;* Theo Brandmüller: *Wie Du unsern Vätern geschworen hast;* Jacob Gilboa: *Chagall sur le Bible*

Gayle H. Martin
001   CD   1997   **Sunday Music**. *Nedělní hudba*. No.3. *Moto Ostinato*, No.4. *Finale*. Gayle Martin (organ). "Prism". [i]

G.face 24 Bit Recording
PRCG-1001   CD   1995   **Windows after Marc Chagall**. *Okna podle Marca Chagalla*. Eisuke Yamamoto (trumpet); Hideyuki Kobayashi (organ). "The Windows – Trumpet and Organ". [ii]

Gothic Records
G 49067   CD   1994   **Windows after Marc Chagall**. *Okna podle Marca Chagalla*. Keith Benjamin (trumpet); Melody Turnquist (organ). "Clarion – New Music for Trumpet and Organ" [iii]
G 49106   CD   **Biblical Dances**. *Biblické tance*. No. 4. *The Wedding at Cana*. "Evensong from Grace Cathedral for the Feast of the Epiphany". [iv]
G 49110   CD   1999   **Sunday Music**. *Nedělní hudba*. Judith Hancock (organ). [v]

Gutingi
gut 226   CD   2000   **Veils and Tears**. *Závoj a slzy*. Franz Bumann (bass clarinet); MädchenChor Hannover; Gudrun Schröfel (conductor). "Wenn sich die Welt auftut". [vi]

HaasClassicCologne
HCC 2000 001   CD   1998   **The Labyrinth of the World and the Paradise of the Heart**. Botho Kurth (speaker); Petr Eben (organ). "Orgelimprovisationen 1998 11. Internationale Altenberger Orgelakademie 9.-15.8.1998". [vii]

---

i   Alexandre Guilmant: *Premiere Sonata Op.42;* Camille Saint-Saëns: *Prelude no.2;* Marcel Dupré: *Prelude and Fugue no.3;* Eugène Gigout: *Ten Pieces – No.8 Scherzo;* Healey Willan: *Chorale Preludes;* Gerald Bales: *Petit Suite*

ii   Paul Huber: *Variations on the Choral 'macht hoch die Tür';* Wolfgang Stockmeier: *Sonata for Trumpet and Organ;* Tamihiro Ozeki: *Kokyoll for trumpet and organ;* Dalibor Vačkář: *Prayer for a dead Soldier;* Otto Ketting: *Intrada;* Benjamin Britten: *Fanfares for St. Edmundsbury*

iii   Václav Nelhybel: *Metamorphosis;* Robert Starer: *Three Preludes;* Peter Hamlin: *Sonata ben melodico;* William Albright: *Jericho - Battle Music*

iv   Johann Pachelbel: *Wie schon leuhtet der Morgnestern. Introit;* Robert White: *Christe, qui lux es et dies;* Leo Sowerby: *Magnificat, Nunc dimittis in D, I was Glad, Christ upon the Mountain Peak;* Felix Mendelssohn: *Excerpts from "Christus" - When Jesus our Lord, Say where is he, There shall a star.*

v   Marcel Dupré: *15 versets sur les Vêpres de la Vierge Op.18*

vi   Max Reger: *Dank saget dem Vater; Im Himmelreich ein Haus steht; Abendgang im Lenz;* Gustav Holst: *Ave Maria;* Francis Poulenc: *Ave Maria; Ave verum corpus; Litanies à le Vierge Noire;* Cammile Saint-Saëns: *Tantum ergo,* Arvo Pärt: *Zwei beter;* Einojuhani Rautavarra: *When the World Opens Up;* Herwig Rutt: *Ballade des äußeren Lebens*

vii   Hans Haselböck: *Choral and Variations "Der Mond ist aufgegangen";* Loic Mallié: *Prelude and Fugue;* Thomasz-Adam Nowak: *Fantasy in Romantic Style on "Schönster Herr Jesu";* Wolfgang Seifen: *Three Symphonic Dances*

Herald
HAVPCD 238   CD   1999   Sunday Music. *Nedělní hudba*. No. 3. *Moto ostinato*. Roger Sayer (organ). "A Classic Selection". [i]

Hope College, Holland, Michigan
CD 1193-02   CD   1993   Verba sapientiae. No. 1, *De circuitu aeterno*. Hope College Chapel Choir; J. Scott Ferguson (conductor). "Ye Shall Have a Song. European Concert Tour". [ii]

Hungaroton
HCD 31840   CD   1998   Catonis moralia. 1. Preludio. Musica Nostra Choir; Zsuzsánna Mindszenty (conductor). [iii]

Hyperion
CDA 66978   CD   1997   Sunday Music. *Nedělní hudba*. No. 3. *Moto ostinato*. Christopher Herrick (Organ). "Organ Fireworks VIII". [iv]
CDA 67194   CD   1993   Programme as Victoria VCD 19080
CDA 67195   CD   1999   (1) Faust.
(2) Biblical Dances. *Biblické tance*. Halgeir Schiager (organ).
CDA 67196   CD   2000-?   Complete organ music of Petr Eben to be played by Halgeir
– 67199?   Schiager. Projected total of five or six CDs.

ICM, Diessenhofen
MKH 40289   CD   1989   Windows after Marc Chagall. *Okna podle Marca Chagalla*. Nos. 3 & 4. Claude Rippas (trumpet); P. Ambros Koch (organ). "Trompete und Orgel Klosterkirche Fischingen". [v]

---

i   Charles Arnaud Tournemire: *Choral-Improvisations sur le 'Victimae paschali'*; Camille Saint-Saëns: *Fantasia in E flat*; Max Reger: *Benedictus*; Johann Sebastian Bach: *Prelude and Fugue in G, BWV541*; Guy Bovet: *Hamburger Totentanz*; César Franck: *Prelude, Fugue and Variation*; Edward Elgar: *Imperial March*; Flor Peters: *Concert Piece Op.52a*; Alec Briggs: *Toccata-Chorale*; Maurice Duruflé: *Prelude et Fugue sur le nom d'Alain*

ii   Heinrich Schütz: *Sing to the Lord a new Song*; Antonio Lotti: *Crucifixus*; Peter Philips: *O beatum et sacrosanctum Diem*; Henry Loosemore: *Why Art Thou So Heavy O My Soul?*; Henry Purcell: *Benedicite omnia opera*; Maurice Duruflé: *Ubi caritas*; János Vajda: *Alleluja*; Georg Schumann: *Yea Though I Wander*; Johannes Brahms: *O Heiland reiss die Himmel auf*; Jeffrey Rickard: *Gloria*; Randall Thompson: *From The Peaceable Kingdom – vii Have Ye not known & viii Ye shall Have a song*; arr. Robert Fountain: *Deep River*; Undine S. Moore: *Danial, Daniel, Servant of the Lord*; William Dawson: *Ain'-a That Good News*; Paul Manz: *E'en so, Lord Jesus, Quickly Come*; arr. George Thalben-Ball: *Lullay, Lord Jesus*

iii Ferenc Farkas: *Missa secunda*; Alberto Balzanelli: *Crux fidelis*; Augustin Kubizek: *Gloria*; Gyögy Orbán: *In the Dawn; Nightmare; Caeli cives; O Gloriosa; Mundi renovatio*; Miklós Sugár: *Lied*; *Cantate Domino*; *Pater noster*; Miklós Kocsár: *In Memory of Love*; Péter Nógrádi: *The Lord's Angel*; *Bethlehem, Bethlehem*; Miklós Mohay: *Song of Thanksgiving*; József Karai: *Evening Prayer*; *Ave Maria*; Erzsébei Szönyi: *Canticum sponsae*

iv   Lemare: *When Johnny comes marching home*; Edward Elgar: *Imperial March* arr. G. Martin; Paine: *Concert Variations on the Austrian Hymn "God Save the King" Op.3 no.1*; Franz Liszt: *Prelude and Fugue on B-A-C-H, S260 v.1*; Max Reger: *Variations and Fugue on "God Save the King"*; Wolfgang Mozart: *Adagio and Allegro in f minor K594*; Hector Berlioz: *Rákóczi March from "The Damnation of Faust"* arr. Best; Maurice Duruflé: *Prelude and Fugue on the name ALAIN*; Marco Bossi: *Étude Symphonique*; Louis Lefébure-Wely: *Sortie in B flat*.

v   Georg Telemann: *Sonata in D*; Johann Sebastian Bach: *"Wenn wir in höchsten Nöten sein"*, BWV 641; *"Nun komm' der Heiden Heiland"*, BWV 659; Georg Händel: *Sonata in d minor*; Antonio Vivaldi: *Largo*; Paul

IFO Musikproduktion

IFO CD 00 5000	CD	1998	**Pictures of Hope.** (Bilder Der Hoffnung). Chamber Choir of the Johann-Wolfgang-Goethe University, Frankfurt; Christian Ridil (conductor). Petr Eben (organ). "Klangbilder der Hoffnung". [i]
IFO CD 000 45	CD	1999	**Biblical Dances.** *Biblické tance.* Hans-Eberhard Roß (organ). "Die große Goll-Orgel St. Martin Memmingen". [ii]

IFO Organ Document

CD 030	CD	1999	**Campanae Gloriosae.** Josef Still (organ). "Faszination Kathedralraum vol. 10. Orgelmusik aus dem Dom zu Trier". [iii]

Image Records

?	CD		**Faust.** Part 9, *Epilogue.* Thomas Ennenbach (organ). "Thomas Ennenbach spielt an der Orgel der St. Andreaskirche der Lutherstadt Eisleben – Lutherchoralbearbeitungen". [iv]

Integral Classics

INT 221107	CD		**Suita Balladica.** Bertrand Braillard (cello); Pierre Dubousset (Piano). "Musical Fairy Tales for Cello and Piano" [v]

Jade Records

JACD 91015	CD	1993	**Four Choruses on Latin Texts.** *Čtyři sbory na latinské texty.* No. 3, *De angelis,* No. 4, *Salve Regina.* Les Petits Chanteurs de Saint-Marc; Nicolas Porte (conductor). "Salve Regina". [vi]

    Huber: *Variations on the Chorale "Macht hoch die Tür";* Henry Purcell: *Suite in D - Prelude - March – Air; Cebell - Trumpet tune*

[i] Daniel Roth: *Choral varié et Finale improvisé; Improvisation über das Gregorianische Pater noster und den Luther-Choral "Vater unser im Himmelreich";* Jehan Alain: *Trois Mouvements;* Johann Sebastian Bach: *Choralbearbeitung "O Lamm Gottes unschuldig" BWV 656*

[ii] Johann Sebastian Bach: *Nun komm, der heiden heila BWV 659; Toccata and Fugue in d minor BWV 565;* César Franck: *Pastorale Op.19; Trois Pièces – Pièce héroïque;* Gabriel Pierné: *Trois Pièces Op. 29;* Louis Vierne: *2nd Symphony – Allegro.*

[iii] Max Reger: *Fantasia and Fugue; Op.135b;* Robert Schumann: *Andantino from Op.56;* Hermann Schroeder: *Toccata Op.5a;* Marcel Dupré: *Symphonie Passion Op.23.*

[iv] Felix Mendelssohn: *Sonate in A op. 65/3;* Bach: *Nun komm der Derden Heiland BWV659; "Gelobet seist du, Jesu Christ" BWV604; "Mit Fried und Freud ich fahr dahin" BWV616; "Christe, du Lamm Gottes" BWV619; "Christ lag in Todesbanden" BWV625, BWV695; "Komm, Gott, Schöpfer Heiliger Geist" BWV651, BWV370; "Gott der Vater wohn uns bei" BWV748, BWV317; "Nun freut euch liebe Christen gmein" BWV734; "Vater unser im Himmelreich" BWV737, BWV90;* Pepping: *3 Choralbearbeitungen über Vom Himmel hoch;* Dietrich Buxtehude: *Ein Feste Burg;* Johann Sebastian Bach: *Ein feste Burg;* Max Reger: *Ein feste Burg*

[v] Leoš Janáček: *Pohádka;* Bohuslav Martinů: *Sonata No. 1 for Cello and Piano; Variations on a Theme of Rossini*

[vi] Franz Schubert: *Psalm 23 D706;* Pablo Casals: *Nigra sum;* Gabriel Fauré: *Salve Regina Op67 no.1; Ave Verum Op65 no.1; Requiem – Pie Jesu;* Felix Mendelssohn: *Motets Op.39 nos.1 & 3;* Godfrey Ridout: *Ave Maria;* Maurice Duruflé: *Motets on Gregorian Themes Op.10 no.2 – Tota pulchra es;* Falconer: *Salve Regina;* Zoltán Kodály: *Psalm 150;* David Falconer: *Salve Regina;* Georges Bizet: *Agnus Dei*

JACD 57942   CD   1993   **Four Choruses on Latin Texts.** *Čtyři sbory na latinské texty.* No. 3, *De angelis*. Les Petits Chanteurs de Saint-Marc. "Carmina Mystica". [i]

JAV Recordings
JAV 107   CD   **Sunday Music.** *Nedělní hudba.* No. 3, *Moto ostinato*. Timothy Smith (organ). "On a Summer's Evening". [ii]
JAV 109   CD   1998   **Sunday Music.** *Nedělní hudba.* No. 3, *Moto ostinato*. Peter Stoltzfus (organ). "Aeolian-Skinner 1937. Saint Mark's Episcopal Church, Philadelphia". [iii]
JAV 112   CD   1998   **Sunday Music.** *Nedělní hudba.* No. 3, *Moto ostinato*. Timothy Smith (organ). "Comes Summertime - Highlights from Riverside Summer Recitals 1998". [iv]

Kammerchor des Instituts für Musikpädagogik der Universität Leipzig
VKJK 00298   CD   1996/98 **Spiritus mundum adunans.** University of Leipzig Chamber Choir; Frank Peter (organ); Michael Reuter (choirmaster). "Spiritus mundum adunans – Chormusik". [v]

Křik
KK102-2   CD   1994   (1) **Prague Te Deum.** *Pražské Te Deum.*
                     and   (2) **Spiritus mundum adunans.**
                     1996   (3) **Missa cum Populo.** Lemka Turková (2, 3) (soloist); Martin Jakubíček (1); Ivo Bartoš (2, 3) (organ); Dan Dlouhý (1, 3) (percussion); Czech Brass Sextet Brno (3); Vox Juvenalis; Jan Ocetek (leader); Academic Choir Žerotín; Pavel Koňárek (leader); Philharmonic Choir Beseda

---

[i] Franz Schubert: *The Lord is my shepherd D.706;* E. Salas y Castro: *Oigan una nueva – Villancico;* Giovanni Palestrina: *Surge, propera, amica formosa mea – Canticum canticorum;* Giuseppe Verdi: *Quatro pezzi sacri – Laudi Alla Virgine Maria;* Pablo Casals: *Nigra sum;* Giovanni Pergolesi: *Quae moerebat – Stabat mater;* Maurice Duruflé: *Introit et Kyrie – Requiem Op.9;* Wojciech Kilar: *Agnus Dei;* Francis Poulenc: *Ave Verum Corpus;* Georges Bizet: *Agnus dei;* Jean-Baptiste Lully: *Regina coeli – Petit motet;* Felix Mendelssohn: *Veni Domine;* Antonio Soler: *Un angel y el demonio – Villancico;* Marc-Antoine Charpentier: *Te Deum H148.*

[ii] Edward Elgar: *Pomp & Circumstance #1;* Johann Sebastian Bach: *Passacaglia and Fugue;* Larry King: *Resurrection;* Paul Manz: *Aria;* Julius Reubke: *Sonata on the 94th Psalm*

[iii] Dietrich Buxtehude: *Fugue in C— "Jig";* Louis Vierne: *Préambule;* Johann Sebastian Bach: *Kommst du nun BWV 650;* Leo Sowerby: *Passacaglia;* Jehan Alain: *Variations Jannequin;* Charles-Marie Widor: *Variations Symphonie VIII;* Max Reger: *Benedictus;* Johann Sebastian Bach: *Passacaglia in c;* Jean Langlais: *Theme & Variations;* Felix Mendelssohn: *Adagio Sonata I;* Max Reger: *Fugue "Wie schön leuchtet"*

[iv] Joseph Bonnet: *Deuxième Légende;* Louis Vierne: *Impromptu;* King: *Revelations of Saint John the Divine;* Ludwig van Beethoven: *Scherzo;* d'Antalffy-Zsiross: *Sportive Fauns;* Samuel Coleridge-Taylor: *Impromptu No. 3;* Ulysses; Kay: *Suite No. 1;* Charles-Marie Widor: *Symphonie VII;* Edward Elgar: *Pomp and Circumstance #1;* Bach-Vivaldi: *Concerto in A minor;* Charles-Marie Widor: *Andante Sostenuto (Gothic Symphony);* Paul Dukas: *The Sorcerer's Apprentice;* Richard Wagner: *Liebestod;* Amilcare Ponchielli: *Dance of the Hours.* 2 CD set.

[v] Patrick Hadley: *My beloved spake;* Jürgen Golle: *Kleines Liebeslied* und *Die Nachtigall;* Joseph Rheinberger: *Ein Stündlein wohl vor Tag* und *Abendlied;* Orlando di Lasso: *Bonjour, mon coeur;* Max Bruch: *Gebet;* Johannes Brahms: *Ach, arme Welt;* Hugo Distler: *Ein Stündlein wohl vor Tag;* Gabriel Fauré: *Cantique de Jean Racine;* George Shearing (arr.): *Lullaby of Birdland;* Max Reger: *Nachtlied;* César Franck: *Chöre nach Texten von Wilhelm Busch;* Dietrich Erdmann (arr.): *Jome (folksong);* Spirituals: *Deep River* and *Sweet Home*

Brněnská; Stanislav Kummer (leader); Kantiléna Mixed Children's Chorus; Valérie Maťašová (director); Ars Brunensis Chorus; Roman Válek (conductor).

Ljubliana
LD 0384   LP   Catonis moralia. No. 6, *Gigue*. Dositej Obradović; M.Veljković (conductor).

Lunarion
LN 0008-1   LP   1992
(1) **Four Choruses on Latin Texts.** *Čtyři sbory na latinské texty.* No. 4, *Salve Regina*.
(2) **Cantico delle creature.**
(3) **Cantica Comeniana.**
(4) **Verba sapientiae.** No. 3, *De tempore*.
(5) **From Life to Life.**
(6) **Vesperae in festo nativitatis.** Vysokoškolský umělecký soubor univerzity Karlovy (SVUK); Jaroslav Brych (conductor). "Petr Eben Musica Spiritualis".

LN 0008-2   CD   Programme as Lunarion LN 0008-1
LN 0008-4   MC   Programme as Lunarion LN 0008-1

Lyrinx
LYR 031/33   LP   1981
(1) **Sunday Music.** *Nedělní hudba.* No. 3, *Moto ostinato*. No. 4, *Finale*.
(2) **Laudes.**
(3) **Windows after Marc Chagall.** *Okna podle Marca Chagalla.*
(4) **Mutationes.**
(5) **Faust.** Susan Landale (1-5) (organ); **Petr Eben** (4) (organs); Konradin Groth (3) (trumpet).

Martech-Corp. s.r.o.
No number   CD   1998   **About Swallows and Maidens.** Five Songs. *O vlaštovkách a dívkách.* Chamber Choir Ambrosius. [i]

MBC
MBC-9603101   CD   1996   **Missa adventus et quadragesimae.** Kyrie; Sanctus; Benedictus; Agnus Dei. Karl Josef Nüschen (organ); Bel Canto Men's Chorus; Men's Chorus of the Wuppertaler Kurrende; Heinz Rudolf Meier (conductor). "Rejoice in the Lord". [ii]

---

[i] Jan Hanuš: *Introdukce a scherzo;* Jiřína Marešová: *Podobenství o vinném kmeni;* Benjamin Britten: *A Ceremony of Carols*

[ii] Heinrich Schütz: *Jauchzet dem Herren (Psalm 100); Also hat Gott die Welt geliebt*; Hans Leo Haßler: *Laetentur coeli;* Johann Sebastian Bach: *Sei Lob und Preis mit Ehren; Christ lag in Todesbanden; Es war ein wunderlicher Tag; Wir essen und wir leben wohl; Gratias agimus tibi;* Sigfrid Karg-Elert: *Wachet auf ruft uns die Stimme; Vom Himmel hoch; Lobt Gott, ihr Christen allzugleich; Lobe den Herren, den mächtigen König; Nun danket alle Gott;* Johannes Brahms: *O Heiland reiß die Himmel auf;* Giacomo Antonio Perti: *Adoramus*

MCPS - Michael Woodward

MW 934	LP	1983	**Sunday Music.** *Nedělní hudba*. Part 3, *Moto ostinato*. Gillian Weir (organ). "Gillian Weir plays the 1861 William Hill Mulholland Grand Organ in the Ulster Hall, Belfast". [i]

Mediason

MEDD 112	CD	1993	Programme as Jade Records JACD 91015

Melantrich

Z1 0001-1	LP	1969	Programme as AR(i)STON issue of 1969.

Melisma Musik

OPUS 7087-2	CD	1994	**Job.** *Hiob*. Andreas Kempin (organ).
ME 7122-2	CD	1994	(1) **Cantico delle creature.**
			(2) **Spiritus mundum adunans.** Kleine Kantorei des Bach-Chors der Lutherkirche Wiesbaden; Klaus Uwe Ludwig (Conductor); Eva Maria Hodel (Organ). "Gott, unser Schöpfer (Motetten und Chorlieder des 20. Jahrhunders)". [ii]

Melodiya

33CM-04409-10	LP	1973	**Laudes.** Leopoldas Digrys (organ). [iii]
33D-030347-48	LP		**Sunday Music.** *Nedělní hudba*. B. Vasiliauskus (organ).
C10 30491 002	LP	1990	(1) **Sunday Music.** *Nedělní hudba*.
			(2) **Two Chorale Fantasias.** *Dvě chorální fantazie*. No. 1. Chorale Fantasia on O Great God. *Chorální fantazie na Ó, Bože veliký*. Galina Bulibenko (organ).

Mitra

16 167	LP	1983	**Faust.** Johannes Geffert (organ).
16 205	CD	1988	**Windows after Marc Chagall.** *Okna podle Marca Chagalla*. Rudolf Linder (trumpet); Joachim Krause (organ). [i]

---

te; Antonio Lotti: *Crucifixus;* Heinrich von Herzogenberg: *Siehe um Trost war mir sehr bange;* Felix Mendelssohn: *Hebe deine Augen auf from "Elijah";* Heinrich August Neithardt: *Frohlocket mit Händen*

i Giacomo Meyerbeer: *Le Prophete – Coronation March;* Felix Mendelssohn: *Variations on "Vater unser im Himmelreich";* Frank Bridge; *Adagio in E;* Antonio Valente: *Lo Balo dell'Intorcia;* Girolamo Frescobaldi: *Toccata for the Elevation;* Zipoli: *Offertorio in C;* John Stanley: *Voluntary in g minor;* Johann Sebastian Bach: *Concerto in d minor BWV596;* Olivier Messiaen: *Joie et Clarte des Corps glorieux;* César Franck: *Choral II in b minor;* Henri Mulet: *Rosace;* François Couperin: *Mess pour les Couvents (Dialogue sur la Voix Humaine); Mess pour les Paroisses (Dialogue sur les grands Jeux);* Marcel Dupré: *Cortège et Litanie. Allegro deciso.* 2 LP set.

ii Zsolt Gardonyi: *Singet dem Herrn ein neues Lied; Der Herr ist mein Hirte; Gott, unser Schöpfer; Erd und Himmel sollen singen;* Ernst Pepping: *Ich bin der Herr; Herr, neige deine Ohren;* Johann Nepomuk David: *Wer Ohren hat zu öhren;* Hugo Distler: *Es ist das Heil uns kommen her Op. 6 No. 2B; Ach, Herr, ich bin nicht wert; Ich wollt, daß ich daheime wär Op. 12 No. 5;* Siegfried Strohbach: *Jesus, der Retter im Seesturm;* Wolfgang Jacobi: *Plange Maria; Tutor dicendi; Lamento mio;* Olivier Messiaen: *O sacrum convivium;* John Rutter: *O Clap Your Hands; The Lord Bless You And Keep You;* Jozef Swider: *Cantus gloriosus*

iii Johann Sebastian Bach: *Fantasia and Fugue in g minor BWV 542/3; Pasacaglia in c minor BWV 582*.

Mixtur
MXT 2005 B LP 1977 **Sunday Music.** *Nedělní hudba.* Susan Landale (organ). [ii]

Motette-Ursina
40151 CD 1990 (1) **Sunday Music.** *Nedělní hudba.* No. 3, Moto ostinato.
(2) Speech by **Petr Eben** (in German).
(3) **Concerto for Organ and Orchestra No 1.** *Koncert pro varhany a orchestr č. 1* (Symphonia gregoriana). Andreas Meisner (1), Paul Wißkirchen (3) (organs); Händel-Festspielorchester Halle; Volker Hempfling (conductor).
20241 CD 1996? **Small Chorale Partita.** *Malá chorální partita.* Irene Greulich (Organ). "Eine Abendmusik in der Wenzelskirche zu Naumburg". [iii]

Multisonic
31 0003-1 LP 1990 **Two Festival Preludes.** *Dvě slavnostní preludia.* **Petr Eben** (organ)."Holy Father John Paul II at Prague". [iv]
31 0003-2 CD 1990 Programme as Multisonic 31 0003-1
31 0065-2 CD 1990 **Suita balladica.** Bohuslav Pavlas (cello); Hana Dvořáková (piano).[v]
31 0095-2 CD 1991 **Job.** *Hiob.* David Titterington (organ); H. Lee (narrator)
31 0097-2 CD 1984 (1) **Laudes.**
(2) **Two Chorale Fantasias.** *Dvě chorální fantazie.*
(3) **Landscapes of Patmos.** *Krajiny patmoské.* Sieglinde Ahrens (organ); Martin Lenniger (percussion).
31 0098-2 CD 1984 (1) **Sunday Music.** *Nedělní hudba.*
(2) **Small Chorale Partita.** *Malá chorální partita.*
(3) **Windows after Marc Chagall.** *Okna podle Marca Chagalla.* Sieglinde Ahrens (1-3) (organ); Rudolf Lodenkemper (3) (trumpet).
31 0347-2 CD 1996 **Windows after Marc Chagall.** *Okna podle Marca Chagalla.* Stanko Arnold (trumpet); Irena Chřibková (organ). "Prague

---

i Anon: *Rostocker Suite;* Tommaso Albinoni: *Concerto in D flat;* John Stanley: *Trumpet Voluntaries;* Hagn Holmboe: *Triade.*
ii Jean Langlais: *Trois paraphrases grégoriennes Op.5.*
iii Hendrik Andriessen: *Theme and Variations for Organ;* Kjell-Mork Karlsen: *Chorale Sonata for Trumpet and Organ No. 3 "Nun freut euch, liebe Christen gmein"* (with Tilman Schneider (trumpet); Peter Planyavsky: *Toccata alla Rumba* ; Johann Sebastian Bach: *Prelude and Fugue in G BWV 541;* Georg Telemann: *Sonata for Trumpet and Organ in D;* Francis Thome: *Fantasia for Trumpet and Organ;* Sigfrid Karg-Elert: *Symphonic Chorale op. 87: Nr. 1 "Ach bleib' mit deiner Gnade"*
iv Bells of St. Vitus Cathedral, Prague; High Mass conducted by Pope John-Paul II; Antonín Dvořák: *The Lord is my Shepherd, Songs of Gladness Shall I Sing to Thee (Biblical Songs);* Jan Evangelista Antonín Koželůh: *Missa pastoralis in D*
v Leoš Janáček: *Pohádka;* Bohuslav Martinů: *Sonata no. 3 for Cello and Piano*

St. James's Basilica Its Organs and Composing Organists".[i]

Musica Intima
MI-001 CD 1996/97 **Christmas Songs.** *Vánoční písně.* No. 2, Koleda (arr. Michael Murray). Musica Intima. [ii]

Musica Organum
MO 20.4009 LP 1984 **Sunday Music.** *Nedělní hudba.* No. 3, *Moto ostinato.* J. Schmitz (organ). "Orgelstad Leiden II". [iii]

Musica Sacra International
No number CD 1994 **Verba Sapientiae.** No. 3, *De tempore.* Kölner Kantorei; Brass Ensemble of the Robert Schumann High School, Düsseldorf; Wolker Hempfling (conductor). "Musica Sacra International, 21. - 26. Mai 1994". [iv]

Musik Centrum Pardubice
MC 017 CD 2000 **Two Songs from the Amsterdam Kancional of Jan Amos Komenský.** *Dvě písně a Amsterdamského kancionálu Jana Amose Komenského.* No. 1, *Ó, Bože veliký;* No. 2, *Smiluj se, Bože.* Mixed Children's Choir Řetízek Železný Brod; Dagmar Vajdíková (organ); Josef Hlubuček (choirmaster). [v]

---

[i] Bohuslav Černohorský: *Fugues in D major and c minor;* Jan Zach: *Prelude and Fugue in c minor;* Josef Seger: *Toccata and Fugue in a minor; Pastoral and Fugue on a Czech Christmas Song;* Bedřich Wiedermann: *Toccata and Fugue in f minor;* Jiří Ropek: *Variations on "Victimae Paschali Laudes"*

[ii] Giovanni Palestrina: *Sicut servus;* Pablo Casals: *O vox omnes;* Francis Poulenc: *Un Soire de Neige;* Orlando di Lasso: *Veni sancte Spiritus;* Anton Bruckner: *Ave Maria; Os justi;* Ralph Vaughan Williams: *Three Sjhakespeare Songs;* Claude Vivier: *Jesus erbaume dich;* Veljo Tormis: *Jaarnilaul;* arr. Osamu Shimizu: *Sohran Bushi;* Ramona Luengen: *Frühlingslied;* Einojuhani Rautavaara: *Credo;* John Wilbye: *Draw on, Sweet Night*

[iii] Johann Kaspar Kerll: *Passacaglia in d minor;* Samuel Scheidt: *De Tabulatura Nova – Da Jesus an dem Kreuze stund;* Franz Tunder: *Jesus Christus unser Heiland;* Georg Böhm: *Allein Gott in der Höh sei Ehr;* Johann Sebastian Bach: Sarabande from Suite 5 BWV 816; Ruppé: *Rondo-Allegro from Huit Pieces pour L'Orgue ou Piano-Forte Op.10;* Philippus Pool: *Sonata in C;* Wim van der Reijden: *Kleine Fantasie über Christ ist erstanden;* Antonio Valente: *Lo Ballo dell'Intorcia*

[iv] Anton Bruckner: *Mass no. 2 in e minor – Sanctus & Benedictus;* Kent Njordr: *Gloria;* Heinrich Schütz: *Calicem salutaris accipiam (Cantiones Sacrae);* Felix Mendelssohn: *Mein Gott, warum hast du michveriassen;* Theodolfus, Bishop of Orleans: *Gloria;* Anon.: *Ascendens Christus, ; Jesu, nostra redemptio;* Etienne de Lengsure: *Veni sanctae spiritus;* Henry Purcell: *Hear my Prayer, O Lord;* Hubert Parry: *There is an old belief (Songs of Farewell);* Olivier Messaien: *Dieu parmi nous (La Nativité du seigneur);* Jehan Alain: *Litanies Op.79;* Trad: *Seigneur nous voici;* *Le Seigneur nous a ;* Kembo; Anon: *Vsyhae dichanie;* Dobrá Chrisov: *Liturgy of St. John Chrysostom - Slava a ninje & Truparison des Hl. Kyrill und Method;* Anon: *Svete tichu;*

[v] Jiří Laburda: *Ecce sacerdos magnus; Beata Dei Genitrix; Missa clara;* Středověký chorál: *Jezu Kriste;* Jacob Arcadelt: *Ave Maria;* Johannes Sebastian Bach: *Jesus bleibet meine Freude;* Karel Blažej Kopřiva: *Salve regina;* Stanislav Šebek: *Cantate o blahoslavené Anežce;* Černošská duchovní píseň: *Pane, chci být dobrý křesťan;* Gerald Kensinger: *Prayer for Pentecost;* Tom Booth, arr. Jan Svoboda: *Profession of Faith*

NCRV
NCRV 9090　　CD　1992　　**Hommage à Dietrich Buxtehude.** Eberhard Lauer (organ). "Organs in Hanse Towns. CD 4". [i]

Neerpelt
6851 173　　LP　198?　　**Catonis moralia.** No. 1, *Prelude;* No. 5, *Air.* Severáček; Milan Uherek (conductor). "Europees Muziekfestival voor de Jeugd Neerpelt". [ii]

Newton Choral Society
AFU-3030　　MC　1990　　**Love and Death.** *Láska a smrt.* Brno Madrigalists; Josef Pančík (conductor). Newton Choral Society; David Carrier (conductor). "Two Psalms and a Proverb". [iii]

Nibiru
NIBIRU 0139-2　CD　1999
(1) **Risonanza.**
(2) **Songs to Lute.** *Písně k loutně.*
(3) **Duettini.**
(4) **Six Love Songs.** *Šestero piesní milostných.*
(5) **Ordo modalis.**
(6) **The Greek Dictionary.** *Řecký slovník.* Kateřina Englichová (harp) (1-6); Jana Tetorová (mezzosoprano) (2, 4); Jaroslav Šaroun (piano) (4); Jana Machat (flute) (3); Radek Hrabě (oboe) (5); Chamber Choir of Czech Radio (6); Štefan Britvík (conductor) (6).

North Arizona University Chorale
NACM 09　　CD　1993　　**An Old-Time Love Incantation.** *Starodávné čarování milému.* Melissa Rose (soprano); Northern Arizona University Chorale; Dr. Jo-Michael Scheibe (conductor). "Songs of Innocence". [iv]

---

[i] Heinrich Scheidemann: *Toccata in G;* Carl Phillipp Emanuel Bach: *Sonata for Organ no. 3.;* Hendrik Andriessen: *Chorale for Organ no. 1* Frank Martin: *Mass – Agnus Dei;* arr. Johann van Dommele: *Variations on Psalm 86;* Anthon van der Horst: *Suite in modo conjuncto – dialogo;* Max Reger: *Sonata no. 2 Op.60 in d minor;* Charles Marie Widor: *Organ Symphony no.6 Op.42 – 2nd movement;* Sigfrid Karg-Elert: *Impression Op.72 – Harmonies du soir*

[ii] Willem Kersters: *Intrada; Tristis est anima mea;* H. Posen: *Das Huhn und der Karpfer;* Etienne Daniel: *Le retour du roi;* Dmitri Bortnianski: *Gloria;* Kostinainen: *Jaakobin pojat;* Hugo Distler: *Ein neu Gebot;* Lajos Bardos: *Elsö nepdalrapszódia;* G. Nuyts: *Toen Hanselijn;* Michael Hennagin: *Walking on the Green Grass;* Y. Nakata: *Lanki ponki;* Philip Koutev: *Diminianka;* Giovanni Palestrina: *Salve Regina;* Vic Nees: *Sine Musica nulla disciplina;* Felix Mendelssohn: *Hebe deine Augen auf*

[iii] Ned Rorem: *Two Psalms and a Proverb;* Martin Amlin: *Time's a Caravan;* Jacob Handl-Gallus: *Ecce quomodo moritur; Musica noster amor;* Olivier Messiaen: *O Sacrum convivium;* Jan Novák: *Exercitia mythologica – selection;* Petr Řezníček: *Tráva;* Anton Bruckner: *Ave Maria; Locus iste;* Oldřich Halma: *Mikulecka Dědina;*

[iv] Martin Shaw: *Sing we merrily unto God our strength;* Stephen Chatman: *There is sweet music - There is sweet music here; Song of the laughing green woods; Music, when soft voices die; Piping down the valleys wild;* René Clausen: *Nocturnes - Tears; As if a phantom caress'd me; A clear midnight;* Edwin Fissinger: *By the waters of Babylon;* Eric Whitacre: *Cloudburst;* James McCray: *A child said;* William Grant Still: *Here's one;* Sam Pottle: *Jabberwocky;* arr. Phillip Wilby: *North country folk songs - II, Marianne ; III, Byker Hill;* arr. K. Lee Scott: *Sometimes I feel like a moanin' dove;* René Clausen: *Set me as a seal.*

Opus
91 2409-2   CD   1992   **Trouvère Mass.** *Truvérská mše.* Mario Fančovič (baritone); Igor Pasek (tenor); Martina Lesná, Juraj Korec (recorders); Julia Csibová (organ); Juraj Struhárik (guitar); Bratislava Boys' Choir; Magdaléna Rovnáková (conductor). [i]

Opus 3
CD 9102   CD   1991   (1) **Laudes.**
                            (2) **Desire of Ancient Things.** *Dech dávno zašlých dnů.*
                            (3) **Cantico delle creature.**
                            (4) **Windows after Marc Chagall.** *Okna podle Marca Chagall.*
                            (5) **Song of Ruth.** *Píseň Ruth.* Helena Ek (soprano); Johannes Landgren (organ); Paul Spjuth (trumpet); Rilkeensemblen; Gunnar Eriksson (conductor).
CD 9301   CD   1992   (1) **Bitter Earth.** *Hořká hlína*
                     1994   (2) **Two Invocations for Trombone and Organ.** *Dvě invokace pro trombon a varhany*
                     1994   (3) **Two Festive Preludes.** *Dvě slavnostní preludia*
                     1994   (4) **Landscapes of Patmos.** *Krajiny patmoské.* Johannes Landgren, Magnus Kjellson (organs); Musica Vocalis; Lars-Göran Carlsson (trombone); Patrik Wirefeldt (recitation); Per Karlsson (percussion)
CD 9302   CD   1994   (1) **Tres iubilationes.**
                            (2) **Four Choruses on Latin Texts.** *Čtyři sbory na latinské texty.* No. 4, *Salve Regina*
                            (3) **Ubi caritas et amor.**
                            (4) **Biblical Dances.** *Biblické tance*
                            (5) **Prague Te Deum.** *Pražské Te Deum.* Paul Spjuth, Börie Westerland (trumpets); Lars-Göran Carlsson, Peter McKinnon (trombones); Johannes Landgren (organ); Varberg Chamber Choir; Musica Vocalis; Roger Carlsson (percussion)

Orfeus
OR 0010-2131   CD   1994   **Prague Te Deum.** *Pražské Te Deum.* Ars Brunensis Chorus; Roman Válek (conductor); Lenka Turková, Zora Jaborníková (sopranos); Dan Dlouhý (percussion); Martin Jakubíček (organ). [ii]

Organum Classics
OGM599035   CD   1999   (1) **Sunday Music.** *Nedělní hudba.* No. 4, *Finale.*

---

[i] Plainsong: *Kyrie; O vere digna hostia;* Jacob Arcadelt: *Ave Maria;* Pierre Certon: *La, la, la;* Paulin Bajan/Tadeáš Salva: *Christmas Pastorale (selection);* Heinrich Schütz: *Sumite psalmum*

[ii] Petr Řezníček: *Haec dies;* Zdeněk Lukáš: *Missa Brevis;* Antonín Tučapský: *Tu ne quaesieris;* Jan Novák: *Exercitia mythologica;* Martin Jakubíček: *Improvisations on a theme from the "Prague Te Deum" by Petr Eben*

(2) **Biblical Dances**. *Biblické tance.* No. 4, *The Wedding at Cana.* Hans-Eberhard Roß (organ). "Mon orgue c'est mon orchestra - Die Goll-Orgel St. Martin Memmingen". [i]

OX Records

OXCD-41	CD	1990	**Sunday Music**. *Nedělní hudba.* No. 3, *Moto ostinato.* David Burchell (organ). "The Organs of Oxford Volume 1". [ii]
OXCASS-41	MC	1990	Programme as Ox Records OXCD-41

Pallas

120	LP		**Sunday Music**. *Nedělní hudba.* M. Sander (organ).

Panton

	EP	1967	**The Piano Goes into the World**. *Piano jde do Světa.* Czech Radio Children's Chorus; Bohumil Kulínský (chorus master). Musicians: **Petr Eben**; A. Sud, Zdeněk Bruderhans, M. Anger, Ivo Kieslich; Singers: Helena Tattermuschová, Libuše Salabová, Karel Berman, Oldřich Lindauer, J. Kepka. [iii]
08 0204	LP		**Autumn is Already Ripening**. *Už zraje podzim.* Kantiléna; Ivan Sedláček (choirmaster).
88 0204	LP		Programme as Panton 08 0204
01 0110	LP		**The Green Twig is Sprouting**. *Zelená se snítka.* No. 6, *Vrbová píšťalka;* No. 3, *Veselá sanice.* Severáček; Milena Uherková, Milan Uherek (directors). "Severáček – dětský sbor ze severních čech". [iv]
01 0277	LP	1971	**Vox Clamantis**. Czech Philharmonic Orchestra; Václav Neumann (conductor); Miroslav Kejmar, Václav Junek, Stanislav Sejpal (trumpets). "Hospodine, pomiluj ny – 1000 Years of Czech Music". [v]
11 0277	LP	1971	Programme as Panton 01 0277

---

i   Eugene Gigout: *Grand choeur dialogue; Pieces for organ – No. 44, Toccata;* César Franck: *Chorale no. 2 in b minor;* Johann Sebastian Bach: *Allein Gott in der Höh she Her' BWV 662;* Louis Vièrne: *Organ Symphony no. 1 – Finale; Fantasiestücke Op.53 – Clair de Lune;* Charles-Marie Widor: *organ Symphony no. 5 – Toccata*

ii   Edward Elgar: *Sonata in G (Op 28) First Movement;* George Thalben-Ball: *Elegy;* Camille Saint-Saëns: *Fantaisie in E flat;* Nicholas Carleton: *A verse (In Nomine);* Thomas Tomkins: *A Fancy for two to play;* Christopher Gibbons: *(Verse) in A (minor);* John James: *Voluntary in A;* Charles Stanford: *Postlude in D minor (Op 106, No 6);* Johann Sebastian Bach: *Chorale and variations on Sei gegrüsset, Jesu gütig (BWV 768);* Nicolaus Bruhns: *Praeludium in E minor;* Louis-Nicolas Clérambault: *Suite du Premier Ton; Basse et Dessus de Trompette ou de Cornet séparé; Dialogue sur les grands Jeux*

iii   56 page booklet and EP record. Text by Kamil Bednář.

iv   Luca Marenzio: *Jaro;* Jacques Ibert: *Fleurs des champs;* Béla Bartók: *Zaklinání stáda;* Artur Honegger: *Píseň kutilů;* Ilja Hurník: *V šírém poli;* Miroslav Raichl: *Brusič mráz;* Věroslav Neumann: *Přání; Věneček;* Nikolai Rimsky-Korsakov: *Kotík;* Kazimierz Szerocki: *Dobrou noc;* Milan Uherek: *D'bravěnka; Zkouška na koncert;* Lubor Bárta: *Jede kuk;* Josef Boháč: *Hrajeme finále;*

v   Anon (Břevnov Monastery): *Hospodine, pomiluj ny;* Anon (Prague University Library): *Hospodine, pomiluj ny;* Anon (Rosa bohemica treatise 1668): *Hospodine, pomiluj ny;* Anon (18th/19th centuries): *Organ improvisations on Hospodine, pomiluj ny;* Antonín Dvořák: *St. Ludmila;* Leoš Janáček: *Hospodine!;* Josef Bohuslav Foerster: *Saint Wenceslas;* Václav Dobiáš: *Gospodine, pomiluj ny*

01 0300	LP	1971	**Vox Clamantis**. Czech Philharmonic Orchestra; Václav Neumann (conductor); Miroslav Kejmar, Václav Junek, Stanislav Sejpal (trumpets). [i]
11 0300	LP	1971	Programme as Panton 01 0300
11 0358	LP	1973	**About Swallows and Maidens**. Five Songs. *O vlaštovkách a dívkách*. Women's Chorus of the Czech Radio Choir; Milan Malý (conductor). [ii]
11 0410	LP	1973	**Duetti per due trombe**. *Dueta pro dvě trubky*. Václav Junek, Josef Svejkovský (trumpets). "Skladby pro dechové nástroje" [iii]
11 0563	LP	1975	**Pragensia**. No. 2, *How Bells are Made*. Prague Madrigalists; Miroslav Venhoda (conductor). "Zlatá brána" [iv]
11 0567	LP	1975	**The Green Twig is Sprouting**. *Zelená se snítka*. No. 7, *Jarní slunce*. Kühn Children's Chorus; Czech Philharmonic Wind Quintet. "Rozkvetlý den" [v]
11 0672	LP	1977	**Windows after Marc Chagall**. *Okna podle Marca Chagall*. Vladislav Kozderka (trumpet); Milan Šlechta (organ). [vi]
01 0719	LP	1977	(1) **Sonata semplice**. 1st movement. (2) **Sonata semplice**. 3rd movement. Radek Malotín (flute) (1); Jaroslav Šaroun (piano) (1); Nothard Müller (clarinet) (2); Robert Hiller (piano) (2). "Concertino Praha 1977". [vii]
8110 0037	LP	1978/79	**Hours of the Night**. *Noční hodiny.*. Czech Philharmonic Orchestra; Václav Neumann (conductor). [viii]
8110 0044	LP	1978	**Two Chorale Fantasias**. *Dvě chorální fantazie*. Alena Veselá (organ). "Skladby pro varhany" [ix]
8111 0044	LP	1978	Programme as Panton 8110 0044
8111 0174	LP	1980	**Tabulatura Nova**. Martin Mysliveček (guitar). "Martin Mysliveček – umělecký portrét". [x]

---

i Jiří Dvořáček: *Ex post;* Pavel Bořkovec: *Symfonietta no. 2;* Josef Boháč: *Fragment*
ii František Kovaříček: *Posmívánky;* Zdeněk Lukáš: *Tváře lásky;* Ivana Loudová: *Kurošio*
iii Jiří Dvořáček: *Due per duo;* Josef Páleníček: *Malá suita pro klarinet a klavír;* Václav Felix: *Wind Quintet Op.35*
iv Václav Felix: *Májový chór;* Ivo Bláha: *Jarní hry;* Ivan Kurz: *Pětilistek;* Miroslav Klega: *Concerto-Partita fro Violin and Orchestra;* Jiří Strniště: *Dětské hry;* František Chaun: *Serenata rabbiosa for violin and four double basses;* František Kovaříček: *Posmívánky;* Ivo Jirásek: *Partita for wind instruments;* Zdeněk Šesták: *Divertimento for wind quintet;* Luboš Sluka: *Země překrásná;* Václav Trojan: *Zlatá brána*
v Ervín Toman: *Směr Praha;* Václav Dobiáš: *Příchod Rudé armády;* Josef Stanislav: *Se zpěvem a smíchem;* Radim Drejsl: *Rozkvetlý den;* Zdeněk Petr: *Zítra;* Ludvík Podéšť: *Má strana;* Jan Seidel: *Kupředu, zpátky ni krok;* Josef Boháč: *Vlak;* Zdeněk Blažek: *Maminčin ráj a Šalvěj;* František Šauer: *Tři dětské písně;* Jiří Srnka: *Dětský rok – Jaro & Otloukej se, píšťaličko;* Zdeněk Marat: *Ztratila Lucinka bačkorku;* Jiří Malásek: *Kolik je, táto;* Václav Felix: *Dny radosti*
vi Ivan Kurz: *Piano Sonata*
vii Jan Křtitel Vaňhal: *Oboe Concerto in F;* Leopold Antonín Koželůh: *Clarinet Concerto in E flat;* Richard Strauss: *Horn Concerto;* Viktor Kalabis: *Bagpipe Suite for Oboe and Piano;* Paul Hindemith: *Sonata for Clarinet and Piano;* Jakub Jan Ryba: *Horn Concerto in E flat;* Jan Hanuš: *Impromptus for Trumpet and Piano*
viii Miroslav Klega: *Mime Show;* Jaroslav Křička: *Northern Nights*
ix Leoš Janáček: *Two Pieces for Organ; Choral Fantasia; Varyto for Organ;* Arnošt Parsch: *Sonata for organ*
x Heitor Villa-Lobos: *Concert Studies Nos.1 & 2;* Leo Brouwer: *Elogio de la Danza;* Joaquin Turina: *Sonata for Guitar;* Petr Fiala: *Epigrams*

8110 0295	LP	1982	**Faust..** Parts 4, 5, 7 & 8. Kamila Klugarová (organ). [i]
8112 0306	LP	1982	**War, A Misfortune.** *Nešťastna vojna.* No.2, *Tatíčku můj starý.* Prague Teachers' Choir; Antonín Šídlo (choirmaster). "Prague Teachers' Choir". [ii]
8110 0391	LP	1983	**Concerto for Organ and Orchestra No 2.** *Koncert pro varhany a orchestr č. 2.* Czech Philharmonic Orchestra; Kamila Klugarová (organ); Libor Pešek (conductor). [iii]
8111 0416	LP		(1) **The Greek Dictionary.** *Řecký slovník.* Nos. 2, 8 & 9. (2) **Spring Ditties.** *Jarní popěvky.* Selection. Martina Pilařová (soprano) (1); Hana Kružiková (alto) (1); Magdalena Spitzerová (harp) (1); Severáček Children's Chorus (1, 2); Instrumental ensemble (2); Milan Uherek (director)(1, 2). [iv]
8112 0426	LP		**An Old Time Love Incantation.** *Starodávné čarování milému.* Alena Sovadinová, Jitka Forstová (soloists); Jitka Koželuhová (soprano); Virginie Walterová (mezzo-soprano); Canticorum jubilo; Oliver Dohnányi (conductor). [v]
81 0037	LP	1978/79	Programme as Panton 8110 0037
81 0044	LP		Programme as Panton 8111 0044
81 0174	LP	1980	Programme as Panton 8111 0174
81 0312-7	LP		**The Greek Dictionary.** *Řecký slovník.* Selection.
81 0391	LP	1983	Programme as Panton 8110 0391
81 0740-1	LP	1988	**Curses and Blessings.** *Kletby a dobrořečení.* Kühn Mixed Chorus; Pavel Kühn (conductor). [vi]
81 0755-1	LP	1987	**Love and Death.** *Láska a smrt.* Brno Madrigal Singers; Josef Pančík (chorus master). "Brno Madrigal Singers". [vii]
81 0794-1	LP		(1) **Desire of Ancient Things.** *Dech dávno zašlých dnů.* (2) **Four Choruses on Latin Texts.** *Čtyři sbory na latinské texty.* No. 4, *Salve regina.* (3) **Ubi caritas et amor.** Canticorum Jubilo; Oliver Dohnányi (conductor).
81 0801-1	LP	1987	**Missa cum Populo.** Josef Kšica (organ); Czech Philharmonic Chorus; Prague Philharmonic Chorus; Chamber Ensemble; Lubomír Mátl (conductor). "Týden nové tvorby 1987". [viii]

i Vítězslav Novák: *St. Wenceslas Tryptych*
ii Giovanni Palestrina: *O domine Jesu Christe;* Jacobus Handl-Gallus: *Ascendit Deus;* Bedřich Smetana: *Festival Chorus;* Josef Bohuslav Foerster: *Great Wide Native Fields;* Leoš Janáček: *The Twilight Goblin;* Miroslav Barvík: *Peace;* Jan Seidel: *Briar Rose;* Ivana Loudová: *Benedetto sia il giorno;* Bohuslav Martinů: *Brigand Songs III & V;* Folksongs: *Should Black Eyes; I'll Buy Myself Black Horses; Little Onion*
iii Milan Slavický: *Terre des Hommes*
iv Orlando di Lasso: *Madrigal;* Adrian Willaert: *Gioia gentil;* Miroslav Raichl: *Stories about Janek and Anička;* Jan Seidel: *We are as many as doves;* Lukáš Matoušek: *Klárka's Nursery Rhymes;* Klement Slavický: *Spring Merry-go-Round;* Arr. Milena Uherká: *Two Folk Songs;* Nikolaj Rubcov: *Verniki;* Zdeněk Petr: *Holiday Song*
v Georg Händel: *Canticorum jubilo;* Paul Hindemith: *Six Chansons;* Bohuslav Martinů: *Three Legends;* Monteverdi: *Sestina; Sfogova con le stelle; T'amo mia vita*
vi Miroslav Raichl: *Six Madrigals for Mixed Chorus;* Zdeněk Lukáš: *Judica me, Deus;* Jiří Kalach: *Lukumo*
vii Bohuslav Martinů: *Czech Madrigals;* Petr Řezníček: *Tráva (Grass)*
viii Svatopluk Havelka: *Poggii Florentini ad Leonardum Aretinum Epistola de magistri Hieronymi de Praga supplicio*

81 0827-1	LP	1987	(1) **Prague Nocturne for Orchestra**. *Pražské nokturno pro orchestr*. Homage to Wolfgang Amadeus Mozart. (2) **Cantico delle creature.** (3) **Four Choruses on Latin Texts.** *Čtyři sbory na latinské texty*. No.4, Salve regina. (4) **Landscapes of Patmos**. *Krajiny patmoské*. Czech Philharmonic Orchestra (1); Wolfgang Sawallisch (1) (conductor); Kühn Mixed Chorus (2,3); Pavel Kühn (2, 3) (choirmaster); Aleš Bárta (4) (organ); Václav Mazáček (4) (percussion).
81 0850-1	LP	1988	**Piano Trio**. *Klavírní trio*. Jiří Hurník (violin); Jiří Bárta (cello); **Petr Eben** (piano). "Týden nové tvorby 1988". [i]
81 0898-1	LP	1989	**Bitter Earth**. *Hořká hlína*. Vratislav Kříž (baritone); Prague Radio Chorus; Jan Hora (organ); Stanislav Bogunia (conductor). [ii]
81 0924-1	LP	1989	**Job**. *Hiob*. Kamila Klugarová (organ). "Týden nové tvorby 1989".
81 0949-1	LP	1989	**The Opponents**. *Protihráči*. Sofia Trio for Contemporary Music. [iii]
81 1141-2	CD	1971	(1) **Vox clamantis.**
		1984	(2) **Concerto for Organ and Orchestra No 2**. *Koncert pro varhany a orchestr č. 2.*
		1987	(3) **Missa cum populo**. Miroslav Kejmar, Václav Junek, Stanislav Sejpal (1) (trumpets); (Kamila Klugarová (2); Josef Kšica (3) (organs); Radovan Lukavský (1) (recitation); Czech Philharmonic Orchestra (1, 2); Czech Philharmonic Chorus (3); Prague Philharmonic Chorus (3); Chamber Ensemble (3); Václav Neumann (1) (conductor); Libor Pešek (2) (conductor); Lubomír Mátl (3) (conductor).
81 1398-2131	CD	1995	(1) **Sonata semplice** (2) **Old Testament Fresco**. *Starozákonní fresky*. Saul and the Prophetess in Én-Dor. *Saul a věštkyně v Én-Dóru*. Jiří Hurník (1), Antonín Novák (2) (violins); **Petr Eben** (1), Jaroslav Šaroun (2) (pianos). "Three Old Testament Frescoes". [iv]
81 9018-2	CD	1963	**Concerto for Piano and Orchestra**. *Koncert pro klavír a orchestr*. František Rauch (1), Antonín Jemelík (pianos); Czech Philharmonic Orchestra; Karel Ančerl (conductor). (From Supraphon SUAST 58594). [v]

---

i   Jiří Pauer: *Sonata for Violin and Piano;* Pavel Jeřábek: *Trio appassionato*
ii Klement Slavický: *Psalmi*
iii Václav Kučera: *Brughelian Inspirations;* Jiří Teml: *The Rite;* Jiří Dvořáček: *Meditations*
iv Viktor Kalabis: *Violin Sonata Op.58;* Oldřich Korte: *Philosophical Dialogues for violin & piano; Elihu contra Job;* Viktor Kalabis: *Hallelujah (Psalm 150)*
v   Pavel Bořkovec: *Piano Concerto no. 2;* Klement Slavický: *Rhapsodic Variations for Large Orchestra*.

Pehy/Atypus
AY 0011 2   CD   1996   **Mare nigrum.** Vladislav Bláha (guitar). [i]

Priory Records
PR 125   LP   **Missa adventus et quadragesimae.** Wakefield Cathedral Choir; Peter Gould (organ); Jonathan Bielby (choirmaster). [ii]
PRC 232   MC   **Two Chorale Fantasias.** *Dvě chorální fantazie.* No. 2, *Chorální fantazie na* Svatý *Václave.* Graham Barber (organ). "The Armley Schulze Organ. Christmas Music played by Graham Barber". [iii]
PRCD 289   CD   1989   **Mutationes.** John Scott Whiteley (organ). "John Scott Whiteley plays the Marcussen Organ of Haderslev Cathedral, Denmark". [iv]
PRCD 485   CD   1996   **Laudes.** John Scott (organ). "Great European Organs Vol. 40. John Scott plays the Reiger organ of St. Giles' Cathedral, Edinburgh". [v]
PRCD 618   CD   1998   **Hommage à Dietrich Buxtehude.** Peter King (organ). "Great European Organs Vol. 51. Peter King plays the Klais organ of Bath Abbey". [vi]
PRCD 643   CD   **Hommage à Dietrich Buxtehude.** John Scott (organ). "Twentieth Century Organ Masterpieces". [vii]

Pro organo
CD 7023   CD   1994   **Sunday Music.** *Nedělní hudba.* Nos. 3, *Moto ostinato;* No. 4, *Finale.*
                           1994   **Faust.** No. 4. Gretchen. No. 5. *Student Songs.*

---

i   Milan Tesař: *Discourses;* Evžen Zámečník: *Introduzione e due toccate;* Antonín Tučapský: *Sonata for Classical Guitar;* Štěpán Rak: *Elegy;* Miloš Štědroň: *Psalterium;* Jiří Matys: *Tuning;* Leoš Janáček: *Waiting for You*
ii Kenneth Leighton: *Magnificat and Nunc Dimittis "Collegium Magdalanae Oxoniense";* Sequence for All Saints; Sidney Campbell: *Sing we Merrily unto God;* Percy Whitlock: *Glorious in Heaven*
iii Johann Sebastian Bach: *In Dulci Jubilo BWV729;* Flor Peeters: *How Brightly Shines the Morning Star;* Sigfrid Karg-Elert: *Choral Improvisations Op.65 – Aus meinem Herzens Grunde; Vachet auf;* Max Reger: *Weihnachten;* Garth Edmundson: *Toccata-Prelude - Von Himmel hoch;* Johann Sebastian Bach: *Schübler Chorales BWV645-50 – Wachet auf, ruft uns die Stimme;* Percy Whitlock: *Four Extemporizations - Carol;* Francis Jackson: *Scherzetto pastorale Op.20;* Marcel Dupré: *Antiennes pour le temops de Noël - Lumen ad Revelationem;* Jean Langlais: *Poèmes évangéliques Op.2 - La Nativité*
iv Bohuslav Martinů: *Vigilia;* Antonín Dvořák: *Prelude and Fugue in g minor;* Leoš Janáček: *Two Adagios for organ; Postlude (Glagolitic Mass);* Vítězslav Novák: *Prelude on a Moravian Song;* Anton Bruckner: *Prelude and Fugue in c minor;* Ludwig van Beethoven: *Adagio for Mechanical Organ;* Peter Planyavsky: *Perpetuum mobile; Toccata alla Rumba*
v   Gyorgy Ligeti: *Musica ricercata – no.11;* Miloš Sokola: *Passacaille quasi Toccata on B-A-C-H;* Frank Martin: *Passacaille;* Judith Weir: *Ettrick Banks;* Jiří Ropek: *Toccata;* Arvo Pärt: *Pari Intervallo;* Anton Heiller: *Fantasia super "Salve Regina"*
vi Dietrich Buxtehude: *Prelude, Fugue and Chaconne in C BuxWV137; Prelude in g minor;* Georg Böhm: *Vater unser im Himmelreich WK ii 138;* Franz Liszt trans. Schaab: *Orpheus S98;* Jesús Guridi: *Triptico del Buen Pastor;* Johann Sebastian Bach: *Pastorale in F BWV590;* Camille Saint-Saëns: *Fantasy in D flat Op.101*
vii Arvo Pärt: *Trivium;* Hendrie: *Le Tombeau de Marcel Dupré;*. Lionel Rogg: *Two Studies for Organ;*. Kenneth Leighton: *Prelude, Scherzo and Passacaglia op.41;* Naji Hakim: *Variations on Two Themes;* Roth: *Final 'Te Deum';* Bovet: *Ricercare; Toccata Planyavska*

		1994	**Job.** *Hiob.* No. 4.
		1994	**A Festive Voluntary**: Variations on "Good King Wenceslas".
		1994	**Biblical Dances.** *Biblické tance.* Janette Fishell (organ).
			"Dances of Death.....Dances of Life: An Eben Anthology".
CD 7026	CD	1999	**Windows after Marc Chagal.** *Okna podle Marca Chagalla.* No.4. *The Gold Window.* The Miller-Lowry Duo: Michael Miller (trumpet); David Lowry (organ) "Breaking Ground".[i]

Psallite
60041	CD		**Small Chorale Partita.** *Malá chorální partita.* Wolfgang Schwering (Organ). "Meisterwerke neuzeitlicher Orgelbaukunst, Vol. 1 (Fleiter-Orgeln)". [ii]

RCA Victor Red Seal
09026 61186-2	CD	1992	**Windows after Marc Chagal.** *Okna podle Marca Chagalla.* Guy Touvron (trumpet); Edgar Krapp (organ). "Music for Trumpet and Organ". [iii]

Regent Records
REGCD114	CD		**Biblical Dances.** *Biblické tance.* Margaret Phillips (organ). [iv]

René Gailly
CD87 108	CD		**Hommage à Dietrich Buxtehude.** Luc Ponet (organ). "The Organs of the Lemmensinstituut at Leuven". [v]

Revilo
F 670 384	LP		(1) **Windows after Marc Chagall.** *Okna podle Marca Chagall.*

---

i   David German: *Festive Trumpet Tune;* Henry Purcell (arr. David Lowry): *Music from "Timon of Athens";* Johann Sebastian Bach (arr. David Lowry): *Charale Prelude "An Wasserflüssen Babylon";* David Ashley White: *Reflections on a Tune;* Robert J. Powell: *Prelude on "Charleston";* Alan Hovhaness: *Sonata Op.200;* David Conte: *Soliloquy;* Giacomo Puccini (arr. David Lowry): *Salve Regina; Sole a amore; Nessun dorma;* Paul Nicholson: *Wondrous Love;* Henri Tomasi: *Variations Grégoriennes sur un "Salve Regina".*

ii Dietrich Buxtehude*: Preludium BuxWV 139 in D; Vater unser im Himmelreich BuxWV 219; Nun bitten wir den Heiligen Geist BuxWV 209;* Giovanni Bernardo Lucchinetti: *Concerto for 2 Organs in B* (with Christoph Seeger); Max Reger: *Pieces for Organ Op. 59: No. 1 Prelude in c minor; Choralvorspiele op. 67: No. 32 "O Lamm Gottes, unschuldig"; Choralvorspiele op. 67: No. 35 "Seelenbräutigam";* Louis Vierne: *Pieces in Free Style Op. 31: No. 1 Preamble, No. 2 Cortege, No. 4 Epitaph, No. 14 Scherzetto;* Charles-Marie Widor: *Organ Symphony no. 2, No. 5 Adagio, No. 6 Finale;* Wolfgang Schwering: *Improvisation on the hymn "Iam Christe sol justitiae"*

iii Harald Genzmer: *Sonata for Trumpet and Organ in C;* Marius Constant: *Alleluias;* Jean Langlais: *Seven Chorales, Nos. 1, 2, 4 & 7;* André Jolivet: *Arioso Barocco*

iv Johann Sebastian Bach: *Fugue in G BWV577 "Jig Fugue";* Johann Pachelbel: *Ciaconna in f minor;* Anon: *Españoleta;* Juan Cabanilles: *Corrente Italiana;* Jan Sweelinck: *Ballo del granduca Sw3/1;* Anton Heiller: *Tanz-Toccata;* Peter Planyavský: *Toccata alla Rumba;* Gaston Litaize: *Prélude et Danse fuguée*

v   Giovanni Gabrieli: *Canzone Quarta;* Giovanni Pergolesi: *Sonata in F, Sonata in G;* François Couperin*: Pièces de trois sortes de mouvement, Sinfonie, Fantaisie;* Michel Corrette: *Hymn Jesu Redemptor, "Les Amants Enchantés";* van Meert*: Travail fugué in G Major and g minor;* Johann Gottlieb Janitsch: *Sonata a tre for Organ in G;* Georg Vogler: *Jesu Leiden, Pein Und Tod*

Rottenburger Dom
280696   CD

(2) **Laudes**. Rudolf Lodenkemper (1) (trumpet); Sieglinde Ahrens (1, 2) (organ).
(1) **Two Chorale Fantasias**. *Dvě chorální fantazie.*
(2) **Landscapes of Patmos**. *Krajiny patmoské.*
(3) **Small Chorale Partita**. *Malá chorální partita.* Sieglinde Ahrens (1-3) (organ); Martin Lenninger (percussion).
(1) **Liturgical Songs**. *Liturgické zpěvy.* (selection)
(2) **Vesperae in festo nativitatis**. Andreas Weil (organ); Children's Choir; Frank Leenen (conductor). [i]

Schóla z Ostrožské Lhoty
No number   CD   1997-98   *Oči všech se upírají*. Schóla z Ostrožské Lhoty. "Já se těším...". [ii]

Signum
SIG X47-00   CD   1993
(1) **Six Love Songs**. *Šestero piesní milostných.*
(2) **Six Songs on the Poetry of Rainer Maria Rilke**. *Písně na slova R. M. Rilkého.*
(3) **Little Sorrows**. *Mále smutky*
(4) **The Most Secret Songs**. *Písně nejtajnejsí.* Michiko Takanashi (mezzo-soprano); Herbert Kaliga (piano).

SIG X79-00   CD   1994
(1) **Momenti d organo**.
(2) **Liturgical Songs**. *Liturgické zpěvy* (selection)
(3) **De nomine Caeciliae**.
(4) **Biblical Dances**. *Biblické tance*
(5) **Song of Ruth**. *Píseň Ruth.* Michiko Takanashi (2,3,5) (mezzo-soprano); Ludger Lohmann (1-5) (organ). "Petr Eben: Sacred Works for Voice and Organ".

SIG X81-00   CD   1997
(1) **Songs from Těšín Region**. *Písně z Těšínska.*
(2) **Spring Ditties**. *Jarní Popěvky. No. 6. Ukolébavka pro dcerku. No. 4. Ukolébavka pro synka.*
(3) **Nursery Songs**.
(4) **Songs to Lute**. *Písně k loutně.*
(5) **Loveless Songs**. *Písně nelaskavé.* Michiko Takanashi (mezzo-soprano) (1-4); Herbert Kaliga (piano) (1-3); Boris Björn Bagger (guitar) (4); Manfred Schumann (5). "Petr Eben: Lieder".

---

i   Guillaume Dufay: *Conditor alme siderum;* Heinrich Scütz: *Heute Christus geboren;* Arnold von Bruck: *Ave Maria;* Georg Telemann: *Hosanna;* Giam Battista Martini: *Tristis est anima mea;* Hugo Distler: *Jesu, deine Passion.*

ii   Private recording, not on general release. Anon: *Emanuel; Otče náš; Ježíši, ty jsi chléb živý; Miluj Pána Boha svého; Stal jsem v tu dobu; Alta Trinita beata, Cum dekore; Vše řidí Bůh; Vás posílám;* Karel Komárek / Josef Hrdlička: *Přijď, Pane, k nám;* Hana Svobodová: *Tichý Betlém;* Spiritual kvintet: *Z Betlém se ozývá; Já se těším do nebe; Žízeň; Někdo pije líh;* Eliška Smolová: *Červíčku Jákobův;* Vít Petrů / Václav Renč: *Nastal čas;* Bob Fliedr: *Rozžíhá;* Josef Veseli / František Trtílek: *Večeříme, Pane, s tebou;* Antonín Burda / Aantonín Šuránek: *Bože, spas Slovany;* Georg Händel: *Hallelujah*

Simax
PSC 1088   CD   1991   **Windows after Marc Chagall**. *Okna podle Marca Chagalla*. Harry Kvebaek (organ) Kåre Nordstoga (trumpet). [i]

Soli Dei Veritas (BMG France)
74321470182   CD   1997   **Windows after Marc Chagall**. *Okna podle Marca Chagalla*. Viviane Loriaut (organ); Pascal Clarhaut (trumpet). "Lumière, trompette et orgue". [ii]
74321470202   CD   1997   **Windows after Marc Chagall**. *Okna podle Marca Chagalla*. No.1, *The Blue Window, Reuben*. Viviane Loriaut (organ); Pascal Clarhaut (trumpet). "Nouvelles Couleurs de l'orgue". [iii]

St. David's Church, Baltimore
SDS 100   CD   1993   **Sunday Music**. *Nedělní hudba*. No. 3, *Moto ostinato*. Randall Mullin (organ). "St. David's Sings". [iv]
No number   MC   1996?   Programme as St. David's Church SDS 100.

St. Olaf Records
OM230   CD   1996   **Vesperae in festo nativitatis**. No. 2, *Psalm 112;* No. 4, *Ave Maria;* No 5, *Magnificat*. St. Olaf College Chapel Choir; Robert Scholz (conductor); Alison Feldt (soprano); Andrew Peters, John Ferguson (organs). "Let the People Praise Thee". [v]

---

[i] Oskar Lindberg: *Old Tune from Dalecarlia;* Alan Hovhaness: *Sonata for Trumpet and Organ op.20; Prayer of St. Gregory Op62b;* Øistein Sommerfeldt: *Elegy op.27;* Norwegian folk tune: *The beloved Jerusalem's longing*

[ii] Philippe Raynaud: *Lumières;* Daniele Zanettovich: *Monterverdiana, ricercare sopra un'aria dell'Orfeo;* Jean Rivier: *Aria;* Robert Planel: *Largo;* Eric Schmidt: *Rhapsodia Sacra*

[iii] 2-CD set. Gabriel Pierné: *Prélude, Op. 29 no 1;* Wolfgang Amadeus Mozart: *Fantasy in f minor K608;* Jean-Jacques Beauvarlet-Charpentier: *Noëls en tambourin;* Claude-Bénigne Balbastre: *Marche des Marseillois et l'Air Ca ira;* Johann Sebastian Bach: *Concerto in d minor BWV596 after Antonio Vivaldi; Toccata, Adagio & Fugue in C BWV564 - Fugue;;* Louis-Nicolas Clérambault: *Premier Livre d'Orgue - Suite du Premier ton;* Johann Sebastian Bach: *Louis-Claude Daquin: Noël sur les jeux d'anches;* Johannes Brahms: *Choral "Mein Jesu, der du mich";* Louis Vierne: *Finale. Allegro;* Maurice Duruflé: *Prélude, Adagio and Choral variations on the theme "Veni Creator", Op. 4 - Andante religioso;* Marcel Dupré: "Résurrection" - Allegro moderato; Nino Rota: *Circus Waltz; Valse Carillon; Extract from "Casanova" by Federico Fellini – the Duke of Wüttenberg; Extract from the film "The Godfather" – The Baptism;* Antonion Soler: *Fandango;* Domenico Scarlatti: *Sonata K255; Sonata in C;* Padre Davide De Bergamo: *Sinfonia;* Trad: *Requiem;* Jean Rivier: *Aria for Trumpet and Organ;* Robert Planel: *Largo for Trumpet and Organ;* Jehan Alain: *Three Movements for Flute and Organ – Andante;* Christophe Willibald Gluck: *Orpheus in the Underworld – Extract;* Béla Bartók: *For Children – Allegro*

[iv] Maurice Duruflé: *Notre Père;* Anthony Piccolo: *Jesus Christ the Apple Tree;* Herbert Howells: *Salvator Mundi;* Alan Gray: *What are these that glow from afar?;* Ned Rorem: *Sing my Soul;* John Rutter: *For the Beauty of the Earth;* Ralph Vaughan Williams: *Prayer to the Father of Heaven;* Healey Willan: *The Three Kings;* Lee Mitchel: *Nunc dimittis;* Charles Callahan: *Drop, drop, slow tears;* Benjamin Britten: *A Ceremony of Carols;* Louis Vierne: *Symphony no.6 – Finale*.

[v] William Mathias: *Let the People Praise Thee, O God;* René Clausen: *Magnificat;* Joseph Ryelandt: *Missa 6 vocibus – Sanctus, Agnus Dei;* Robert Young: *There is No Rose;* Hugo Distler: *Sing Anew a Song of Joy;* John Rutter: *What Sweeter Music;* Edward Elgar: *The Apostles – Prologue, Part 1*

Styltón
RS0548200   CD   1999/00 **Greek Dictionary**. *Řecký slovník*. Permoník Youth Choir; Willy Postma (harp); Eva Šeinerová (conductor). "Permoník and the Golden Harp". [i]

Suisa
MKH 40289   CD   **Windows after Marc Chagall**. *Okna podle Marca Chagalla*. Nos. 3 & 4. Claude Rippas (trumpet); A. Koch (organ).

Supraphon
4784-M   78   **The Green Twig is Sprouting**. *Zelená se snítka*. No. 1. *Sníh*. Jana Nováková (singer); Czech Radio Children's Chorus; Bohumil Kulínský (conductor). [ii]
4786-M   78   **The Green Twig is Sprouting**. *Zelená se snítka*. No. 2. *Písnička o vrabci;* No. 9. *Padej, dešti (Déšť)*. Jana Nováková (singer); Czech Radio Children's Chorus; Bohumil Kulínský (conductor). [iii]
                 EP   **Differences and Opposites**. *Rozdíly a protiklady*. ? (piano). Given with a book on the musical cultural movement.
04 109   45   **Six Love Songs**. *Šestero písní milostných*. (Selection). Soňa Červená (soprano); Karel Patras (harp); **Petr Eben** (piano). "Pět písní na středověké texty".
04 205/06   LP   **In the Grass**. *V trávě*. Children's Chorus of the Czechoslovak Radio; Rejcha Wind Quintet; Bohumil Kulínský (conductor).
0 42 0107   LP   1967   **Orff's School**. *Orffova škola*. (Adapted from Carl Orff's "Schulwerke" by Petr Eben and Ilja Hurník). Czech Radio Children's Chorus; Instrumental ensemble; Bohumil Kulínský (conductor).
1 42 0107   LP   1967   Programme as Supraphon 0 42 0107
0 41 0119   LP   1968   **Quintetto per Stromenti a fiato**. Rejcha Wind Quintet.
1 41 0119   LP   1968   Programme as Supraphon 0 41 0119
0 11 0429   LP   1967   **Ordo Modalis**. Czech Chamber Duo – Libuše Váchalová (harp); František Hanták (oboe). [iv]
1 11 0429   LP   1967   Programme as Supraphon 0 11 0429
0 28 0443   LP   **Wind Quintet**. *Dechový kvartet*. Members of the Prague Wind Quintet.
0 29 0446   LP   **The World of Children**. *Svět malých*. No. 1, *Dlaždiči*. Jan Vrána (piano).
0 11 0470   LP   1967   **Laudes**. Petr Sovadina (organ). "Musica Nova Bohemica et Slovaca". [v]
1 11 0470   LP   1967   Programme as Supraphon 0 11 0470

---

i   Benjamin Britten" *?;* Christian Sinding: *?;* Edvard Grieg: *?;* Oskar Merikanto: *?;* Henning Sommerro: *?.*
ii   Ilja Hurník: *Světriček — Posvícení v pekle; Kam Běžíš, potůčku*
iii Jiří Srnka: *The Children's Year*
iv   Alois Hába: *Suite for Cymbalom;* Jan Rychlík: *Hommaggi Gravicembalistici;* Zdeněk Pololáník: *Preludi Dodici*
v   Klement Slavický: *Invokaction;* Miloslav Kabeláč: *Preludes for organ;* Miloslav Ištvan: *Musica aspera*

0 19 0558	LP	1968	**Apologia Sokratus.** Libuše Márová (alto); Antonín Švorc (baritone); Czech Radio Children's Chorus; Bohumil Kulínský (chorus master); Czech Radio Chorus; Milan Malý (chorus master); Vít Nejedlý Men's Chorus; Miroslav Košler (chorus master); Prague Symphony Orchestra; Zdeněk Košler (conductor). "Týden nové tvorby Pražských skladatelů 1968". [i]
1 19 0558	LP	1968	Programme as Supraphon 0 19 0558
1 12 0613	LP	1969	**Bilance.** Prague Teachers' Chorus; Jan Kasal (conductor). [ii]
0 18 0630	LP	1968	**Letters to Milena (Kafka).** *Dopisy Mileně.* Radovan Lukavský, Jaroslava Adamová, Martin Růžek (narrators); **Petr Eben** (piano improvisations). "Dopisy Mileně".
0 18 0753	LP		(1) **Ordo Modalis.** (part of the work). Czech Chamber Duo. (2) **Suita Balladica.** (part of the work). František Smetana (cello); Jiří Hubička (piano).
1 18 0753	LP		Programme as Supraphon 0 18 0753
0 12 0880	LP	1968 1970	(1) **Apologia Sokratus.** (2) **Ubi caritas et amor.** Libuše Márová (1) (alto); Antonín Švorc (1) (baritone);Czech Radio Chorus (1 & 2); Milan Malý (1 & 2) (chorus master); Czech Radio Children's Chorus (1); Bohumil Kulínský (1) (chorus master); Vít Nejedly Men's Chorus (1); Miroslav Košler (1) (chorus master); Prague Symphony Orchestra (1); Zdeněk Košler (1) (conductor). "Gramofonový Klub 1970".
1 12 0880	LP	1968	Programme as Supraphon 0 12 0880
1 19 0946	LP	1970	**Brass Quintet, Variations on a Chorale Theme.** *Žesťový kvintet.* Prague Brass Quintet. "Týden nové tvorby Českých skladatelů". [iii]
1 19 1054	LP	1971	**Music (Trio) for Oboe, Bassoon and Piano.** *Hudba (trio) pro hoboj, fagot a klavír.* Jiří Kaniak (oboe); Lumír Vaněk (bassoon); **Petr Eben** (piano). "XV Týden nové tvorby 1971". [iv]
1 19 1192	LP	1972	**The Green Twig is Sprouting.** *Zelená se snítka.* No. 7, *Jarní slunce.* Kühn Children's Chorus; Markéta Kühnová (director); Members of the Czech Philharmonic Orchestra; Martin Turnovský (conductor). "Umění poslouchat hudbu" *"The Art of Listening to Music"*. [v]

[i] Věroslav Neumann: *Invitation to a Cocktail*
[ii] Jan Klusák: *Bez náziru;* Bohuslav Martinů: *Brigands' Songs;* Giovanni Palestrina: *O Domine Jesu Christe;* Lodovico da Viadana: *Ave verum corpus;* Johannes Ockeghem: *Agnus dei;* Jacobus Handl-Gallus: *Ecce quomodo moritur justus;* Hans Leo Hassler: *Cantate Domino;* Grzegorz Gerwazy Gorczycki: *Sepulto Domino;* Carl Orff: *O lux beata Trinitas*
[iii] Jan Hanuš: *Centemplazioni per organo*
[iv] Zdeněk Lukáš: *Variations for Piano and Orchestra;* Václav Kučera: *Argot;* Marek Kopelent: *Zátisí*
[v] An 8-record set with text and speaking by Ilja Hurník. 115 musical examples by some 43 composers.

1 19 1194	LP	1972	**Orff's School.** *Orffova škola*. (Adapted from Carl Orff's "Schulwerke" by Petr Eben and Ilja Hurník). Czech Radio Children's Chorus; Instrumental ensemble; Bohumil Kulínský (conductor). "Umění poslouchat hudbu" *"The Art of Listening to Music"*. [i]
1 19 1397	LP	1973	**Pragensia.** Prague Madrigalists; Miroslav Venhoda (conductor). "Týden soudobé tvorby 1973". [ii]
1 12 1484	LP	1974	**Songs to Lute.** *Písně k loutně*. Roman Cejnar (singer); Jiří Tichota (lute). "Ohlasy dávných dob". [iii]
1 18 1528	LP	1975	**Piano Improvisations.** Dagmar Sedláčková, Radovan Lukavský, Milan Friedl (narrators); Zuzana Riedlbauch-Matulková, Petr Brock (flutes); Milan Zelenka (guitar); Ivo Kieslich (percussion); Kühn Mixed Chorus; et al; Zdeněk Zahradník (conductor); **Petr Eben** (piano). "Tisíc let české poezie". [iv]
1 12 1607	LP	1975	**Pragensia.** Prague Madrigalists; Miroslav Venhoda (conductor).[v]
1 12 2315	LP	1977	**Catonis moralia.** *Katonova mudrosloví*.. Kantiléna; Ivan Sedláček (choirmaster). "Kantiléna". [vi]
1 19 2408	LP	1978	**Greek Dictionary.** *Řecký slovník*. Magdalena Spitzerová (harp); Kühn Women's Chorus; Pavel Kühn (choirmaster). "Týden nové tvorby 1978". [vii]
1 12 2425	LP	1978	"Písně německých romantiků". Jiří Bar (baritone); **Petr Eben** (piano). [viii]
1 29 9844	LP	1973	**Elce, pelce, kotrmelce.** Nos. 1-26, 28-38, 40-49. Severáček Children's Chorus; Milena Uherková (choirmistress); Milan Uherek (conductor); Instrumental ensemble; Pavel Jurkovič (conductor). [ix]
0 29 9889	LP		(1) **Antiphons and Psalms.** *Antifony a Žalmy*.
0 29 9891	LP		(2) **Religious Songs for Folk Singer.** *Duchovní písně pro lidový zpěv*. Men's church choir (1, 2); B. Kejř (1, 2) (conductor); J. Novák (1) (singer);
0 89 9988	EP	1967	(1) **Sunday Music.** *Nedělní hudba*. Part of No. 4, *Finale*.

---

i See footnote to 1 19 1192. Full set: 1 19 1191-98.
ii Jiří Pauer: *Musica da Concerto*
iii Oldřich Korte: *Troubador's Songs;* Luboš Sluka: *Renaissance Songs;* Václav Trojan: *Czech Patorellas*
iv Luboš Sluka and Zdeněk Zahradník: other music to accompany recital of 59 Czech poetic works from a thousand year period.
v Bohuslav Martinů: *Madrigals; Part-Song Book*
vi Pavel Řezníček: *Atoms in the Service of Peace;* Josef Boháč: *Drobné Zpěvy;* Ctirad Kohoutek: *Skalické zvony;* Arnošt Parsch: *Válka s mloky*
vii František Šauer: *Žalm naděje;* Jiří Pauer: *Madrigals;* Evžen Zámečník: *Music for Pablo Casals*
viii Franz Schubert: *Frühlingslauge; Sei mir gegrüsst!; Der Musensohn;* Robert Schumann: *Es treibt mich hin, es treibt mich her; Du bist wie eine Blume; Mit Mythen und Rosen;* Johannes Brahms: *Wir wandelten; Feldeinsamkeit; Meine Liebe ist Grün;* Hugo Wolf: *Mörike-Lieder nos. 12, 17, 9 & 6;* Richard Strauss: *Traum durch die Dämmerung; Zuegnung; Heimliche auffordung*
ix 60 page booklet with LP record. Text by Václav Fišer.

			(2) **Concerto for Piano and Orchestra**. *Koncert pro klavír a orchestr*. 2nd part of 1st movement.
			(3) **Loveless Songs**. *Písně nelaskavé*. No. 6, *Stesk*.
			(4) **An Old Time Love Incantation**. *Starodávné čarování milému*. Prague Madrigalists (4); Miroslav Venhoda (4) (conductor); Milan Šlechta (1) (organ); František Rauch (2) (piano); Czech Philharmonic Orchestra (2); Karel Ančerl (2) (conductor); Věra Soukupová (3) (soprano); Violists of the Czech Philharmonic Orchestra (3).
11 0480-1	LP	1988	**Ordo Modalis**. Selection. Czech Chamber Duo – Libuše Váchalová (harp); František Hanták (oboe). "William Shakespeare - Venus and Adonis". Ilona Svobodová, Milan Friedl (recitation).
11 0564-1	LP	1990	(1) **Hommage à Dietrich Buxtehude**.
			(2) **Laudes**.
			(3) **Sunday Music**. *Nedělní hudba*. Kamila Klugarová (organ)
11 0564-2	CD	1990	Programme as Supraphon 11 0564-1
11 1205-4	MC	1989	**Antiphons and Psalms**. *Antifony a Žalmy*. Cantores Pragensis; Josef Hercl (choirmaster); Amici musicae antiquae; Jaroslav Orel (choirmaster). "Pocta svaté Anežce České". [i]
11 1438-1	LP	1990	(1) **Missa adventus et quadragesimae**.
			(2) **Vesperae in festo nativitatis**.
			(3) **Prague Te Deum**. *Pražské Te Deum*.
			(4) **Two Invocations for Trombone and Organ**. *Dvě invokace pro trombón a varhany*.
			(5) **Song of Ruth**. *Píseň Ruth*. Czech Philharmonic Chorus (1-3); Lubomír Mátl (1 – 3) (chorus master); Prague Trumpeters (3); Josef Svejkovský (3) (director); **Petr Eben** (1), Josef Kšica (2, 5), Jan Kalfus (4) (organs); Dagmar Mašková (2) (soprano); Jaromír Bělor (2) (baritone); Pavla Bušová (5) (mezzo-soprano); Jan Votava (4) (trombone). "Musica Nova Bohemica".
11 1438-2	CD	1990	Programme as Supraphon 11 1438-1
11 1438-4	MC	1990	Programme as Supraphon 11 1438-1
11 2224-2	CD	1995	**Prague Te Deum**. *Pražské Te Deum*. Czech Philharmonic Chorus; Lubomír Mátl (chorus master); Prague Trumpeters; Josef Svejkovský (director). "Welcome to the world of Supraphon". [ii]

---

[i] Ceremony *(Pope John-Paul II)*; Anon: *In hac praecelsa sollemnitate; Sonet vox ecclesidae; Responsorium: Audi filia; Alleluja, quinque prudentes; Hospodine, pomiluj ny; Martir dei Wenceslaus; Svatý Václave; Lux vera lucis radium;* Mass: *Cardinal Archbishop Tomášek;* J. Snížková: *Agnes;* Sermon: *Pope John-Paul II;* Jan Hanuš: *Matka Chudých*

[ii] Antonio Vivaldi: The Four Seasons (1-3); Johann Sebastian Bach: English Suite No. 3 in G minor, BWV 808; Violin Concerto; Bedřich Smetana: String Quartet no. 1 – mvmt. No. 4; Joaquin Rodrigo: Concierto de Aranjuez for Guitar and Orchestra – mvmt. 2; Leoš Janáček: ? Hans Leo Hassler: ? Rudnev: ? Wolfgang Amadeus Mozart: String Quartet ?

10 3019-1	LP	1981	**Windows after Marc Chagall.** *Okna podle Marca Chagalla.* Miroslav Kejmar (trumpet); Milan Šlechta (organ). "Musica Nova Bohemica". [i]
10 3375-1	LP	1983	**Mutationes per organo grande e piccolo.** Věra Heřmanová (organ). [ii]
10 3377-1	LP	1983	**String Quartet.** *Smyčcový kvartet.* Smetana Quartet. [iii]
11 3997-1	LP	1982	**Elce, pelce, kotrmelce.** Selection. Severáček Children's Chorus; Milena Uherková, Milan Uherek (directors). [iv]
1112 2455	LP	1979	(1) **Three Quiet Songs.** *Tři tiché písně.* (2) **Greek Dictionary.** *Řecký slovník.* (3) **Six Songs on the Poetry of Rainer Maria Rilke.** *Písně na slova R. M. Rilkého* (all except No. 1). Jiří Bar (3) (baritone); Women's Chorus of the Czechoslovak Radio Choir (2); Eva Bromová (2) (soprano); Maria Mrázová (2) (alto); Milan Malý (2) (choirmaster); Libuše Váchalová (2) (harp); Václav Žilka (1) (flute); Jana Jonášová (1) (soprano); **Petr Eben** (1, 3) (piano). [v]
1119 2766	LP	1980	**Sonata for Flute and Marimba "Wood and Wind".** *Sonáta pro flétnu a marimbu.* Jan Riedlbauch (flute); Miroslav Kokoška (marimba). "24 Týden nové tvorby 1980". [vi]
1119 2938	LP	1981	**Tabulatura Nova.** Martin Mysliveček (guitar). "Týden nové tvorby 1981". [vii]
1111 3019	LP	1981	**Windows after Marc Chagall.** *Okna podle Marca Chagalla.* Miroslav Kejmar (trumpet); Milan Šlechta (organ). "Musica Nova Bohemica". [viii]
1117 3200	LP	1986?	**Curious Songs.** *Zvědavé písničky.* No. 4, *Barevný svět.* Koťata, Children's Chorus of the Nursery Schools of Chlumec and Ústí nad Labem; Jana Horáková (piano); Eva Koupilová (soprano & conductor). "Děti dětem". [ix]
1111 3375	LP	1983	Programme as Supraphon 10 3375-1.
1111 3377	LP	1983	Programme as Supraphon 10 3377-1.
1119 4623	LP	1986	**Curious Songs.** *Zvědavé písničky.* No. 4, *Barevný svět.* Koťata; Children's Chorus of the Nursery Schools of Chlumec u Chabařovic and Ústí nad Labem; Jana Horáková (piano); Eva

---

i   Václav Trojan: *Divertimento;* Jan Hanuš: *Tower Music*
ii   Jiří Teml: *Tři ritornely;* Milan Slavický: *Monolit;* Ctirad Kohoutek: *Rapsodia eroica*
iii Jiří Pauer: *Three Episodes for String Quartet;* Othmar Mácha: *String Quartet No.2*
iv   61 page book with 4 records.
v   Viktor Kalabis: *Pět romantický písně o lásce*
vi   Jiří Bažant: *Piano Sonata no.4;* Karel Reindeer: *Panels;* Miroslav Hlaváč: *Impulsioni*
vii Pavel Jeřábek: Sonatina; Jiří Válek: *Koncertantní meditace;* Ivan Kurz: *Notokruh*
viii Václav Trojan: *Divertimento;* Jan Hanuš: *Tower Music*
ix   Pavel Kvapil: *Kočka;* Jan Oliva: *Jak se volá na písničku; Oženil se mraveneček; Žížala; Písnička jen tak; Tiše, tiše; Dokolečka, dokola; Ozvěna;* Anon: *Kdes kukačko, kdes kukala; Konvalinka; Jenom ty mně; Zahraj ně hudečku; Měla sem milého sokolíka; Marjánko, Marjánko; Vyjdu si já na vršíček; Spadla ně šablička; Když sem šel ráno cestičku; Štyry koně ve dvoře; Koulelo se koulelo; Na tej lúce zelenej; Voženil se brabeneček; Pod tým naším okénečkem; Holka modrooka; Komáři se ženili;* Petr Sistil: *Noty;* L. Švagera: *Pavouček;* Slavoj Princl: *Majdelena*

			Koupilová (conductor). "Hudba ke společenským událostem. Vítání občánků, promoce". [i]
1119 9749	LP		**Liturgical Songs.** *Liturgické zpěvy.* No. 1, *Introit.* Prague Mixed Chorus; V. Kubový (organ).
DM 5638	LP		**The Green Twig is Sprouting.** *Zelená se snítka.* Kühn Children's Chorus; Markéta Kühnová (director); Members of the Czech Philharmonic Orchestra; Martin Turnovský (conductor). [ii]
DM 5703	LP	1959	**The Green Twig is Sprouting.** *Zelená se snítka.* No. 1, *Sníh;* No. 7, *Jarní slunce;* No. 2, *Písnička o vrabci.* Kühn Children's Chorus; Markéta Kühnová (director); Members of the Czech Philharmonic Orchestra; Martin Turnovský (conductor). "Gramofonovy Klub Školní Řada. Vybrané skladby pro 1. Ročník". [iii]
DM 5715	LP		**Sunday Music.** *Nedělní hudba.* Milan Šlechta (organ).
DM 5911	LP	1963	(1) **In the Grass.** *V trávě.* No. 9 *Klubko;* Children's Chorus of the Czechoslovak Radio; Rejcha Wind Quintet; Bohumil Kulínský (conductor).
			(2) **One Hundred Folk Songs.** *Sto lidových písní. Za hory, za lesy; Kačena divoká.* "Gramofonový Klub. Vybrané skladby pro 1. Ročník". [iv]
DM 5912	LP	1963	(1) **The Green Twig is Sprouting.** *Zelená se snítka.* No. 13, *Písnička pro maminku;* No. 1, *Sníh.*
			(2) **In the Grass.** *V trávě.* No. 7, *Behám, behám;* No. 14, *Vlak;* No. 12, *Když si hrajeme s míčkem.*
			(3) **One Hundred Folk Songs.** *Sto lidových písní. Já nechci žádného; Černé oči jděte spát; Já mám koně; Pásla ovečky.* "Gramofonový Klub. Vybrané skladby pro 2. Ročník". [v]
DM 5913	LP	1963	(1) **The Green Twig is Sprouting.** *Zelená se snítka.* No. 13, *Písnička pro maminku;* No. 9, *Padej dešti, deštíčku.*

---

i Zdněk Fibich: *Poème;* Jan Seidel: *Deťátko;* Jan Oliva: *Tiše, tiše; Dokolečka, dokola;* Suk: *Hra dětí;* Bedřich Smetana: *Má hvězda; Pochod Pražské studentské legie z r. 1948;* Antonín Dvořák: *Bagatelles (1-3); Lento (String Quartet Op.51);* Pavel Vejvanovský: *Ingressus;* M. Menzl z Kolsdorfu: *Univerzitní zdravice;* Václav Dobiáš: *Slib věrnosti ridné zemi;* Anon.: *Gaudeamus igitur*
ii Jiří Srnka: *The Children's year Op.10.*
iii Arr. Karel Hába: *Kočka lezeďitou; Holka modrooka; Pec nám spadla; Tluče bubeníček;* arr. V. Mišurčová and M. Klement: *Chytil táta sojkou;* arr. Václav Trojan: *Okolo Třeboně; Travička zelená;* arr. Otakar Jeremiáš: *Muzikanti co děláte; Tancuj, tancuj;* Karel Bendl: *Ten náš pes; Žežulka;* Vladimír Sommer: *Do školy;* Peter Ilyich Tchaikovsky: *March of the Wooden Soldiers; The Skylark*
iv Karel Hába: *Houpací židle; Lokomotiva; Lenošný Ondřej; Elektrika;* Ilja Hurník: *Svetřícek;* Jaroslav Křička: *Mašimová Op. 49/1 – Kocour;* Dezider Kardoš: *Milý ty mój kamarát; Čo sa stala v nedelu;* Peter Ilyich Tchaikovsky: *Op. 39 – Polka;* J. Verberger: *Byla jedna kočka* R. Kubernát: *Čtvrtek – Kolíbačka*
v Ilja Hurník: *Posvícení v pekle; Co si zpívá dlaždič;* Viktor Kalbis: *Sněhulák;* Folk Song from Těšín: *Pytala sa kočka;* Jaroslav Smolka: *Hajej, spinkej;* Peter Ilyich Tchaikovsky: *Op. 39 – Italian Song;* Jiří Šlitr: *Sluníčko;* E. Strašek: *Májová;* Miloš Smatek: *Baroch – Rozpočítadlo*

DM 6157	EP	1965	(2) **One Hundred Folk Songs.** *Sto lidových písní. Kdes, kukačko, kdes kukala; Okolo Frýdku.* "Gramofonový Klub. Vybrané skladby pro 3. Ročník". [i] **Six Love Songs.** *Šestero písní milostných.* Věra Soukupová (soprano); **Petr Eben** (piano). [ii]
DM 10155	LP		**Spring Ditties.** *Jarní popěvky.* The Pioneer Headquarters Choir; J. Mikeš (choirmaster). "Lullabies for Daughters".
DM 10189	LP		**Roundabouts and Stars.** *Kolotoč a hvězdy.* Severáček Children's Chorus; Milan Uherek (director). "The Musical Tomcat".
DM 15181	LP		**The Dissatisfied Prince.** *Nespokojený králíček.* Children's Choir of Czechoslovak Radio; Václav Voska, Ivanka Fišerová, Jan Bor (readers); Jiří Korn, Antonín Jedlička (singers); Miroslav & Karel Klement (recorders); **Petr Eben** (piano); Bohumil Kulinský (conductor). [iii]
DV 5194	LP		**Arrangements of Folk Songs** (1963/65). *Úpravy lidových písní.*
DV 5195	LP		**Arrangements of Folk Songs** (1963/65). *Úpravy lidových písní.*
DV 5522	LP		**Suita Balladica.** František Smetana (cello); Jiří Hubička (piano). [iv]
DV 5638	LP		Programme as Supraphon DM 5638
DV 5755	LP	1963	**Love and Death.** *Láska a smrt.* Czech Children's Choir; Josef Veselka (choirmaster). [v]
DV 5988	LP	1963	**Concerto for Piano and Orchestra.** *Koncert pro klavír a orchestr.* František Rauch (piano); Czech Philharmonic Orchestra; Karel Ančerl (conductor). [vi]
DV 5995	LP	1963	**An Old Time Love Incantation.** *Starodávné čarování milému.* Prague Madrigal Singers; Miroslav Venhoda (conductor). "Musica Nova Bohemica et Slovenica No.24 – New Czech and Slovak Madrigals". [vii]
DV 6113	LP	1964	**Epitaph.** *Epitaf.* Moravan Academic Choir; Josef Veselka (choirmaster). [viii]
DV 6194	LP	1965	**Loveless Songs.** *Písně nelaskavé.* Věra Soukupová (soprano); Violists of the Czech Philharmonic Orchestra; Martin Turnovský (conductor). "Musica Nova Bohemica". [ix]

---

[i] Vladimír Sommer: *Májová koťata;* Bedřich Nikodem: *Jdeme na výlret;* Josef Suk: *Bagatela "S kytici v ruce";* William Byrd: *La Volta;* R. Kubernát: *Čtvrtek - Kapitán;* Jan F. Fischer: *Atomová pohádka;* Ilja Hurník: *Na piano; Na bubínek Ráda, ráda můj zlatej Honzíčkou;* Czech Folk: *Až já pojedu přes ten les; Měla jsem holoubka;* Slovak Folk: *Dievča, čo robíš; Lúčka zelená;* Karel Reiner: *Pojďte, jiskry*
[ii] Jan Hanuš: *Sonnets*
[iii] Text by Marie Majerová
[iv] Ivan Jirko: *Sonata for Cello and Piano;* Jindřich Feld: *Two Compositions for Cello and Piano*
[v] Ilja Hurník: *Maryka*
[vi] Iša Krejčí: *Symphony No. 2 in Csharp*
[vii] Klement Slavický: *Madrigals on Words from Folk Poetry;* Eugen Suchoň: *Two Lyrical Songs;* Jan Kapr: *Seaman's Dreams;* Bohuslav Martinů: *Part-Song Book;* Pavel Bořkovec: *Madrigals About Time*
[viii] Osvald Chlubna: *Hornická balada;* Václav Kalík: *Navrat do vlasti;* Ilja Hurník: *Sbory o matkách;* Jaromír Podešva: *Symfonietta přírody*
[ix] Jan Novák: *Passer Catulli;* Ilja Hurník: *Shulamite*

DV 10137	LP		**Spring Ditties.** *Jarní popěvky.* Severáček Children's Chorus; Milan Uherek (director). "Little Songs for an Outing".
DV 10208	LP		**Roundabouts and Stars.** *Kolotoč a hvězdy.* Šlapanický Children's Choir; K. Šiktanc (piano); Jaroslav Smýkal, Ivan Sedláček (conductors). "Roundabouts and Stars". [i]
DV 15046	LP		**Chamber Music on Seifert's Collection of Poems "Maminka".** *Komorní hudba k básnické sbírce J. Seiferta Maminka.* Chamber instrumental group; Zdeněk Košler (conductor).
DV 15190	LP	1964	**Verses about Love.** *Sloky lásky.* (most of the work). Jiřina Petrovická, Dagmar Sedláčková, Václav Voska, Josef Chvalina, Bohumil Švarc (recitation); Beno Blachut (tenor); Milada Boublíková (soprano); Men's Chorus of the Czechoslovak Radio Choir; Josef Veselka (conductor). [ii]
FLPM 396	LP		Ludmilla Komancová (mezzo-soprano); Jiří Bar (baritone); František Rauch, **Petr Eben** (piano). [iii]
SP 20307	LP	1963	Programme as Suphraphon DV 5755.
SU 0181-2	CD	1995	**Job.** *Hiob.* Moshe Yegar (narrator); Tomáš Thon (organ)
SU 3011-2	CD	1996	(1) **The Most Secret Songs.** *Písně nejtajnější.* (2) **Songs from Těšín Region.** *Písně z Těšínska.* (3) **Loveless Songs.** *Písně nelaskavé.* (4) **Six Love Songs.** *Šestero piesní milostných.* (5) **Six Songs on the Poetry of Rainer Maria Rilke.** *Písně na slova R. M. Rilkeho.* Ivan Kusnjer (baritone) (1, 2); Dagmar Pecková (mezzo-soprano) (3, 4, 5); **Petr Eben** (piano) (1, 2, 4, 5); Jan Pěruška (viola) (3).
SU 3177-2	CD	1995	**Job.** *Hiob.* Radovan Lukavský (narrator); Tomáš Thon (organ).
SU 3288-2	CD	1996	**De sancto Adalberto.** No. 1, *Adalbertus et nullus alius.* No. 3, *O sanctam et beatissimum virum.* Schola Gregoriana Pragensis; David Eben (director). "Anno Domini 997". [iv]
SU 3373-2	CD	1997	**Suita liturgica.** Schola Gregoriana Pragensis; David Eben (director); **Petr Eben** (organ)."Antica e Moderna". [v]
SU 3384-2	CD	1998	**Curses and Blessings.** *Kletby a dobrořečení.* Kühn Mixed Chorus; Pavel Kühn (conductor). "Curses and Blessings". [vi]
SUA 10073	LP		**Suita Balladica.** František Smetana (cello); Jiří Hubička (piano). [vii]
SUF 20 098	LP		Programme as Supraphon DM 5715
SUF 20 344	LP		Programme as Supraphon FLPM 396

i   Selection of Children's Choruses
ii Text by Štěpán Ščipačov
iii Robert Schumann: *Lieder - selection*
iv Anon. Gregorian: *Aquisgranum (Aachen); Praga (Praha); Vratislavia (Wroclav); Ad missam (Commune martyrum Tempore Paschali)*
v   Gregorian Chant: *Missa in Dedicatione Ecclesiae*
vi Johannes Brahms: *Fest und Gedenksprüche;* Vítězslav Novák: *Twelve Lullabies;* Oliver Messiaen: *Cinq rechants pour 12 voix mixtes;* Bohuslav Martinů: *Dandelion Romance*
vii Ivan Jirko: *Sonata for Cello and Piano;* Jiří Feld: *Two Pieces for Cello and Piano*

SUA 1 ?	LP	1963	Programme as Supraphon DV 5755
SUA 18 506	LP	1963	Programme as Supraphon DV 5995
SUA 18 594	LP	1964	Programme as Supraphon DV 5988
SUAST 58 594	LP	1964	Programme as Supraphon DV 5988
SUA 18 751	LP	1965	Programme as Supraphon DV 6194
SUAST 587 51	LP	1965	Programme as Supraphon DV 6194
SUA 10 892	LP	1968	Programme as Supraphon 0 41 0119
SUAST 50 892	LP	1968	Programme as Supraphon 0 41 0119
SV 8161	LP	1963	Programme as Supraphon DV 5988
SV 8233	LP	1964	Programme as Supraphon DV 6113
SV 8275	LP	1965	Programme as Supraphon DM 6157
SV 8308	LP	1965	Programme as Supraphon DV 6194

Svatopluk

L1 34519226 CD 1999
(1) **Oči všech se upírají k Tobě**
(2) **Dobrý a upřimný jest Pán**
(3) **S touhou**
(4) **Nic ať tě neděsí**
(4) **National Songs for Mixed Chorus**. *Národní písně pro smišený sbor*. No. 2, *Galanečko starodávná*. Mixed Chorus Svatopluk Uherské Hradiště; František Šimek (conductor). "Kořeny". [i]

Teldec

66 22 038-01 LP 1985 **Sunday Music**. *Nedělní hudba*. No. 3, *Moto ostinato*. K.H. Herrmann (organ).

66 23 410-01 LP **Laudes**. Gwyn Hodgson (organ).

Thorofon

CTH 2107 CD 1990 **Greek Dictionary**. *Řecký slovník*. Mädchenchor Hannover; Ellen Wegner (harp); Ludwig Rutt (conductor). [ii]

T.O.G.

No number CD **Windows after Marc Chagall**. *Okna podle Marca Chagalla*. John Aley (trumpet); John Chappell Stowe (organ).

---

[i] Arr. Jiří Laburda: *Hospodine, pomiluj ny; Svatý Gorazde;* Adam Michna: *Nebeští kavalérové;* J.A. Koželůh: *Tristis est anima mea;* Jan Zach: *Salve Regina;* Bedřich Smetana: *Modlitba;* Antonín Dvořák: *Hospodin jest můj pastýř; Slyš, ó Bože modlitbu mou;* Jiří Laburda: *Ave Regina coelorum;* Jan Slimáček: *Jubilate Deo; Modlitba; Adesto Domine; Magnificat;* Dimitrij Bortniansky: *Tebe poem; Cheruvimskaja pěsň;* Anon: *Blagoslav duše moja;* Sergei Rachmaninov: *Bogorodice Děvo;* Peter Tchaikovsky: *Svjatyj Bože;* Leoš Janáček: *Na tych fojtových lukach; Ty ukvaldsy kostelíčku; Láska opravdivá;* Arr. Antonín Tučapský: *Co to máš děvečko; Kole Jarošova; Mám já v Hodslavicách;* Arr. Karel Dýnka: *Teče voda, teče*.

[ii] Benjamin Britten: *A Ceremony of Carols;* Heinrich von Herzogenberg: *Mädchenlieder*

Tonstudio Weikert

TW 993032	CD	1999	**A Collection of Foreign National Songs**. *Úpravy lidových písní cizích národů*. No. 6. *What shall we do with a Drunken Sailor?.* Chor des Borg Spittal; Peter Elwitschger (conductor). "Chor des BORG Spittal". [i]
TW 993102	CD	1999	**A Collection of Foreign National Songs**. *Úpravy lidových písní cizích národů*. No. 6. *What shall we do with a Drunken Sailor?.* Chor des Borg Spittal; Peter Elwitschger (conductor). "4th Kärntner Chorwettbewerb 1999 in Feldkirchen". [ii]

Univerzita Karlova v Praze

No number	CD	1998	**In Honour of Charles IV**. *Pocta Karlu IV*. Men's Chorus of the Kühn Mixed Choir. Pavel Kühn (conductor); Czech Philharmonic Orchestra; Vladimir Ashkenazy (conductor). [iii]

Ultravox

UCD 005	CD	1991	**Missa adventus et quadragesimae**. Prague Men's Chorus; Miroslav Košler (conductor); Karel Hron (organ). "Musica Sacra". [iv]

Ventus

DSV 001	CD	1995	**Four Choruses on Latin Texts**. *Čtyři sbory na latinské texty*. No. 2, *De Angelis*. Ventus Children's Chorus; Jiří Slovík (choirmaster); Hana Heidrová (piano). "Ventus". [i]

---

[i] Gerhard Glawischnig / Günther Mittergradnegger: *Übar dö Stapflan;* Günther Antesberger: *Ehr sei Gott;* Folk songs: *Srdce je zalostno; Du redst allweil vom Scheidn; Då draußn in Wåld; Auf da Schåttseitn; Kommt, ihr Gspielen;* Ottilie von Herbert / Peter Elwitschger: *De Liab is a Traman;* Hans Leo Haßler: *Feinslieb, du hast mich g'fangen;* Joseph von Eichendorff / Felix Mendelsohn-Bartholdy: *Abschied vom Walde;* Cesar Bresgen: *Der Wind;* Negro Spiritual / Peter Elwitschger: *This little light of mine;* Spiritual / Audrey Snyder: *Michael, row the boat ashore;* E. Hawkins / G. Helbling: *O happy day;* Jan Groth, Tore W. Aas: *You are the light;* Zulu Traditional / Markus Detterbeck: *Nginesi ponono;* Xhosa / Zulu Traditional / Markus Detterbeck: *Jikela emaweni hamba;* Ballard MacDonald, Buddy G. De Sylva, George Gershwin, Hawley Ades: *Somebody loves me;* Jacub Jacubs, Jakob & Sammy Cahn, Saul Chaplin, Sholom Secunda, Roger Emerson: *Bei mir bist du schön;* George David Weiss, George Shearing, Carl Strommen: *Lullaby of Birdland*.

[ii] Felix Mendelssohn-Bartholdy: *Mailied;* Johannes Brahms: *Wach auf, meins Herzens Schöne;* John Farmer: *Fair Phillis I saw;* Thomas Morley: *April is in my mistress' face;* Cesar Bresgen: *Der Wind;* I. Marton: *Kosiv kosar sino;* arr. Fritz Dietrich: *Der Jäger längs dem Weiher ging;* Thomas Koschat: *Vorbei;* arr. Anton Anderluh: *Srecno, srecno, ljub'ca moja; Still träufelt milder Tau hernieder;* Danilo Bucar: *Srce je zalostno;* Josef Hopfgartner / Hellmuth Drewes: *Vawaht is lång da Håslstab;* Erasmus Widmann: *Wohlauf, ihr Gäste; Vinum schenk ein;* arr. Helmut Wulz: *Der Streit zwischen Wein und Wasser;* M. Claudius / I. A. P. Schulz: *Der Mond ist aufgegangen;* Joze Leskovar: *Pri farni cerkvici;* arr. Alois Leiler: *Dekle na vrtu;* Thomas Koschat: *I håb dir in die Äuglan gschaut;* Günther Steyrer: *Da Summa lahnt her;* arr. Lorenz Maierhofer: *This little light of mine;* John Dowland: *Come Again;* arr. H. Pommer: *Ich hört ein Sichelin rauschen;* Maria Kendi / Gretl Komposch: *Ziagt a Wettar übarn Kogl;* arr. Erwin Tränkle: *Kein schöner Land*.

[iii] Opening address by Charles University Rector, JUDr. Karel Malý DrSc.; Albert Roussel: *Bacchus and Ariadne* Op.43; Antonín Dvořák: *Symphony No.8*.

[iv] Peter Tchaikovsky: *Trisvjatoje; Blažen muž;* Pavel Tchesnokov: *Spasi Bože; Veličt duša moja Hospoda; S nami Boh;* Sergei Rachmaninov: *Tebe pojem; The Lord's Prayer; Prijdite, poklonomsja; Topář Veličanije; Sergiu i German;* Johann von Gardner: *Blažený;* Dimitrij Bortniansky: *Hospody uslyši; Cheruvimskaja;* Bohuslav Martinů: *The Mount of Three Lights*.

Vergara
14013-SL   LP   1968   **Vesperae in festo nativitatis.** Capella I Escolanía de Montserrat; Father Gregori Estrada (organ); Ireneu Segarra (conductor). "Encuentro internacional de compositores en e Monasterio de Montserrat, Septiembre de 1968". [ii]

Victoria
VCD 19080   CD   1993   (1) **Laudes.**
                                  (2) **Job.** *Hiob*
                                  (3) **Hommage à Dietrich Buxtehude.** Halgeir Schiager (organ).

Vista
VPS 1062   LP   1977   (1) **Sunday Music.** *Nedělní hudba.* No. 3, *Moto ostinato.*
                                  (2) **Ten Chorale Preludes.** *Deset chorálnich předeher. No. 4. Umučni N.P. Jezu Krista.* Jiří Ropek (organ). "Czech Organ Music from All Souls". [iii]

VUS Pardubice
VUS 001-2   CD   1997   **Cantica Comeniana.** No. 6, *Otče náš.* VUS Pardubice. "Souznění". [iv]

VUS UK
VUS UK 1997   CD   1997   **Love and Death.** *Láska a smrt.* Charles University Choir, Prague; Jaroslav Brych (choirmaster). [v]

Wedum Gård Records
WGRCD0497   CD   1997   **Sunday Music.** *Nedělní hudba.* Gro Årsvoll Ryen (organ). [vi]

---

i Jacob Gallus: *Regnum Mundi;* Orlando Lasso; *Madrigal no.IX;* Anon: *Du Mein Einzig Licht;* Johannes Brahms: *Adoramus;* Franz Schubert: *Heilig, Heilig;* Pavel Hanousek: *Sv. Anežka Česká;* Francis Poulenc: *Ave Verum Corpus;* Vladimír Šainskij: *Veselá Fuga;* Spiritual: *Babylon's Falling;* Leonard Bernstein: *I Feel Pretty; Somewhere;* Jaroslav Ježek, Jiří Voskovec, Jan Werich: *Medley of songs;* Dobroslav Lidmila: *Až Budu Mít Na Dešť; Honzíčkovi;* Miroslav Raichl: *Tancuj, Tancuj;* Stefan Klimo: *Travnice;* Zdeněk Lukáš: *Jede Sedlák do Mlejna; Kravarky;* Václav Hálek: *Dolino, Dolino;* Antonin Tučapský: *Dyž Verbujú*
ii Ernst Křenek: *Propi de la missa a la feste de la Nativitat de la Mare de Deú*
iii Bedřich Wiedermann: *Nocturne; Impetuoso;* Leoš Janáček: *Glagolitic Mass – Postlude;* Josef Klička: *Concert Fantasia on the St. Wenceslas Chorale*
iv Robert Ray: *He Never Feiled Me Yet;* Duke Ellington arr. Nancy Wartsch: *Hit Me With A Hot Note;* Bodleaux Bryan arr. Tomáš Havlín: *All I Have To Do Is Dream;* Andrew Lloyd Webber arr. Jiří Kožnar: *Vše psát od prvních řádků;* Otto Ceral arr. Jiří Kožnar: *Čas návratů;* Orlando di Lasso arr. Ward Swingle: *Bon jour, mon coeur;* Marc Shaiman arr. Jiří Kožnar: *Hail Holy Queen;* Johann Sebastian Bach arr. Ward Swingle: *Suite in D – Air;* Antonín Tučapský: *Pod dubem, za dubem;* Zdeněk Lukáš arr. Miroslav Košler: *Missa Brevis – Sanctus; Benedictus;* Kryštof Harant: *Missa quinis vocibus - Sanctus;* Miroslav Raichl: *Chodský den;* Josef Schreiber: *Ó lásko, lásko;* Francis Poulenc: *Exultate Deo;* Charles Gounod: *Ave verum corpus;* Johann Sebastian Bach: *Die Nacht ist kommen;* S. African spiritual: *Thuma Mina*
v Bohuslav Martinů: *Czech Madrigals; Four Madrigals;* Leoš Janáček: *The Wild Duck;* Miroslav Raichl: *Loving Without Seeing;* Vítězslav Novák: *Ballads*
vi Jean Langlais: *Hymne d'Actions de Graces;* Johann Sebastian Bach: *Sei gegrüsset, Jesu gütig BWV768;* J.N. Haff:*Ach Gott, vom Himmel sieh darein; Ein fester Burg ist unser Gott*

Weston Woods
No number   MC   1972   **Leopold the See-Through Crumpicker.** Wiliam Bernal (narrator); Musical performer? [i]

Wheldrake Sound Recordings
WSR 96001   MC   1996   **Sonata Semplice.** Louisa Creed (flute); Ludmila Kwan (piano). "A Recital of Czech Music for Flute & Piano". [ii]

Wuppertale Kurrende
WK0011   CD   1996   Programme as MBC CD MBC-9603101

York Ambisonic
YORKCD108   CD   1996   **Sunday Music.** *Nedělní hudba.* No. 3, *Moto ostinato.* David Flood (organ). "The Canterbury Collection - The Organ of Canterbury Cathedral". [iii]
YORKMC108   MC   1996   Programme as York Ambisonic YORKCD108

2. (b) Recordings of Uncertain Status

Evidence for some recordings of the music of Petr Eben has been found but without definite proof of their existence. Details of some other recordings are either incomplete or indefinite. Proof of their existence or otherwise and supply of missing details would be invaluable.

?
?   CD   1999   **Missa adventus et quadragesimae.** Foerster Female Chamber Choir; Gaudium Jihlava Children's Choir; Jiří Jakeš (conductor). [iv]

Artia
AP 185   LP   **Sunday Music.** *Nedělní hudba.*

---

i   1 sound cassette with a book, by James Flora.
ii   Jan Křtitel Vaňhal: *Sonata in G Major;* Bedřich Smetana: *Four Sketches Op.5;* Bohuslav Martinů: *Sonata no.1 for flute and piano;* František Benda: *Sonata in G Major for flute and piano;* Antonín Dvořák: *Dumka and Furiant for piano; Humoresque*
iii   Louis Vierne: *Pièces de fantasie Suite no. 3 Op.64 6th movement, Carillon de Westminster;* Johann Sebastian Bach: *Schübler Chorales BWV645-50 - Wachet auf, ruft uns die Stimme; Leipzig Chorales BWV651-68 – Schmücke dich, o liebe Seele;* Henry Purcell: *Trumpet Tune and Air in C ZT698;* César Franck: *Pièces héroïques in b minor;* Johann Pachelbel: *Canon and Gigue in D for 3 violins and basso continuo trans. For organ;* Camille Saint Saëns: *Fantasy for Organ in E flat;* Joseph Jongen: *Chant de May Op.53 no.1;* Henri Mulet: *Byzantine Sketches for Organ – no.10, Tu es Petra*
iv   Anon: *Veselými hlasy;* Benjamin Britten: *Hymn to the Virgin Mary;* Claudio Casciolini: *Panis angelicus;* Anon: *Chtíc, aby spal;* Antonín Tučapský: *Omnis mundus iocundetur;* Jan Evangelista Kypta: *Pastorela Nr. 2 -for children; Sem pastýřové; Ejhle opět;* B. Pernica: *Moravské pastorely;* National song: *Píseň ponocného;* J. Schreier: *Pastorela in D major;* J.A. Čok: *Veselme všichni zpívejme;* Spiritual: *Bim, bam;* Jacob Arcadelt: *Ave Maria;* P. Šandera: *Lidové zpívání – závěr;* Jan Jakub Ryba: *Czech Christmas Mass "Hej mistře".*

AP 3112   LP   Laudes

Bonton
?   MC   1994   ?. Václav Renč. "Perníková chaloupka".

Christophorus
LC 0612   ?   ?

Dětské pěvecké sbory Opava
?   CD   1997   **Kocour muzikant.** Mixed children's choirs from Opava: Sluníčka; Cvrčci; Domino. [i]

Klub přátel poezie
?   LP   **Poetry by Vítězslav Nezval.** Piano improvisations (?) by **Petr Eben.**
?   LP   **Poetry Recital by Eduard Cupák and Miroslav Florian.** Piano improvisations (?) by **Petr Eben.**

Multisonic
31 0116-1   LP   1991   **One Hundred Folk Songs.** *Sto lidových písní.* ?. The Heuréka Group. "Vzhůru pastýři". [ii]
31 0116-4   MC   1991   Programme as Multisonic 31 0116-1.
31 0116-2   CD   1991   Programme as Multisonic 31 0116-1.

Pavel Schnabel Filmproduktion
?   VC   1993   ?. "Der böhmische Knoten". [iii]

Salón Lyry pragensis
?   MC   1971   ? P. Höger, K. Jurkovič (speakers); Jana Jonášová, Věra Soukopová (singers); **Petr Eben** (piano).

Supraphon
?   LP   1969   Poetry by Jaroslav Seifert. Otakar Brousek, Václav Broska, Věra Kubánková (reciters). Piano improvisations (?) by **Petr Eben.**
?   LP   1971   Writings of Vladislav Vančura. František Smolík, Karel Höger, Clasts Fabianová, Václav Voska, Radovan Lukavský (reciters). Piano improvisations by (?) **Petr Eben.**

---

[i] František Kumpera: *Pět ježibab;* Přemysl Kočí: *Koncert v botách;* Folksongs: *Zpívala bych,zpívala; Okolo javora; Před susedovym; Ej,rano; Dyž verbuju; Chodila po roli; Oj,včerajky; U suseda dobra voda; V kolaji voda; Vyjechala z okenka; Prší,prší; Žádnyj neví jako já; Do gala,do gala;* Miloš Smatek: *Zimní čača;* IvanaLoudová: *Páni kluci;* Přemysl Kočí: *Medvěd;* Folksongs: *Jean qui pleure; I am a poor wayfaring stranger;* Adam Michna z Otradovic: *Magnet a střelec; Vánoční roztomilost; Již jest spadla rosička;* Bohuslav Martinů: *Koleda*

[ii] Václav Holan Rovenský: *Nové hvězdy;* Adam Michna: *Chtíc, aby spal; Vánoční roztomilost;* Arrangements of carols by Petr Eben, Milan Uherek and Miroslav Raichl.

[iii] Includes music by Dvořák, Eben, Janáček, Ježek and Smetana.

| ? | | LP | 1979 | Poetry by D. Šajner, J. Urbánková and K. Boušek. Piano improvisations (?) by **Petr Eben**. |
| ? | | LP? | 1990 | ?. "Hovory v Lánech '90". [i] |

SURF, Blansko
| ? | | MC | 1997 | ?. "Skřivánek zpívá". Josef Slavíček. |

Venkow Records
| ? | | CD | 1998 | Stýskání. Marek Eben. "Folk and Country – Hity 98". [ii] |

World Music Press
T26	MC			The Green Twig is Sprouting. *Zelená se snítka*. No.24, *Snow. Snih*.
T27	MC			The Green Twig is Sprouting. *Zelená se snítka*. No.25, *A Song About a Sparrow. Písnička o vrabci*.
T29	MC			The Green Twig is Sprouting. *Zelená se snítka*. Nos. 24, 25 & 21, *If There Were Nothing Else. Kdyby tu nic nebylo*. "Three Czech Songs". [iii]

Žatecký příležitostní sbor
| CD1 | | CD | 1997 | **Cantica Comeniana**. No. 8, *Bože Otče, buď s námi*. Žatecký příležitostní sbor. Anežka and Anna Urbancová (choirmistresses). "Žatecký příležitostní sbor". [iv] |
| CD2 | | CD | 1999 | **Cantica Comeniana**. No. 1, *Ach, smutku můj*. . Žatecký příležitostní sbor. Anežka and Anna Urbancová (choirmistresses). "Žatecký příležitostní sbor". [v] |

---

[i] Works by Bohuslav Martinů, Bedřich Smetana, Jaroslav Ježek, Petr Eben, Petr Skoumal, Jan Vodňanský, Jaroslav Hutka, Jaromír Nohavica.

[ii] Jaromír Nohavica: *Až to se mnou sekne;* Robert Křesťan & Druhá tráva: *Tanečnice;* Vlasta Redl: *Dvakrát;* Pavel Žalman Lohonka: *Kóta 8000;* Kamelot: *Zachraňte koně;* Pavlína Jíšová: *Já písnička;* Spirituál kvintet: *Co prej bude s mojí duší;* Hana Ulrychová: *Modlitba;* Klíč: *Mince;* Českomoravská Hudební Společnost: *Janošek;* Helena Maršálková: *Ranec plnej písní;* Wabi Daněk: *Las Palmas;* AG Flek: *Carpe diem;* Věra Martinová: *Jako dřív;* Karel Plíhal: *Tři andělé;* Příbuzní: *Horo, horo;* Pavel Dobeš: *Seděli jsme v zadní lavici;* Duo Cis: *Šílená Lenka a blázen Jan;* Slávek Janoušek: *Fernetovka*

[iii] Demonstration tapes intended to accompany the sheet music. T29 to be with songs 1 and 2 bound together. Not yet released. Dates to be announced.

[iv] Spirituals: *Walk in Jerusalem; Swing Low, Sweet Chariot* arr. *Anders Öhrwell; Go Down Moses; Freedom is Coming;* Bob Carlton: *Ja-Da;* Moravian folksong arr. A. Urbancová: *Eh Janku, Janíčku;* Jacques Berthier: *Zpěvy z Taizé;* Anon: *Wait for the Lord;* Orlando di Lasso: *Exaltabo te; Christus resurrexit; Nade te turbe; Galans qui par terre;* Johannes Sebastian Bach: *Da nobis pacem Domine;* Carol: *Deťatko se narodilo;* Adam Michna: *Vítej, Ježíšku milý*

[v] C. Carter: *Good Night;* Lionel Bart: *Where is Love;* Ukrainian folksong: *Starenkij Tramvaj;* E. Maschewitz: *Nightingale;* Adam Michna: *Vítej, Ježíšku milý;* Carols: *Vánoční rosíčka; Chtíc aby spal; Vánoční vinšovaná pošta; Vánoční roztomilost;* Spirituals: Walk in Jerusalem; *Swing Low, Sweet Chariot; I Pharadisi; Go Down, Moses; Freedom is Coming; Ja-Da;* Moravian folksong arr. A. Urbancová: *Eh Janku, Janíčku;* ; Jacques Berthier: *Zpěvy z Taizé;* Orlando di Lasso: *Exaltabo te; Christus resurrexit; Nade te turbe; Galans qui par terre;* Johannes Sebastian Bach: *Da nobis pacem Domine;* Carol: *Deťatko se narodilo*

ZUŠ Česká Lípa (?)
?   CD   **Trouvère Mass**. *Truvérská mše*. Komorní pěvecký sbor; Sbor mladi ZUŠ Česká Lípa. [i]

2. (c) Other Recordings

The libraries of some schools of music, especially American universities and colleges, house privately made recordings, often of graduation or guest recitals. These are usually available on loan but are not otherwise commercially available. The following is a summary of items whose existence has been discovered on the Internet. Rather than record number, the first column represents the library's accession number. Only the work by Petr Eben is listed here.

Eastman School of Music

26145709   RT   1991   **Sunday Music**. *Nedělní hudba*. No. 4, *Finale*. Esther Chang (organ). "Candidate for the degree of Master of Music in Performance and Literature".

41491869   CD   1999   **Two Chorale Fantasias**. *Dvě chorální fantazie*. No. 2, *Chorale Fantasia on Saint Wenceslas*. *Chorální fantazie na Svatý Václave*. Sonia Kim (organ). "Sonia Kim, Organ".

Indiana University

15607751   RT   1987   **Sunday Music**. *Nedělní hudba*. Cheryl Hamilton (organ). "Graduate Recital".

31159474   RT   1994   **Two Chorale Fantasias**. *Dvě chorální fantazie*. No. 2, *Chorale Fantasia on Saint Wenceslas*. *Chorální fantazie na Svatý Václave*. Wendy Markovsky (organ]. "Graduate Recital"

40650059   MC   1998   **Sunday Music**. *Nedělní hudba*. R. Ward Scott (organ). "Graduate Recital".

Norges musikkhøgskole

KD 781   RT   1990   **Windows after Marc Chagall**. *Okna podle Marca Chagalla*. No. 4, *Zlatá okno*. Kåre Øistein Nordstoga (organ); Harry Kvebaek (trumpet). "Orgelinnvielseskonsert".

KD 895   MC   1991   **Laudes**. Hallgeir Schiager (organ). "Hallgeir Schiager".

KD 1060   MC   1993   **Landscapes of Patmos**. *Krajiny patmoské*. Carl Andreas Næss (organ); John Ivar Knutzen (percussion). "Orgel, slagwerk og blåsers".

---

i   Antonín Hradil: *Česká vánoční mše*

KD 1416	MC	1996	**Windows after Marc Chagall.** *Okna podle Marca Chagalla.* Ole Johannes Kosberg (organ); Hilde Prestrud (trumpet). "Hovedfagskonsert".
KD 1524	MC	1998	**Windows after Marc Chagall.** *Okna podle Marca Chagalla.* Andreas Karlsen (trumpet); Anders E. Dahl (organ). "Diplomkonsert".
KD 1662	MC	2000	**Two Invocations for Trombone and Organ.** *Dvě invokace pro trombón a varhany.* Marius Hesby (trombone); Anders E. Dahl (organ). "Diplomkonsert".

Oberlin College

25376168	RT	1991	**Sunday Music.** *Nedělní hudba.* No. 4, *Finale.* Bruce R. Frank (organ). "Honors Recital".
26979666	RT	1992	**Sunday Music.** *Nedělní hudba.* No. 4, *Finale.* Bruce R. Frank (organ). "Orientation Recital".
27905601	RT	1993	**Laudes.** No. 2, *Fantastico.* No. 3, *Gravimento.* Erik William Suter (organ). "Honors Recital".

Southern Baptist Theological Seminary

42453704	MC	1973	**Sunday Music.** *Nedělní hudba.* No. 4, *Finale.* Karel Paukert (organ). "Guest Recital".
9938790	MC	1982	**Sunday Music.** *Nedělní hudba.* No. 3. *Moto ostinato.* Roger W. Wischmeier (organ). "Doctor of Musical Arts degree recital".
15565689	MC	1986	**Song of Ruth.** *Píseň Ruth.* Daniel Edward Lawhon (organ); Rebecca Jean Prater (meezzo-soprano). "Master of Church Music degree recital".
43713358	MC	1999	**Song of Ruth.** *Píseň Ruth.* Robert Munns (piano); Sally Johnson (soprano). "Guest Recital, 1999".

2. (d) Spurious Recordings

The following recordings appear on a number of Internet websites, and claim to contain works by Petr Eben. They do not.

Laserlight
B00000ARVN	CD	"Dance Little Lady".

VOX Cameo Classics
8731	CD	"A Latin Guitar Festival".

Plate 4   Petr Eben during the recording of *Faust*, 1981

Plate 5   Petr Eben rehearsing *The Labyrinth of the World and the Paradise of the Heart*, Greyfriars Kirk, Edinburgh, 1990

> *Petr Eben,*
> COMPOSER
> *The perfect gift for the world of music would be for people to start to sing. They are no longer singing. People have CDs, radio, TV, they aren't singing, even in pubs. We have such a rich, beautiful treasury of folk tunes. If they would go back to this treasure... For church music, a return to Gregorian chant. There is nothing more spiritual...*

Plate 6   Cartoon drawing of Petr Eben by Nenad Vitas. Reproduced with the permission of the artist and *The Prague Post*. © Nenad Vitas 1993.
The drawing was published as part of a larger cartoon group of artists in the December 22-28 1993 issue of The Prague Post.

Plate 7

Petr Eben at the organ in his study in Prague, 1998

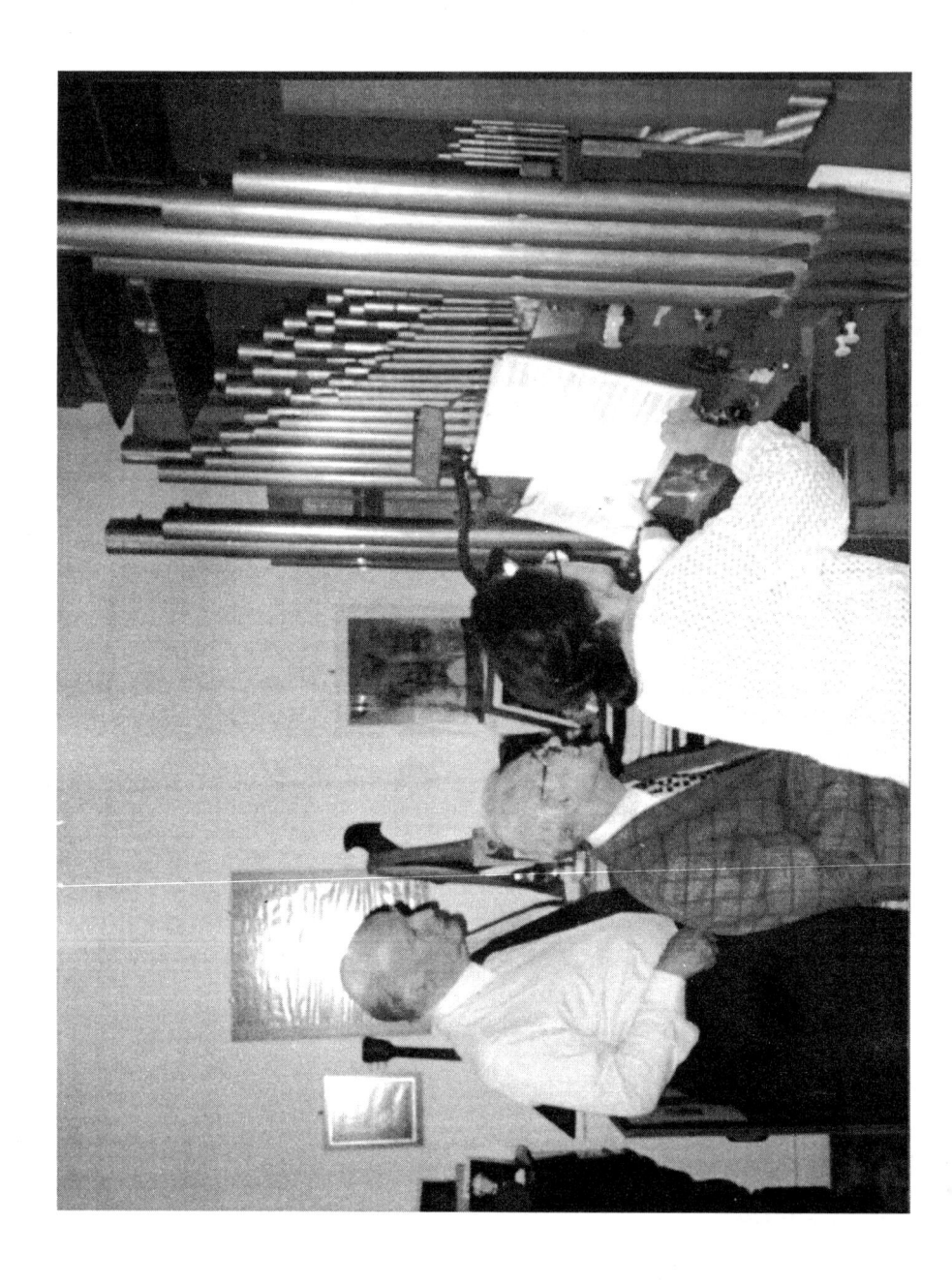

Plate 8   Petr Eben with Graham Melville-Mason and Susan Landale, Paris 1999, playing through *Campanae gloriosae,* while stil a "work in progress"